Tony Buzan - aged 31.   Painted by Lorraine Gill

What they are saying about Tony Buzan

"...Mind Mappers are taking our information democracy to the next stage"

Bill Gates

"We recognise the importance of Mind Mapping as a useful tool in helping individuals carry out their everyday activities with many of our staff using Mind Mapping techniques"

Lord Peter Mandelson, House of Lords

"Mind Mapping uses the brain in the way it was designed, saves time, improves results and is fun. How can any business person be without this powerful tool?"

Stephen C Lundin, author of the five-million-copy bestselling book, *Fish*

"Tony Buzan is a man on an impressive mission – to unlock the power of our brains and show us how to tap into and use our creative genius with ease and effectiveness"

His Excellency Dr Abdul Hussein Ali Mirza, Minister for Gas and Oil, Bahrain

"Tony Buzan deserves a medal for coming up with the sanity-saving concept of Mind Maps, which makes difficult mental tasks possible, even pleasurable."

Time Out Magazine

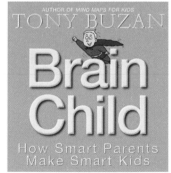

"Tony was the keynote speaker at our annual L&D conference. He held the audience spellbound as he challenged, confronted and tested our collective assumptions about how adults learn. His complete mastery of his subject shone through, and the audience would clearly have loved him to continue not just for another few hours, but for several days! He is an extraordinary teacher and communicator..."

Ann Ewing, Head of Learning & Development, HSBC Bank plc

"Tony appeals to the disenfranchised in education.

Mind Mapping helps you to become the best version of yourself. Tony's methods take the mystery out of being clever.

They put education back into the hands of the possible.

They are relevant to readers and their kids.

Kids who speak many languages such as Swahili or Urdu are clever/smart without realising it.

People are being encouraged to learn but not think. Tony reverses this syndrome."

All of the above from Jeremy (Jezz) Moore

"The use of Mind Mapping is an integral part of my Quality Improvement Project at Boeing. This has provided savings of over $10 million for my organisation."

Mike Stanley, Boeing Corporation, USA

"mens sana in corpore sano"

a healthy mind in a

healthy body;

a healthy body

in a healthy mind

Tony Buzan

About the Author

Raymond Keene OBE is the UK's senior Chess Grandmaster, Master of Arts from Trinity College, Cambridge, correspondent for *The Times*, *The Sunday Times*, *The Spectator*, *The Gulf News*, *The Australian* and *The Daily Yomiuri* in Tokyo. He holds the world record for authoring 164 books on Mind Sports, thinking and genius. He has organised three world championships involving Garry Kasparov. Ray was twice the winner of the Oscar for world's best writer on chess.

Her Majesty Queen Elizabeth II awarded Ray the title Officer of the British Empire (OBE) in person for services to chess and charity. He organised, along with Tony Buzan, the very first Man v Machine World Championship in any thinking sport (Dr. Tinsley v Chinook London 1992 World Draughts Championship).

Ray was the first western chess grandmaster to compete in China (1981). He also is the holder of the Gold Medal of the Chinese Olympic Association. He is the Chairman of the English Chess Association and of the Howard Staunton Society.

Amongst Ray Keene's 164 books are biographies of the Chess Grandmasters: Howard Staunton, Aron Nimzowitsch and Leonid Stein. He also organised and founded with Tony Buzan the World Memory Championships, which reached its 21st event in 2012.

More about the author, Raymond Keene OBE, can be found at www.keeneonchess.com. You can follow him on Twitter @times_chess

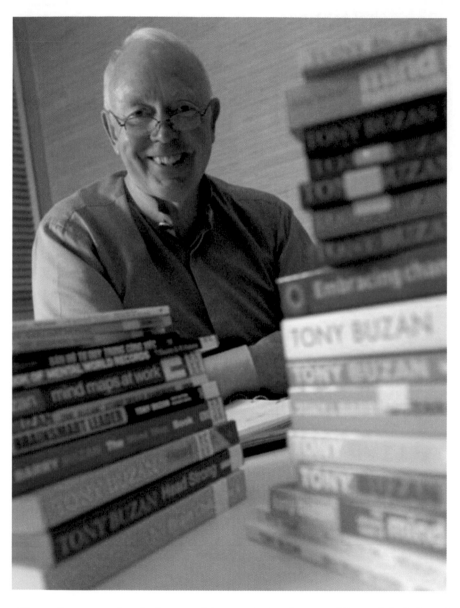

There is no one book that could ever do justice to a life as rich, full and diverse as that of Tony Buzan, so to learn more about him, visit his personal website www.tonybuzan.com

Follow Tony Buzan on Twitter at @TonyBuzan

To find out more about iMindMap™ visit www.thinkbuzan.com

Foreword by Nicky and Jonathan Oppenheimer

When Raymond Keene first asked us to write the foreword to this book, we did not hesitate. As Raymond's research has developed, we have grown increasingly aware that this is not just a book about a close friend, but also an important record of an unusual life, one that it is essential to record. It has not only been a life of ground breaking thought, but also one of great personal friendships.

Tony came into our lives over 25 years ago, first through Strilli, (Nicky's wife and Jonathan's mother) who was introduced to him by a friend, whilst Tony was in South Africa. It was the beginning of a friendship that will last a lifetime. Since then Tony has regaled us with many a humorous tale, enjoyed many of our family's highs and lows and always provided great advice. This term does not do Tony's insight justice, but when it comes to advice there is no one better.

Raymond's exploration into Tony's life has provided us with a greater understanding of his work, but also with some solid reminders of what Tony is about. One contributor remarked that we should "thank God that Tony is in the world" and indeed they are right. The context of this

comment refers to far more than his work as an educator and an author; it is personal. His innovative thinking cannot be questioned, but many will not know about the character that lies beneath, a character that Raymond has done well to uncover.

Naturally, the focus must be on Tony's remarkable achievements; to merely comment that he has sold more than 7 million books worldwide would only be a snap shot. He has written over 120 books, *Use Your Head* being the first and biggest seller, and these books have been translated into 40 languages, which gives some indication of his reach. These figures provide us with an easy metric, but Tony has also had an extremely varied advisory role over the years too, a long list of successful companies and governments being two strings to this particular bow.

Like the millions who have read his great works, Tony has enriched our lives in many ways. To describe Tony as the "Neil Armstrong of the mind", as one old friend did, by no means overstates the achievements of this pioneer; and we are very pleased that his amazing journey is finally being told in this book.

Nicky and Jonathan Oppenheimer

. . . .

"Your brain is like a sleeping giant"

Tony Buzan

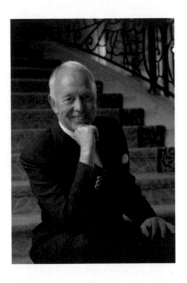

The Official Biography of

TONY BUZAN

The man who introduced the world to

Mind Maps ™

by

Raymond Keene OBE

Published by Filament Publishing Ltd

16, Croydon Road, Waddon,

Croydon, Surrey, CR0 4PA UK

Telephone +44 (0)20 8688 2598

Fax +44 (0)20 7183 7186

info@filamentpublishing.com

www.filamentpublishing.com

Filament Australia 24 Tamworth Drive, (P O Box 3588),

Helensvale, Qld 4212   FreeCall 1800 060 982

Office 07 5502 6570

info@filamentpublishing.com.au

Contents

• • • •

Author's Foreword:

According to Jonathan Case, of the prestigious Branding Laureate Group, Tony is a living legend in the sphere of education, a true pioneer and an innovator in every sense of the word. This book is based on over two decades of knowing Tony and working with him, plus thousands of hours of conversations as well as numerous recorded interviews. Many of the stories, already famous, are recounted again here, often in his own words, as part of the legend of Tony Buzan.

As one of the world's foremost educational and business gurus of the past four decades, Tony's techniques have inspired many to maximise the potential of their mind and thus to experience richer and more meaningful lives. Having invented the Mind Mapping technique in the 1960s, his subsequent *Use Your Head* series, which aired on the BBC, popularised his ideas and helped people to comprehend the true capacity of the mind. He did not stop there, and has since authored over 120 books, with translations into forty languages.

Having left a major footprint in so many areas, Tony Buzan's legacy has transcended his own work to enter the realm of becoming a cultural phenomenon. Since his initial leap to fame, he has lectured across the globe and has advised the governments of over 10 nations on educational policy, in addition to spreading his wisdom to many Fortune 500 companies as a consultant. That his ideas have been so readily accepted and integrated into our existing knowledge of education speaks volumes about the power of his work. Tony can point to the millions he has enabled, empowered and inspired as evidence of the deep impact he has left on the world.

Tony's core message has been to liberate and unlock the potential of every human being, a crusade to demonstrate that everyone has talents, which can be deployed, if given the right tools and taught how to become mentally literate. His insights did not come easily, though, and not everyone applauds his assertion that we must question who decides who is intelligent – and who is not. Who guards the guards? "Quis custodiet ipsos custodes?" as Socrates asked and Juvenal formulated.

In an ideal and mentally literate world, improvements in thinking, IQ, Speed Reading, Creativity and Memory Power would be welcomed with open arms by all. This has, paradoxically, proved not to be the universal case. Indeed, Tony's career has been an endless, Homerically epic battle against the enemies of Mental Literacy. Against political leaders who are apathetic about education, and push it to the back-burner, against rigid methods of education, wedded to the notion of linear, black and white reductionism, against regimes and organisations which wish to crush independent thinking, against government jobsworths, who sometimes casually and sometimes for reasons of political correctness, reject Mental Literacy, and against rivals who have hijacked his ideas and have sought to portray harmful and stunting alternatives as superior pathways to mental achievement.

In 2009, for example, the Welsh Assembly's Department for Children, Education and Lifelong Learning (DCELL), rejected approaches from Tony concerning Memory training, claiming that their brand new guidelines were focusing on process-based education rather than information delivery and memorisation. Just the sort of jargon, which helps kids to learn, of course! And where was the vision for educating the young in the political programmes of either of the two US Presidential aspirants in their campaigns of 2012?

Then there are the University Professors who combined to accuse young Tony of cheating in exams, when his brilliantly devised Memory systems should rightly have earned him a Summa cum Laude (highest honours).

In contrast, it will come as no surprise to learn of the huge triumphs of China in the World Memory Championships, which Tony co-founded in 1991, given the acute Chinese hunger for learning and their notable successes on the general education front.

In 2008, Tony was granted his personal Coat of Arms by The Royal College of Heralds. The original point of a Coat of Arms was to identify, with an immediately recognisable individually crafted, visual symbol, each member of your army in mediaeval battle; the battle now being fought is for the Brain and Planetary Mental Literacy.

From personal experience, I can relate an anecdote connected with our first literary collaboration: on the nature of Genius. I had expected Tony to be in thrall of great minds, born, as it were with superhuman powers direct from the divine intelligence. Not a bit of it – Tony's emphasis was on the ordinary, humble, just like you and me, nature of the Genii, and how their hard won comprehension of the secrets of mental literacy had led to their stunning successes. Tony was determined to prove that you do not need to be born from a ruling family, or in a den of artists, to aspire to the heights of human mental achievement. Einstein, it transpired, was a patent clerk with no early discernible aptitude for mathematics; Leonardo was the son of a notary; Bach was so impoverished he had to walk tens of miles to Buxtehude's concerts; Shakespeare was once jailed for poaching; Goethe was a bourgeois lawyer, and on it goes…

In the course of his personal Odyssey, Tony has remained true to his vision, and its expression in the ideals of the Renaissance Academy.

With Newton, Tony can say he is a friend of Plato, a friend of Aristotle and, above all, a friend of the truth.

The power of social conformity is great, established dogma yields with reluctance, as the obstructive jobsworths and doubting professors amply demonstrated. Yet as the celebrated chess Grandmaster and ultimate chess strategist, Aron Nimzowitsch wrote in his book *My System*:

"Ridicule can do much, for instance embitter the existence of young talents; but one thing is not given to it, to put a stop permanently to the incursion of new and powerful ideas. The old dogmas…who bothers themselves today about these? The new ideas, however, those supposed byways, not to be recommended to the public, these are become today highways, on which great and small move freely, in the consciousness of absolute security."

And in a final, further and utterly apt parallel, Tony Buzan, where Mental Literacy is concerned, has, like Nimzowitsch on the chessboard, been described as "the embodiment of all sapient virtues!"

Ray Keene OBE

London, May 2013

"The soul is a kind of rough diamond, which requires Art, Labour, and Time to polish it. For want of which, many a good natural Genius is lost, or lies unfashioned, like a Jewel in the Mine."

Richard Steele
The Spectator, London 1712

• • • •

Tony Buzan

A Chronology

"Whatever your discipline,
become a student of
excellence in all things.
Take every opportunity to
observe people who manifest
the qualities of mastery.
These models of excellence
will inspire you and guide you
toward the fulfilment of
your highest potential."

Tony Buzan

Tony Buzan Chronology

1942: June 2, born in London to Jean and Gordon Buzan

1949: First literary endeavour: *The Book of My Pets.*

1952: Whitstable School for Boys, Kent; Simon Langton Grammar School for Boys, Canterbury, Kent. Identifies necessity for re-evaluation of criteria for assessing both intelligence and knowledge.

1954: Emigrated to Vancouver, Canada.

1959: Captain, winning school chess team, Provincial Schools Chess Team Championship, British Columbia representing Kitsilano High School, Vancouver, British Columbia.

1959/60: Head Boys Prefect, Kitsilano High School.

1960: Valedictorian High School Graduation, Kitsilano High. Commencement of invention of Mind Maps. Perceives need for operational manual for the brain.

1961/62: Feature Journalist, University of British Columbia student newspaper.

Tony, Jean, his mother, and brother Barry Buzan

1964: University of British Columbia; graduated with Double Honours in Psychology, English, Mathematics and General Sciences. (BA Hons Arts with Science). First job: agriculture - working in the field with Gallus Gallus Domesticus (the common chicken!).

1964/66: Masters Student, Psychology, English and Creative Thinking, Simon Fraser University.

1965/66: Inaugural President, Simon Fraser University Student Council.

1966: Returned to London, UK. Special Assignment Teacher for three years, Inner London Education Authority.

1969: Co-founded Salatticum Poets with John Carder Bush and Jeremy Cartland.

1969 - 1971: Edited *The International Journal* of MENSA, the High IQ Society.

1970: Continued development of the theory of Mind Mapping.

1970/1974: National Union of Journalists (NUJ), editing and writing for Haymarket Publishing and Daily Telegraph Travel.

1971: Founder, Buzan World/Think Buzan. Spore One (collected poems, limited edition). *The Speed Reading Book*, 1st edition.

1973/74: Launch of first BBC ten-part television series with accompanying book: *Use Your Head*.

1974: First publication of The Seminal Work: *Use Your Head*. Theory of Mind Maps in more detailed development. Prime time TV feature documentary on the future of education and the brain, *The Enchanted Loom*.

1974 and ongoing to the present day: Advising governments, including those of Australia, Bahrain, China, UK, Jamaica, Malaysia,

Mexico, Scotland, Singapore and South Africa. Advising Fortune 500 companies, including Apple Computers, BBC, Disney, HSBC, IBM, Intel, Microsoft, Stabilo, Telefonica, The Kuwaiti Oil Company, The National Bank of Malaysia and Vodafone. Global lecturing connected with all of the above.

1981: Initiated the 'Super Class', teaching two thousand Soweto schools students in the government-backed 'Soweto 2000'.

1984: Founded the World Speed Reading Championships. Made Freeman of the City of London.

1986: *Use Your Memory* published.

1988: *Master Your Memory* published. Member of coaching team for the Great Britain Olympic Rowing squad, Korean Olympics.

1989: Founded the Brain Trust Charity, No. 1001012. Founding Editor in Chief of Synapsia, the worldwide Brain Club magazine.

1990 and ongoing: Mental Toughness coach, Marlow Rowing Club, one of the most prestigious clubs in the world. Develops techniques of TEFCAS and Meta-Positive Thinking.

1991: The Eagle Catcher Award, presented by Electronic Data Systems (EDS), "for attempting the impossible and achieving it". Inaugurates first Brain Trust Charity Brain of the Year Award to Garry Kasparov, World Chess Champion. Originated and subsequently co-founded the World Memory Championship at The Athenaeum, London, with author Raymond Keene, OBE. Many subsequent initiatives were planned and executed together, such as…

1992: The first ever Man vs. Machine World Championship in any thinking sport; Dr Marion Tinsley defeats the Chinook Draughts Computer, Park Lane Hotel, London. Member of coaching team for the Great Britain Rowing squad, Barcelona Olympics.

1993: Second World Memory Championship, London. Publication of *The Mind Map Book* with Barry Buzan, then Professor of International Studies at University of Warwick and Project Director at the Centre of Peace and Conflict Research, Copenhagen. Tony's books now published in fifty countries and have been translated in over 30 languages. Sales of *Use Your Head* exceed global sales of 1 million.

1994: Third World Memory Championship, London. Publication *Buzan's Book of Genius*, with Ray Keene OBE. Tinsley vs. Chinook rematch, Science Museum, Boston, USA. Attends Star Trek International convention at London's Royal Albert Hall as "IQ".

1995: Created Grandmaster of Memory title with Royal endorsement from the Princes of Liechtenstein (Hanbury Manor, UK). Co-founded the World Mind Mapping and Creativity Championships with Raymond Keene, OBE. Fourth World Memory Championship, London. Appointed Dean Liechtenstein Global (Renaissance) Academy (co-created with Prince Philip of Liechtenstein). Co-founded the Festival of the Mind with Raymond Keene, OBE, at London's Royal Albert Hall.

Inaugural Grandmaster of Memory Awards sanctioned by the Princes of Liechtenstein, Hanbury Manor, UK.

1996: Fifth World Memory Championship, London.

1997: Honorary Black Belt in Aikido awarded for services to, and knowledge of, the Martial Art. Sixth World Memory Championship, London. First Mind Sports Olympiad, Royal Festival Hall London. Publication Buzan's *Book of Mental World Records* with Ray Keene OBE.

1998: Seventh World Memory Championship, London. Second Mind Sports Olympiad, London.

1999: Eighth World Memory Championship, London. Third Mind Sports Olympiad, Olympia.

Inaugural Festival of the Mind Royal Albert Hall

2000: *Head First*, 1st edition. Ninth World Memory Championship, Alexandra Palace, London. Chairman match committee, World Chess Championship, London between Garry Kasparov and Vladimir Kramnik. Member of coaching team for the Great Britain Rowing squad, Sydney Olympics.

2001: Tenth World Memory Championship, University of Manchester. *The Power of Intelligence* (series of 5), 1st editions,

2002: Eleventh World Memory Championship, University of Manchester.

2003: *Mind Maps for Kids* (series of 3), 1st editions. Twelfth World Memory Championship, Kuala Lumpur, Malaysia. *Brain Child*, first edition.

2004: Thirteenth World Memory Championship, University of Manchester.

2005: Extended 'Super Class' concept, teaching 9,000 school children at the Royal Albert Hall. *Happy Dictionary* television feature on Mind Maps and Memory for 300 million people in Central China TV.

2005: Featured in BBC's documentary, *In Search of Genius*, transforming the cognitive skills of young children, described by the BBC as "a unique social experiment". Fourteenth World Memory Championship, University of Oxford. Special Recognition Award by President Vicente Fox of Mexico for length and excellence of service in helping Mexico with educational and good governance initiatives. *The Ultimate Book of Mind Maps*, 1st edition. *Embracing Change*, 1st edition.

2006: Fifteenth World Memory Championship, Imperial College London.

2007: *Requiem for Ted* (Hughes) (poetry), 1st edition. *Concordea* (poetry), 1st edition. *Age-Proof Your Brain*, 1st edition. Sixteenth World

Memory Championship, Kingdom of Bahrain. *The Study Skills Handbook*, 1st edition. Won the Great Education Debate, National Teachers' Education Conference, Mermaid Theatre, London.

2008: Seventeenth World Memory Championship, Bahrain. Lifetime Achievement Award, The American Creativity Association, for services to global creativity and innovation. Granted Armorial Bearings, College of Arms, by the Royal College of Heralds. Thinker in Residence at Wellington College, Berkshire, England.

2008/2009: *Collins Language Revolution Beginners / Beginners Plus* (Spanish, French, Italian), 1st editions.

2009: Freeman of the Guild of Educators. Thinker in Residence, Wellington College. Honorary Fellow of the Academy for Leadership in Higher Education, Ministry of Higher Education, Malaysia. Founding Member of the Inaugural International Board of Advisors, University Putra Malaysia. Developed and launched new taxonomy for reading and learning. Eighteenth World Memory Championship, London.

2010: Nineteenth World Memory Championship, Guangzhou China. Appointed Visiting Professor, Stenden University, 2010. *Mind Maps For Business*, 1st edition.

2011: Twentieth World Memory Championship, Guangzhou China. Nominated by UK History Faculty Head and Professor for Nobel Peace Prize, after lecturing to Nobel Laureates in Amman at the personal invitation of King Abdullah II of Jordan. Promulgation of the Magna Memoria, or Great Memory Charter.

2012: Recovers in phoenix-like style from a serious illness to be pronounced a certain centenarian by his medical advisers. 70th birthday attended by Princes, Lords, Captains of Education, Industry and Brain Stars. Twenty-first World Memory Championship, Lilian Baylis School, London.

Publication of *The Most Important Graph in the World* with Jennifer Goddard and Jorge Castaneda. Publication of *Brain Training with Kids* with Jennifer Goddard. Tony has now authored and co-authored over 120 books on Learning, the Brain, Memory, Mind Sports, Creativity and Intelligence, as well as books of poetry, dreams and his personal epics AMAN AND STUDIS. Receives Brand Laureate Trophy in Kuala Lumpur.

2013: Tony's Brain Trust Charity makes the Brain of the Year award at Simpson's-in-the-Strand to Prof Michael Crawford, the world's leading expert on Brain Chemistry and Human Nutrition, Director of the Institute at London's Imperial College.

Presented with the Lifetime Achievement Award by Dr Lothar Seiwert of Deutscher Redner Preis. Awarded the inaugural Avicenna Gold Medal by Prof Dr Ahmed Ali Khan, Dean of MIQ Academy Mexico, under the patronage of the new Academus, former President Vicente Fox.

• • • •

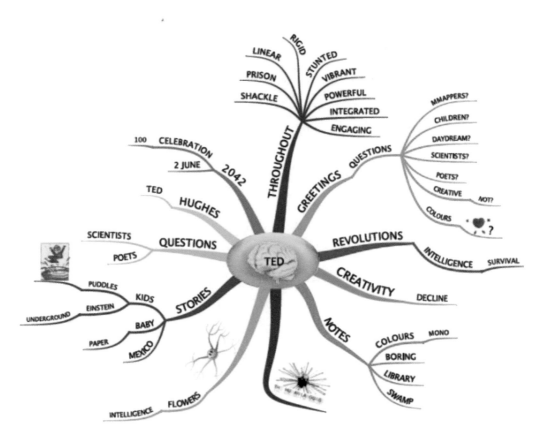

Spoke at TEDx (Technology Education and Design) using the following Mind Map to lecture to potentially millions of viewers globally.

Mind Map drawn by Phil Chambers, twice (and reigning) World Mind Mapping Champion and six times medallist.

To watch go to http://bit.ly/TtlJQE

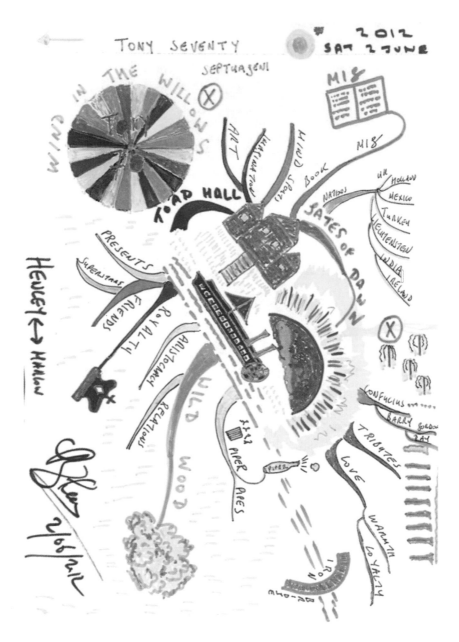

This is a page from Tony's UPO or Universal Personal Organiser, a mentally literate form of Uber Diary. This page records, in Mind Map form, Tony's 70th birthday celebration on June 2nd 2012.

How Tony Met Ray

On the first evening of a two-day seminar in 1990, Tony had booked an international Chess Master to play 20 simultaneous games of chess against the delegates, in order to demonstrate to them the power and potential of the human brain, with particular reference to the powers of concentration, work, ethic, memory and creative thinking.

Tony continues: "Five days before the event, the international Master came down with flu and was told by his doctor that there was no way he would be able to make the event. The organiser telephoned me in a panic because there was 'no time' to find a replacement. Of course, there was time – there were five days.

"I told her to pursue every avenue – and in the end the solution came from a most surprising source. Over afternoon tea with some friends, at which her seven-year-old son, Simon, was present, she explained, almost tearfully, her dilemma. Suddenly her son piped up, 'Mummy, why don't you try Raymond Keene?'

"Not having the faintest idea who Raymond Keene was, and egged on by her son who had become enamoured of chess at his school chess club, she contacted Raymond Keene and asked him if he could possibly fill in for the missing international Master. Mr. Keene said that he could.

"She then nervously telephoned me and asked if I would be willing to accept this unknown chap called Keene as a substitute. I nearly fell off my chair. I told her that it was as if she was asking me whether I would mind, instead of having the amateur lightweight boxing champion from Scunthorpe, having Mohammed Ali as his substitute.

"Raymond Keene was one of the world's leading chess Grandmasters, the chess correspondent for *The Times*, *The Sunday Times* and *The*

Spectator, the former British Chess Champion, the author of over 160 books on chess, and the chess writer whom I had been following for many years!

"Raymond took on twenty of the delegates, thrashed them all, and then randomly demonstrated that he had memorised every single move of every single game, including his own thoughts as he was considering each of his own next moves – the demonstration of the power of the brain was complete, and a new Mind Sports partnership had been formed."

Author, Chess Grandmaster and Head of the Mind Sports Faculty in the Renaissance Academy, Ray Keene OBE, as depicted by a Graduate of Tony Buzan's Liechtenstein Global Trust Academy.

• • • •

Part One

Enigma and Solutions

"Did you know that you use less than 1% of your brain? The good news is that Mind Mapping can help you to access the other 99%!"

Tony Buzan

Chapter 1
Dodging The Doodle-Bugs

Tony's Early Life

Tony's own first memories were at the end of 1944 and the beginning of 1945, during the closing stages of the Second World War, when he was between two and two-and-a-half years old. He remembers vividly standing between the thick velvety curtains in his living room, sandwiched between their warmth and texture and the cold panes of glass that looked out on to his back garden.

Coming over the horizon, accompanied by an increasing, rumbling roar that eventually shook the foundations on which he was standing, came a giant squadron of Royal Air Force bombers. To his young eye, they looked mysterious, fantasmagoric and awesome.

Shortly after the flight of the bombers, his second and equally vivid memory was of the shrill and tantalizing whistle of a doodlebug bomb, which thundered overhead and which, as was their wont, suddenly went silent before plummeting to earth, one knew not where.

After the mandatory few seconds of silence, the doodlebug struck earth some few hundred yards from his family house. The impact sent tremors through the building, and the force of the explosion shattered the thick and corrugated glass of their front door. The glass had been bomb-blown into the front hall and now lay shimmering on the hallway floor.

Tony recalls: "I remember looking with delight and enchantment at this cascade of reflected and refracted rainbows and beautifully clean-cut edges. I picked them up gently, as one would a delicate animal, already knowing at that early age that glass and sharp edges were dangerous. The texture of the glass, the beauty of the multi-coloured light, and the magic of the whole splintered fairyland are etched as vividly in my mind today as the reality was in my eyes at the time."

Both his media and travelling career started at the age of eight. During that year he travelled to his first foreign country, and spent a wonderful summer holiday with his classmates, somewhat ironically, in Germany along the River Rhine. These were halcyon days that began to open his eyes to the wider world. During the same year, he experienced his first media appearance, being interviewed in the *Whitstable Gazette* for his second prize in the town's pet show, and for his opinions on animals.

In 1954, after severe floods in England, he, his parents and his brother Barry emigrated to Vancouver, British Columbia, Canada where he was to experience a very different culture from that in which he had been brought up.

One of the first major revelations was the fact that England, which, because of the pink pervading the world maps, he had come to believe was 'the biggest country in the world' was so tiny that you could fit five of them into the province of British Columbia alone! Further revelations were to follow in rapidly accelerating succession first, though, comes a story from his early years in England.

• • • •

Chapter 2

The Redefinition Of Intelligence And The Re-Evaluation Of Knowledge

We are at the dawn of young Tony Buzan's encounter with Learning, Knowledge, Memory and Intelligence, and an amazingly insightful and significant story is about to be told.

In Tony's own words:

"When I was seven years old, my family moved to Whitstable, a small seaside fishing village, near Canterbury, on the northern coast of Kent. I was in the first year of Whitstable Primary Boys School, my best friend was called Barry, and our only and all-consuming interest was nature.

At the end of the day we could not wait to get out of school in order to play in the woods, fields, and by the rivers and dykes, studying and exalting in the glory of nature, and collecting living things for our homes' mini zoos.

Barry had an amazing capacity: he could run into a field, make birds and butterflies fly away, and, as they flew over the horizon, could identify them all by flight pattern alone, while I was mumbling Cabbage White, Sparrow, by which time they had all gone. His perceptual and identifying abilities were phenomenal. One day in school, we boys were informed that we were going to be divided into four different classes: 1A, 1B, 1C and 1D. We were also told that it made no difference to which class we were assigned. It took us a microsecond to realise that

1A was for the academic 'A 'student, and that 1D was for the dunces, dimwits, dullards, and dense boys.

I was put in class 1A; my best friend Barry in class 1D.

In each class, the seat in which you sat was determined by the result of the last test you had taken. The top boy sat in the back right hand seat, the second in the seat next to that, and so on along the back row, then snaking down the class to the front row where the bottom student in that test sat in the front right hand seat."

Where, in general, sat little Tony Buzan?

"Never in seat 1 or seat 2. Those prestigious locations were always reserved for either Mummery or Epps, who always came first or second, no matter what the subject. Little Tony Buzan was somewhere else along the back row, or in the middle of the class.

One day our teacher, Mr. Hake, was asking us some pretty dull questions including such as:

- Name two fish you could find in an English stream (there are over a 100!)
- What is the difference between an insect and a spider (there are over 15!)
- What is the difference between a butterfly and a moth (again there are over 15!)

A few days later, our teacher came into the class and announced: 'Boys, someone has scored a perfect mark in a test!' Everyone, including me, looked at Mummery and Epps to see which one of them had done it again.

The teacher then announced, to my stunned and total surprise, 'Buzan!'

I knew that he had made a mistake, because I knew that in every test we had taken I had either left answers out, or had definitely given incorrect answers.

Nevertheless, we all had to take our books, pens and writing materials out of our little wooden flip top desks, and move to our new position. For the first time in my life, I was sitting in seat number 1, looking, for the first time, at the right profiles of Mummery and Epps!

Pleasing as this all was, I knew that my triumph was going to be short-lived, because Mr. Hake would quickly discover that he had made a mistake.

He then began to hand out the papers, eventually coming to me. He plonked a paper in front of me, and to my surprise it had 100%! Well done Boy!

"Top marks! Points for your team! And my name in my handwriting!

"When I looked at the paper, I realised that it was filled with the answers. I had casually written down to the dull questions he had asked about nature a few days earlier.

My immediate thought and reaction was: that wasn't a test! I could have named him 50 fishes from English rivers; many differences between insects and spiders; many differences between butterflies and moths, so it wasn't a test.

After a few minutes, it began to dawn on me that it was a test, and that when Mummery and Epps got their high and perfect scores, it was because they had the same relationship with the subjects, in which they were scoring well, as I had with nature. So it was a test! And I was, for the first time in my life, Number One!

It felt good. For about five minutes. Then the realisation dawned on me that would, over time, transform the direction of my life.

The realisation was that the system had identified me as number one, while, sitting at the very bottom of the combined snake of 1A, 1B, 1C and 1D, was my best friend Barry. And who knew more about nature little Barry? Or little Tony? Little Barry, by far! He could identify, by flight pattern alone a butterfly, moth or bird. In the real and comparative knowledge of nature, Barry should have been sitting half a mile to the right of me in terms of his excellence. He was the real number one, and yet the system was identifying him as all the Ds."

From the moment of that realisation on, little Tony became an intellectual delinquent, asking:

Who has the right to say who is smart?

Who has the right to say who is not smart?

What is smart anyway?

And how can my teachers and school get it so absolutely, and antipodally, wrong?!

"The pain and discomfort of being named number one at the expense of the real number one, who also happened to be my best friend, which made it even more painful, grew over the years into a passion for the identification and nurturing of the multiple intelligences that we all have."

Tony's reactions to this unexpected triumph veered between the suspicions that there must have been a flaw in the marking system, to the belief that somehow he was an impostor. Both of these gnawing doubts were not true.

So, as he accustomed himself to his new found esteem, a fresh nagging thought burgeoned in his mind. Officially he was now the school kid possessed of the greatest knowledge of nature. There, though, languishing and marooned at the lowest ebb of the worst class, was his mate Barry. Barry was, in Tony's estimation, the greatest expert on nature that he knew. Barry's nature IQ was phenomenal as, indeed, was his accumulated knowledge of nature and his ability to recall nature facts at will.

This level of IQ and this store of knowledge was, however, not officially recognised, not least because Barry's skills exceeded, by such an enormous margin, what the school required children to know about nature, that it travelled beneath the radar of their conventional antennae. This leads us to the ancient Socratic question in a new and provocative format: "Quis custodiet ipsos custodes?" Who guards the guards?

Who, and by what right, decides who is intelligent and who is not, and who decides which repositories of knowledge itself are relevant and which to be denied? The implications, not lost on the young Buzan brain, were, and remain, momentous, not to say monstrous.

Modern mass systems of education are designed, as with so many contemporary institutions, to create one-size-fits-all assessments and solutions. In gigantic state-led organisations, the needle of genius may be mislaid in the proverbial haystack of mediocrity. Just consider the extent to which immense reserves of individual, but nonconformist, talent might be overlooked and wasted in such juggernautical operations.

In Tony's staggeringly precocious insight into this anomaly of evaluation, assessment and selection, one observes the very roots, the primeval stirrings of what was destined to become a redefinition, even more, a revolution in the perception and drawing out of the varying and radiantly divergent capacities of the human brain. It led on to alternative methodologies for note-taking and creativity, such as The Mind Map, to the BBC documentary, *In Search of Genius*. In this ground -breaking documentary, failing school kids were offered parameters for recognising their own hitherto dismissed potential.

Tony's early insight had formed the basis for the belief that geniuses are not born fully armed, like Pallas Athene from the head of Zeus, but nurtured through a gradualistic process which welcomes their talents and which both fosters and rewards their determination to succeed. Versions of defining intelligence have varied since IQ tests were first introduced in the early twentieth century, but Tony's definition of intelligence as 'the ability to handle the second by second challenges which life throws at you', has always struck me as the most satisfactory, and is the reason that I have described him as the modern Aristotle, as Dante put it of the original, "The master of the men who know!"

Years later, further events were to add similar power, conviction and impetus to Tony's desire to bring about tectonic shifts in the way that children are both appreciated and educated.

When Tony was young he was continually questioning authority, asking, 'Who says who is intelligent or not?' and 'What is intelligence?', and 'Can it be trained and improved?' He admits that he was also singularly un-athletic, and hated all forms of physical sports, which were obligatory at school!

Tony continues: "At the age of 13, my life and attitudes were transformed. I had vaguely begun to comprehend that a fit body was attractive to girls! An athletic friend of mine introduced me to push-ups, chin-ups and sit-ups.

"In the cooperative/competitive nature of friends, we began to compare notes and I tried to match him. At first my performances were pathetic!

"Gradually though, as I persisted, my results improved. Then came the 'Wow!' When checking in the mirror, I could see, for the first time in my life, the faint outline of my abdominal muscles (the 'six-pack') and the first definition of the muscles in my chest, shoulders and arms.

"I was transforming!

"And I was transformed....

"I began to grasp that the body with which I had been blessed was not simply 'there' – it was a flexible 'machine' which would respond to the way I treated it. It was mine to abuse, lose or use. Suddenly a whole new world opened up to me, and I embraced with gusto. Physical training was not the pain, agony and torture that I had imagined it to be in my earlier years. It was energising, stress-reducing, and had made me both look and feel good.

If you exercise your brain, you will positively influence your body. If you exercise your body, you will positively influence your brain.

"I qualified as a lifeguard, studied the martial arts of ju-jitsu, karate and eventually the 'King of the Martial Arts' – aikido, and became an enthusiastic runner and rower. In conjunction with this, I became a trainer in a health club, and kept myself further in shape by taking up disco and ballroom dancing (among the hardest physical sports there are!) This eventually led me to assist in the coaching of Olympic athletes.

The power to change your body lies in knowing how to use the power of your mind.

"As I began to notice the first changes in my body as a young teenager, I began to ask the next question: 'If I can transform my body's strength and power, then why cannot I transform my brain's strength and power too?'

"The answer, of course, is that I could!

"Not only that – the two were linked.

"In harmony with my own physical development and self-exploration, including my many learning mistakes, I understood that those thinking tools that I had yearned for did exist; that I could convert stress and anger into energy and excitement; that there were thinking tools which could help guarantee me greater success; that there were techniques for improving all levels of physical and mental performance; and there was always a 'brighter side'."

When Tony was fourteen, his school class was given a battery of tests to measure their mental skills.

Concealed among them was a speed reading test. A few weeks later, the pupils were given their results, and Tony found that he had scored an average of 213 words per minutes (wpm). His first reaction was elation, because 213 sounded like a lot! However, his joy did not last long, for the teacher soon explained that 200 wpm was fairly average, and that the fastest student in the class had scored 314 wpm – just over 100 wpm faster than Tony's score.

This demoralising piece of news was to change his life: as soon as the class ended he rushed up to the teacher and asked him how he could improve his speed. The teacher answered that there was no way of doing so, and that one's reading speed, like your IQ, our adult height and the colour of your eyes, was fundamentally unchangeable.

This did not quite ring true. Why?

Over to Tony: "I had just started a vigorous physical training programme, and had noticed dramatic changes in nearly every muscle of my body within a few weeks. If knowing the right exercises had enabled me to bring about such physical transformation, why shouldn't the appropriate visual and mental exercises allow me to change my reading speed, comprehension and memory of what I had read?

"These questions launched me on a search that soon had me cracking the 400 wpm barrier, and eventually reading comfortably at speeds of over 1000 wpm. Through these investigations, I realised that, on all levels, reading is to the mind as aerobic training is to the body."

"Once again, the authorities seemed to have got it wrong! We now know the radius of your eyes is extraordinarily wide, you can see far further to left or right then you might imagine. Try using a pointer, pen or pencil when you read, take in chunks at a time, all of these techniques will increase your reading and comprehension speed.

"By learning about the miracle of my eyes and the extraordinary capacity of my brain, I not only increased my speed, comprehension and memory; I also found myself able to think faster and more creatively, to make better notes, to pass exams with relative ease, to study more successfully, and to save days, weeks and even months of my time."

"Now consider your brain as a massive bio-computer. We already know about the miracle of the dormant power of your eyes. As you read on, try to guess what activity is being described.

"Wanting to approach a horizontal line that theoretically stretches to infinity in both directions, your super bio-computer manipulates an unbelievably complex system composed of millions of levers and pulleys, and directs them through three-dimensional space to that desired line.

"Your super bio-computer then swivels to the left, and takes in, at billions of units of information per second, the entire three-dimensional plane before it. It notices hundreds of three-dimensional objects, of different sizes and of every imaginable shape and colour. A few are not moving. Most are. Those that are moving are moving in different directions and are of multiple sizes, masses and shapes. Each one is travelling at its own unique velocity.

"In a split second your super bio-computer registers this entire geometry-in-motion scene and extrapolates precisely where every moving object will be within the next two-to-five seconds. It then swivels to the right, and with an entirely new three-dimensional vista composed at its own static and moving multi-varied geometric shapes, performs exactly the same kind of geometric calculations and predictions.

"Having completed these immensely complex calculations, matched them together, swivelled to the left to double check that all the multi-billion facets of reality are acting as they were predicted to do, your super bio-computer instructs the million-fold system of levers and pulleys to dance through the moving geometric shapes that are hurtling across the three-dimensional plane your brain wishes to traverse.

"Having successfully completed this action, your bio-computer brain then manipulates the lever/pulley system perfectly into one of the more rectangular geometric structures, and by subtle manipulation engineers it to move amongst the to-and-froing geometric landscape.

"Your super bio-computer brain then unerringly manipulates its own three-dimensional cube through tens to hundreds of miles of geometric space, magically avoiding any contact with the tens of thousands of objects that are coming at it from all directions, and at infinitely different angles and varying speeds.

"Through this entire time your super bio-computer brain has monitored and negotiated symbols, signals, flashing lights, sounds, right-angles, circles and semi-circles, gradients and innumerable impediments and obstacles.

"Upon reaching its destination, millions of such super bio-computer brains have been known, inexplicably, to exclaim, 'I can't do maths!'

"Having just done what?!

"Having just completed a non-stop series of billions-faceted geometric and algebraic equations with unerring accuracy! And all in aid of what? The common daily routing of walking across a busy street, getting into your car and driving home!

"Your day-to-day accomplishments in simply surviving this geometric world in which we live demonstrate that you are, by nature, a genius in the arts and sciences of geometry and spatial awareness."

• • • •

Einstein said
"There are no straight lines in the Universe"

Buzan said
"There are no straight lines in the
Mind Map Universe!"

Use CURVILINEAR branches in your Mind Maps,
NOT straight lines.

Don't waste your time and your life fighting both
Einstein and The Universe.

"Normal linear note taking and writing will put you into a semi-hypnotic trance, while Mind Mapping will greatly enhance your left and right brain cortical skills."

Tony Buzan

Chapter 3
Mightier Than The Sword

The Pen Is Taken Up

Tony's writing career began at the age of 8!

Tony's first book was a little tome: *The Book of My Pets*. This resulted in his first contact with the media as a result of the book winning second prize in his town of Whitstable's Pet Competition. *The Book of My Pets* also gave him his first taste of public notoriety, as he made himself none too popular by innocently proclaiming from the pages of the *Whitstable Gazette* that the world would be a far better place if all the humans were removed, leaving the animals and plants to live their lives undisturbed by us!

While at school, Tony contributed the occasional article to the school newspaper, and while at the University of British Columbia became a feature columnist for the University newspaper, *The Ubyssey*. He wrote an investigative and observational column titled *Indagatio* – 'the art and science of tracking down'.

When he returned to London in September 1966, his writing career began to blossom. He became a member of the National Union of Journalists (NUJ), a travel writer for *The Daily Telegraph*, and the Assistant Editor for *Nursery World* in the Haymarket Media Group. From 1969-1971, he was privileged to be the Editor of the International Journal for MENSA, the high IQ Society, which, with the approval of the Society, he renamed: *Intelligence*.

During this prolific period, he was asked by Anthony Cheatham, Director of Sphere Publications, and one of the rising young lions in the publishing world, if he could write two books, one on speed reading, and the other on memory. To 'seal-or-sink' the deal, Anthony gave Tony a surprise memory test. Tony applied the memory techniques he used at that time in his teaching and was able to memorise everything in the test immediately and perfectly. "Done deal!" said Anthony Cheatham, and within a year Tony's first two formally published books, *Speed Reading* and *Speed Memory*, were released in 1971. During that same period, he had been prolifically writing poems, and in the same year his first edition of poetry, *Spore One*, was published.

Since those early days, Tony has exploded into being a prolific author of world renown. He is the author/co-author of over 120 books on the brain, the body and learning, including the BBC's classic *Use Your Head*, as well as four volumes of poetry. *Use Your Head* was selected, at the turn of the century, by Waterstones bookshops, the Express Newspaper Group, and their advisors as one of the thousand greatest books of the previous millennium. The group recommended it as an essential part of the thousand-book library for the current millennium – the Millennium of the Mind.

As of 2013, Tony's 120+ books have been translated into all the main languages with a current total of 40, and are published and distributed throughout the globe, in over 200 countries. In total, they have sold over 7,000,000 copies. These works are published by over 100 publishers around the world, numbering among them most of the publishing giants. These include: BBC, Pearsons, Harper Collins, Collins Language, Simon & Schuster, Penguin, Foreign Language Teaching & Research Press (China), Gower, Hodder & Stoughton, Bertelsmann, Shanghai 99, Jarir, Utusan and Popuri.

The multi-million sales of all Tony's classic BBC Mind Set books (*The Mind Map Book, Use Your Head, The Speed Reading Book, Use Your Memory*) have made him BBC's most widely read international author.

Every book Tony writes, he first Mind Maps! The Mind Mapping of his books is the secret behind his extraordinary literary productivity.

Newspapers And Magazines

In addition to authoring over 120 books, Tony has edited major magazines, has written thousands of articles for both magazines and newspapers, and has designed articles for journalists writing about the brain, thinking, intelligence, Mind Maps and Tony's work and Thinking Systems.

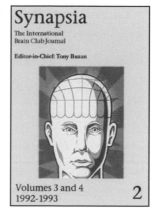

In 1989 he founded *Synapsia*, the first magazine devoted entirely to the brain and its functions, and both edited and wrote much of the magazine from the founding date.

Tony and/or his work have appeared in most of the world's leading newspapers and magazines, including *The Times*, where he contributed the obituary of World Draughts Champion Dr Marion Tinsley, as well as a major feature on his language learning courses. Also *The Telegraph*, *The Guardian*, *The Independent*, *The Daily Mail*, *The Daily Express*, *The Shimbun*, *The Straits Times*, *Newsweek*, *The Times*, *The New Yorker*, *Management Today*, *Human Resource*, *Leadership Magazine*, and *Excellence Magazine*.

Use Your Head – A Publishing Phenomenon

By 1973, the success of Tony's books, his work with underprivileged children and lecturing led to him being asked to do a ten-part television series for the BBC entitled *Use Your Head,* and a one-hour feature documentary on the brain for Thames Television entitled *The Evolving Brain*. In conjunction with these two television features, he was asked to write the programmes' accompanying books: *Use Your Head* and *The Evolving Brain*.

Within a week of being published, *Use Your Head* had sold out!

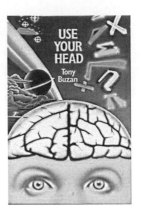

The book was immediately reprinted, and this reprinting sold out within the week!

And so it has continued to this very day with seven new revised and updated editions published in the years of 1982, 1989, 1995, 2000, 2003, 2006 and 2010, and over 50 printings appearing in the same time period.

The book has been labelled, 'a modern classic' by the BBC and still, after four decades, is an international best-seller.

Use Your Head, which formally introduced the global audience to Mind Mapping and to Tony's thinking systems for memory, creativity, speed reading, note-taking, note-making, and study skills (the Buzan Organic Study Technique) immediately led to requests for more books and articles, and for him to give lectures and presentations on all major continents.

The Children Of Use Your Head

Among the 120 authored and co-authored books produced after *Use Your Head* and up to the turn of the century, were:

Use Your Memory, a massive expansion of the original Speed Memory, presenting all the major memory systems, including the "new kid on the block": Mind Maps.

Master Your Memory, an advanced memory systems book, introducing Tony's second major memory invention after Mind Maps: The Self Enhancing Master Memory Matrix (SEM3).

The Mind Map Book (Fully Illustrated) with Tony's brother Professor Barry Buzan. The first comprehensive guide to Mind Maps and the theories behind them.

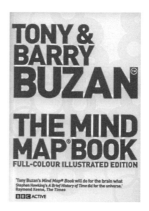

Buzan's Book of Genius with Raymond Keene, the complete analysis of the qualities of genius and a provocative ranking, based on those (teachable!), qualities, of the world's top 100 geniuses.

The Teach Yourself Revision Guides, GCE Level in 17 subjects; A Level in 8 subjects; thus introducing Mind Maps and Mental Literacy to the formal school study curriculum.

The Teach Yourself Literature Guides (28 titles), applying Mind Mapping and Mental Literacy to the study and appreciation of great literature.

Buzan's Book of Mental World Records with Raymond Keene, the first book to present all the major world records for the brain, including those in memory, creativity, IQ, chess, bridge, Go, IQ, crosswords, etc.

The New Millennium – A New Writing Explosion

The first decade of the new millennium saw an unprecedented acceleration in Tony Buzan's writing. As the century turned, his new book, *Head First*, was published. *Head First* introduced the definitions of, and how to develop, the newly identified multiple intelligences.

This book gave birth in 2001-2003 to *The Power of Intelligence* series: *The Power of Creative Intelligence, The Power of Physical Intelligence, The Power of Social Intelligence, The Power of Spiritual Intelligence,* and *The Power of Verbal Intelligence.*

As the last of *The Power of Intelligence* series was being published in 2003, so too was Tony's new book, *Brain Child*, a polemic/controversial argument on how to bring up a baby from the baby's brain's point of view!

Through 2003-2005, the revolutionary *Mind Maps for Kids* series was published, and began to change the way children around the world thought about themselves and about learning and study. The series included: *Introduction*, *Max Your Memory and Concentration*, and *Study Skills*.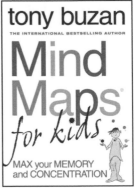

As 2005 drew to a close, more minds were opened with the publication of *The Ultimate Book of Mind Maps*, an in-depth look at the mental and physical theory behind the art and science of Mind Mapping.

In 2005 and 2006, Tony's new book, *Embracing Change*, expanded on TEFCAS, providing guidelines and the essential steps to 'make your future today'.

Throughout the decade, he had been working on, in addition to the aforementioned books, two volumes of poetry: *Requiem for Ted* and *Concordea*. These were published in limited hard-bound first editions, in 2007.

In this same year, the *BBC Study Skills Handbook* was published, and was described on the website www.ukparentslounge.com as: 'the perfect guide for any student who wants to get more from their studies, improve their brain power, consolidate their concentration and learn from the master of memory'. Also in 2007, Tony's new book *Age-Proof Your Brain* appeared, giving guidelines on life-long care for your brain, so that its cognitive skills and intelligences, as you get older, get better.

For a number of years Tony had been thinking about, and answering questions about, Mind Mapping and the application of Mental Literacy and Mind Maps to the learning of languages.

In 2008 and 2009, *Collins Language Revolution* was born, with Beginner and Beginner Plus Level courses in Spanish, French and Italian. Each *Collins Language Revolution* book comes in a pack which includes 2 CDs, and access to an interactive website specifically designed to use Mental Literacy and Mind Mapping techniques to review and reinforce the learning. These were followed in 2010 by new books for each language on the development of vocabulary, and the enhancing of grammar.

A major new publishing event for 2010 was the publication of *Mind Maps for Business* (with Chris Griffiths), the first comprehensive survey of the application of Mind Maps at all levels of, and for all functions in, businesses around the world. *Mind Maps for Business* is the first book to feature throughout Tony's new Mind Mapping software iMindMap. The book also features a specially dedicated website in which Tony Buzan and his co-author guide the reader in a series of personal video presentations into further theory, extensions and applications for each chapter. Within three months of publication, *Mind Maps for Business* was being translated into 16 different languages!

In 2012, Tony wrote *The Most Important Graph In The World* with Jennifer Goddard and Jorge Castaneda, *Brain Training with Kids* with Jennifer Goddard, *Modern Mind Mapping for Smarter Thinking* with Chris Griffiths and James Harrison.

Since 1971, Tony Buzan has written over 120 books – an average of three books per year! For four decades, the sales of his books have been accelerating exponentially.

"Tony Buzan is to the world of training the mind what the top boxing trainer is to the boxing champion."

Barry McGuigan
Champion

Barry McGuigan: Youngest ever Irish and British Boxer to be elected to the Boxing Hall of Fame

When I was at the height of my boxing career, it never occurred to me that the knowledge and use of words would become so important to me. At that time, my life was all about rigorous training, dedicated fitness regimes, total discipline and keeping my wits about me in the ring!

After retiring, I started a new and exciting career: that of a commentator for television coverage of boxing. It was then that I realised that my enormous enthusiasm for the sport I was watching needed a much wider range of words and expressions to convey its action and excitement. My every other word being 'terrific' didn't quite do the job. I determined to do something about it.

Inspired by the work of my dear friend Tony Buzan, I began a new path of discovery, which has grown into a real passion in my life. I set myself the task of improving my memory and vocabulary and of learning ten new words a week and then applying them, first in conversation, and then in my commentary work. I felt liberated! All the thoughts that I had wanted to convey but which were trapped within me were suddenly there,

I have followed Tony's work for many years, read many of his books and attended his lectures, Tony is to the world of training the mind what the top boxing trainer is to the boxing champion. I still keep to the discipline of learning ten new words each week. I am also determined to help my children have this fundamental ability."

• • • •

"The world is historically

mentally illiterate."

Tony Buzan

Chapter 4.

Praeceptor Orbis Terrarum - Teacher of the World

Tony Buzan has become one of the world's leading and most recognised educators and educational innovators. He has been the recipient of many educational awards, titles and positions, and for 50 years has taught at schools, universities, businesses and governments globally, and lectured in over 70 countries.

His educational inventions and innovations, including new approaches to reading, learning, memory and creativity, and featuring the ultimate learning and thinking tool, the Mind Map, have positively influenced the lives of hundreds of millions of people. Surprisingly, his first love as a boy was nature, with education nowhere on the screen. However, as we have seen, it was this love of nature that led to his growing passion for, and realisation of, the importance of education as a global force.

Tony: "In my second year at University, I strode purposefully into the library, and asked the librarian where I could find a book on my brain and how to use it. She immediately directed me to the medical section of the library!

"When I explained that I did not wish to operate on my brain, but to use it, I was politely informed that there were no such books.

"I left the library in astonishment.

"Like others around me, I was going through the typical student's 'pilgrim's progress', the slow realisation that the volume of academic work is increasing and that the brain is starting to buckle under the strain of all the thinking, creativity, memory, problem-solving, analysis and writing required. Again, like others, I had begun to experience not only diminishing returns but accelerating non-returns. The more I took notes and studied, the less, paradoxically, I seemed to succeed!

"The logical progression of either situation led me to catastrophe. If I cut down my studying, I would not absorb the necessary information and would consequently do progressively badly; if I were studying harder, making more notes, putting in more time, I was similarly spiralling into failure.

"The answer, I assumed, must lie in the way I was using my intelligence and thinking skills – thus my visit to the library.

"As I walked away from the library that day, I realised that the 'problem' of not being able to find the books I needed was actually a blessing in disguise. For if such books were not available, then I had happened upon virgin territory of the most staggering importance.

"I began to study every area of knowledge I felt would help shed light on the basic questions:

- How do I learn how to learn?
- What is the nature of my thinking?
- What are the best techniques for memorising?
- What are the best techniques for creative thinking?
- What are the best current techniques for faster and efficient reading?
- What are the best current techniques for thinking in general?
- Is there a possibility of developing new thinking techniques or one master technique?

"As a consequence of these questions, I began to study psychology, the neuro-physiology of the brain, semantics, neuro-linguistics, information theory, memory and mnemonic techniques, perception, creative thinking and the general sciences. Gradually I realised that the human brain functioned more effectively and efficiently if its various physical aspects and intellectual skills were allowed to work harmoniously with each other, rather than being divided.

"The tiniest things produced the most significant and satisfying results. For example, simply combining the two cortical skills of words and colours transformed my note-taking. The simple addition of two colours to my notes improved my memory of those notes by more than 100 per cent, and perhaps even more importantly, made me begin to enjoy what I was doing.

"Little by little, an overall architecture began to emerge, and as it did, I began to coach, as a hobby, pupils who had been described as 'learning disabled', 'hopeless', 'dyslexic', Educationally Sub Normal, 'backward', and 'delinquent'. All these so-called 'failures' very rapidly changed into good students, a number of them rising to the top of their respective classes.

"One young girl, Barbara, had been told that she had the lowest IQ her school had ever registered. Within a month of learning how to learn, she raised her IQ to 160, and eventually graduated as the top student from her college.

"Pat, a young American of extraordinary talent, who had been falsely categorised as learning disabled, subsequently said (after having shattered a number of creativity and memory tests), 'I wasn't learning disabled, I was learning deprived!'

"By the early 1970s, artificial intelligence had arrived and I could buy a megabyte computer and with that computer I could receive a 1,000-page operating manual. Yet, in our supposedly advanced stage of civilisation, we were all coming into the world with the most astounding complex bio-computer, quadrillions of times more powerful than any known computer, and where were our operating manuals?

"It was then that I decided to write a series of books based on my research: *An Encyclopaedia of the Brain and Its Use*. I started in 1971, and as I did so the image on the horizon became ever clearer – it was the growing concept of Radiant Thinking and Mind Mapping.

"In the early stages of its development, I envisaged Mind Mapping being used primarily for memory. However, after months of discussion, my brother Barry convinced me that creative thinking was an equally important application of this technique.

"Barry had been working on the theory of Mind Mapping from a very different perspective, and his contribution enormously accelerated my development of the Mind Mapping success.

"In my fourth year of university, by which time my knowledge of investigations into learning and study skills and memory had led me to improve my own capabilities, I began, on both a charitable and small-income-earning basis, to coach younger students who were having problems at school.

"One day I was approached about the possibility of teaching an ineducatable young girl. Her problems were many, including the fact that she was, and had always been, the bottom student in her class, a problem compounded by the fact that she had an elder sister at university who was intelligent, blonde and beautiful, popular and athletic. I was asked if I wanted to take on the challenge of such an impossible student, and obviously said yes.

"A few days later, I was knocking on the large wooden door of a house in the suburbs, which was answered by a blonde, very blue and bright-eyed young girl.

"'My name is Tony Buzan, and I have come here to see your sister Barbara,' I said by way of introduction.

"'I'm Barbara,' she said with a big smile.

"I had obviously assumed that she was the elder sister, and now assumed that she was joking.

"'So you're the one who's having difficulty at school?' I said, with a slight tinge of irony.

"'Yes,' she said directly and brightly. 'Come up to my study and we can get to work.' I followed her up the stairs, already aware that somehow things were out of joint.

"Our first hour together was spent overviewing the subjects she was studying, discussing and confirming the fact that she was usually at or near the bottom of the class, and spending some time preparing her for a geography exam she was taking in a few days time. During our discussion time, she informed me, among many things, that the headmistress of her school had told her that she had scored the lowest mark on an IQ test ever recorded for that school.

"Firstly, even though I had been with her for such a short time, I found that utterly implausible, and secondly found it appalling that authority would lay such a monstrous burden on a child's intelligence. Distant bells rang and when we were going through her geography, Barbara immediately understood everything I explained to her, and when I tested her at the end of our session, she was virtually perfect. I left confident that the change had been made, and that her test results would confirm my estimates of her real intelligence.

"The following week I returned full of positive expectations, and asked her cheerily how she had done in the exam.

"'Bottom again,' she said matter-of-factly, and I exclaimed, 'How could you?'

"'I don't know,' she said. 'I just came bottom again.'

"'OK, let's move on,' I said and we began to go over her other subjects' preparation for her next set of tests. As before she learnt everything I taught her at an incredibly rapid pace, and seemed to be able to remember it very clearly as well. During our conversations she constantly riddled them with wit, and on two occasions totally out-smarted me, a bit embarrassing, as I was a number of years older than her, in my final year at university, and a member of the debating team! She couldn't be as unintelligent as her life-time performance and teachers' and parents' reports were confirming she was.

"In the middle of one of our discussions, she suddenly grabbed my arm, moved her mouth close to my ear, and said, in a whispered, very confidential tone, 'Can you hear that music?'

Faintly in the background there was a violin concerto playing.

"'Yes, I can,' I said.

"'Do you like it?' she said, again in a whisper and very confidentially.

"'Yes, I do,' I said.

"And whispering even more quietly and more confidentially she whispered, 'So do I.'

"I said, 'Barbara, you don't have to whisper about that. You can just say it.'

"'But isn't that kind of music only for very special people who live in very big houses or palaces?' she said.

"'No, it's classical music, and it's for everybody.'

"'But when I say I like it, people say that I am crazy,' Barbara said.

"A picture was beginning to form and on the third week, again expecting that her performances would have improved, I was once again met with the almost cheerful news that she'd failed again!

"I knew something was majorly wrong, yet couldn't put my finger precisely upon what it was. That evening I was invited to dinner with her mother, father and elder sister and had both a delightful meal and delightful conversation. The conversation was slightly marred for me by the fact that whenever Barbara contributed either an insightful comment or a witty observation, she was immediately dismissed by the other members of the family and sideways comments were made about her, as the not-so-bright one of the family.

"The next week, I came back and she had once again done badly in school.

"There had to be a reason, other than her lack of intelligence of which she certainly did not have a lack.

"Like Poirot or Sherlock, my mind searched for the solution to the *Case of the Brilliant Moron*! Suddenly, an inspiration flashed its presence. I immediately initiated a three-pronged investigation: Firstly, I asked, 'How many different schools did you go to between the ages of five and ten?'

"'Quite a few,' she said. 'My parents moved around a lot when I was very young.'

"Suspicion one confirmed.

"Secondly, I asked her to read a page from one of her history texts while I prepared some other work and games for her. My interest was not in preparing work or games for her; it was in how long she took to read the page. After five minutes, she still had her finger on the page less than three quarters of the way down.

"Suspicion two confirmed.

"Thirdly, I asked her to read me one of the short essays she had written for English, and for which, as with everything else, she had received bottom marks. She first showed me the one page essay, and I observed that it was total gibberish. There were no proper words, and the page was filled with strange scrawl. Rather than commenting on this, I asked her to read it to me. She read it with total aplomb and made it sound completely sensible.

"I had already come to the conclusion that she was clever, but this was super-creativity: to create a comprehensible and immaculate story from meaningless scribble was a pretty creative accomplishment!

"I thanked her, and we went on to study other work. In the meantime, I had more or less memorised by the essay she had recited, and near the end of the lesson asked her to read it to me again. To my utter amazement, she did! And not only again, but exactly the same essay as she had read before. I felt as if I were in the presence of a miracle story unfolding.

"Next, I pointed to different words on the page and asked her what they were, and she told me immediately the same words as she had read in that section of her recitation. The astounding conclusion, which went far beyond any of my initial theories was the following: Barbara, having been to nearly twenty different schools while she was learning to read, had been taught many different methods of reading, each one of which was stopped almost before it began and substituted for the next method. Her brain, as happens with many young children in such transitional situations, had quite logically and sensibly decided that learning this stuff was a waste of time, because firstly you never finished it, and secondly it was always wrong by the time you got to your next school. Therefore, don't waste time on it.

"Barbara couldn't read but was intelligent enough to pretend that she could. Further, and this is what truly astounded me and affects me to this very day, because she couldn't make head or tails of the standard alphabet and its language, she had made up her own language!! The reason why she had been able to read her essay perfectly once and then perfectly again later, was not because she was cleverly creating on the spot and then remembering what she had said; she was reading her own language.

"I had a genius on my hands!

"I asked her if she wanted to learn to read the English language, to which she answered 'Yes'. In the next few lessons I taught her, and she absorbed it almost instantaneously. Once she had mastered the basics, I asked her what kind of book she would first like to read, and suggested simple stories about stewardesses, or girl's sports teams, or light romances.

"She listened to my suggestions with a slight look of bemusement on her face, and then asked. 'Are there any books on how different people think about God and Heaven?'

"The first ever book that Barbara wanted to read was not light adventure or light romance, it was comparative religion! After I had momentarily recovered from my embarrassment at having so grossly and prejudicially underestimated her, I asked her what she thought Heaven was. She paused, placed her forefinger on her cheek, raised her eyes thoughtfully sideways to the ceiling, and said... 'I think...that Heaven is a place where everybody is the same as you are (sic).'

"Within a few months, Barbara was the top student in her class. She had also written her first essay, a twenty-five page report on dental health, a subject that had always fascinated her. She was given another battery of IQ tests, and turned out to have a real IQ of over 145, one of the highest the school had ever recorded! She graduated from school, was accepted into a top dental hygienists' college, graduated from that, bought herself an apartment in the countryside by a lake, and filled that apartment with shelves and shelves of guess what? Classical music!

"Barbara's story had sharpened and refined the impressions and conclusions I had formed because of the school nature story, conclusions which were neatly summarised in Gray's poem *Elegy in a Country Churchyard* in which the poet muses, while looking at the grave of a common man."

> ### *Elegy in a Country Churchyard*
>
> Full many a gem of purest ray serene
> The dark unfathom'd caves of ocean bear:
> Full many a flower is born to blush unseen,
> And waste its sweetness on the desert air.
> Some village-Hampden, that with dauntless breast
> The Little tyrant of his fields withstood,
> Some mute inglorious Milton here may rest,
> Some Cromwell, guiltless of his country's blood.
>
> *Thomas Gray, 1750*

A further story emphasises how easily mediocrity and conformity can smother budding genius:

One day Tony was travelling by train through the London Underground. He had been making the same journey for a number of months, knew the time it took, and had established a reading/working/resting/people-watching routine.

As Tony recalls: "On this particular day I was sitting behind a mother and her very young daughter. Halfway through the journey I noticed, with some alarm, that the train seemed to be travelling faster than usual, and seemed still be accelerating.

I rapidly went into panic-thought mode, envisioning us hurtling increasingly faster out of control towards a demolition destination.

"As my mind was being gripped by a rising fear, the little girl in front of me, who had obviously become aware also of the train's speed, turned to her mother, and grabbing excitedly on her sleeves said: 'Mummy, wouldn't it be amazing if this train could keep going faster, until it was going so fast it could take us into the next day, because then when we got home we could tell Daddy what was going to happen tomorrow!'

"The mother's reaction was to turn around and shout: 'Don't you ever say stupid, crazy things like that to me again! Now be quiet, and sit still.'

"The little girl retreated into her shell, the genius who had already, before her first days at junior school, launched her imagination into those wonderful realms that had so intrigued all the great physicists of the nineteenth and twentieth centuries. Had she been encouraged appropriately, I am sure we would have seen her as one of the Nobel Prize winners in the early part of this century.

"In my young life, I had encountered several educational situations in which exactly the opposite of what had been assumed, was true.

"How many millions, tens of millions, hundreds of millions or even billions of such stories were there where the innate intelligence and brilliance of the child had either not been appreciated, or had been actively suppressed?"

The Frightening Grip of Social Conformity

Tony had been asked to help in an experiment on human behaviour, to show the incredible and unknown power each of us have over others.

The experiment was originally designed by an insightful investigator of human social interaction by the name of Professor Asche. It was performed as follows:

"Picture a small, fairly bare room. At the front is a plain desk with one chair behind it. About 10 feet in front of the desk, and facing it, is a row of three chairs. The whole arrangement is much like a mini theatre. There is nothing else in the room. The experiment involved five people: two 'psychologists' in 'official' white scientific coats, and three observers.

In the experiment, one of the 'psychologists' stood and presented 'visual tests' to the observers, while the other 'psychologist' recorded the results and described the experiment to the observers. Tony's role was as the recorder and this is what he had to say to the three students:

"You are going to be shown a number of cards. On each card there will be three vertical black bars. Each bar will be labelled 'A', 'B' or 'C' at the top of it. Your task is to state, in order, the letter of the tallest, middle and shortest bar. The order of the bars on each card will vary throughout. The person to the left will always go first, the person in the middle second and the person to the right, last."

"However, there was a mischievous twist to the plot! Unknown to the observer sitting on the right, the other two observers were in on the experiment! The cards had been especially arranged and the two false observers had both rehearsed giving predetermined incorrect answers.

"To the first two cards presented, both 'One' and 'Two' shot back the correct answers. To the third card 'One', with a mix of correct and incorrect responses, feigned anguish but eventually stated that the medium was the tallest, the tallest the medium and the shortest, the shortest. 'Two, ummed and ahhhed on cue, rocked back and forward in his chair, voiced his indecision, and then finally decided, 'Yes, yes I agree....' And gave the same answers as 'One'.

"You can guess the state of mind of poor 'Number Three', and imagine how you would react in that situation.

"This procedure was repeated for a total of 17 cards. 'One' increasingly giving more wrong answers, and 'Two' always agonizing before agreeing with him when he was wrong. On the rare occasions when 'One' answered correctly and immediately, 'Two' always responded with similar conviction and speed.

"We repeated this same experiment with 20 different 'Number Threes', conscientiously recording all their responses. What do you think they were?

Do you think they all disagreed with 'One' and Two'?

Do you think some of them did?

Do you think none of them did?

"The results were stunning, shook me to the core, and made me realise for the first time in my life just how powerful our social conformity over each other truly is.

"Over 60 percent of 'Threes' totally agreed with everything that the misleading numbers 'One' and 'Two' said! When the 'Threes' were retested on the same cards in isolation, they scored 100 per cent accuracy. When confronted with their test results and asked to explain the discrepancies, they said that they had physically seen the correct relationships. They had, however, been so persuaded by the responses of numbers 'One' and 'Two' that they felt they must have somehow been wrong in what they saw and so decided to 'go along with the crowd'.

"Astonishingly, a small percentage of this 'agreeing group', when confronted with their two massively different results on the same tests, said that they had 'called it as I saw it!'

"This suggests that the power of social interaction is so great that it can actually completely distort our perceptions.

"Even those rugged individualists who stuck to their true perceptions against the socially persuasive power of 'One' and 'Two', went through either agonies or violent emotions. One individual began increasingly to look quizzically at the others, and in the later tests took out his comb and measured the bars much like an artist measuring for a picture!

"Another, when number 'One' stated flatly the shortest was the longest and the longest the shortest on one card, exploded in fury at him, exclaiming, 'What's the matter with you, you idiot, can't you SEE?'

"At least this reaction indicates that some people adhere to their beliefs, no matter what the crowd is saying.

"Asche's experiment, which has been repeated thousands of times with similar results, underlines the fact that even basic social interactions have the power to produce in us strong emotions, to make us consider our own truths doubtful, and even to change the very way in which we see – not to mention demonstrating the hold social conformity has over us!

Indeed, as a teenager Tony made an effort to conform with his social peers in order to become more popular. How to win friends and influence people? It is said that on his deathbed the atheistic 18th century French philosopher, Voltaire, was visited by a Catholic priest who begged him to renounce sin and The Devil. Voltaire responded: 'This is no time to be making new enemies!'

In his teens, Tony thought that the way to become popular was to be 'smart' and fit. He went to parties and social events flaunting his high IQ, analysing the faults in others, getting into discussions in which he always tried to prove that his 'opponents' were wrong and he was right, and showing off his good (but rigid!) physique.

Having been told that a high IQ and a fit body were the paths to success, he was taken aback by the number of enemies he was unintentionally making, and the lack of friendship his 'smart/tough/correct' presence was generating.

Tony: "My realisation that simply winning debates was not the way to social success was helped along by my father. Once, when I had won the battle – the argument – and lost the war in a social situation, my father gave me a little poem that he said would help me improve my social awareness. The poem went as follows:

Here lies the body of Jonathan Grey,
Who died defending his right of way,
He was perfectly right as he sped along
But he's just as dead as if he'd been wrong!

"I began to look around at those who were obviously more socially successful than me. I noticed that they were doing many things that at that time were alien to me, and the opposite of what I had been taught was 'acceptable behaviour' in my school life.

"The most popular (and most happy) people were always smiling and laughing and telling jokes. (I couldn't!); they were expressive and open, helpful and considerate of others, and tended to avoid arguments. To make matters even worse for my sensitive teenage soul, they were much more relaxed, much more confident, and much more successful in attracting romance!

"Gradually the light began to dawn. My IQ and muscles were not the only strengths I had to develop if I wished to be socially successful: I had to pay attention to the vitally important skills – of Social Intelligence.

"When I was still in the 'Mighty Muscle/Mighty Vocabulary' stage of developing my Social Intelligence, I would tend to 'dominate the airwaves'.

This was because I thought that the more brilliant points I made, the more brilliant the conversation was. This was a very one-sided and limited view. Nature stepped in and taught me a very valuable lesson.

"Just before an important social occasion, I contracted an irritating throat infection. To my chagrin, I could hardly utter a word. At the party, I met someone who was passionate about many things. We began an animated conversation, but because of my weakened voice, I was soon reduced to nodding, massaging the conversation with well-placed 'uhuhms' and very occasionally asking a question, which gave my companion the opportunity to launch into another five minute conversational journey.

"When we eventually parted, I assumed that he would consider me an utter bore, as I had contributed probably less than 5 per cent to the conversation, and he comfortably more than 95 percent. To my amazement, I heard later that he considered me a fascinating conversationalist!

"How could this be so?

"We had had a wonderful conversation. He had entertained me with delightful stories and provocative concepts; my body, rather than my voice, had 'spoken back to him', indicating that I was interested, was involved and, by my supportive presence, I had allowed him to explore his own thoughts in good company, and therefore not only to have a conversation with me but also with himself.

"I realised that listening gave me this wonderful opportunity to be completely relaxed in a conversation, to be entertained with wonderful tales and thoughts, as well as allowing me to give someone else the opportunity to be freely expressive. Up to that time, I had been guilty of social crime which Leonardo da Vinci had castigated: that most people 'listen without hearing'.

The Sensei

"By the time I was in my mid twenties I had become, what I thought, was physically fit. I had gone from being the traditional 'seven-stone weakling' to a swimmer, runner, budding karate exponent, weightlifter and physical fitness coach, and I had learned to listen. I thought I had arrived. Not so – as I was soon to find out!

"At that time I had a friend, Kurt, who engaged in similar activities, and who was also an accomplished horseman, all-round athlete and stuntman. We had heard about the 'new' Japanese martial art of aikido, so one evening we went to a beginners' class to find out what it was all about. A motley group of about 14 individuals shuffled nervously on the side of the dojo, waiting for the class to begin. Our instructor, the Sensei, a five-foot Japanese 5th Dan, dressed in the traditional black 'skirt' of the Samurai warrior, strolled up and down in front of us, examining us all intently.

"Finally, he came up to Kurt and myself, and said, 'Haawww, you two look velly fit, velly strong!' and he beckoned us onto the mat with a flick of his head. We both thought how perceptive he was to recognise the superb state of our physical fitness. How little did we know.....

"The Sensei walked into the middle of the mat, and knelt down, his shins resting on the mat, his buttocks resting on his heels and his body perfectly relaxed and poised. He calmly held out both his arms so that they were straight, parallel to the mat, and extended them directly to his left and to his right. He then gestured that Kurt and I should stand on either side of him.

"'Glab lists!' he said, 'and make me fall over!'

"Kurt and I looked at each other in disbelief. Did he really want two powerhouses like us to make a fool of him in front of a beginners' class? Surely there could be nothing easier than pulling a small man off balance when two much bigger men had two hands on each of his wrists? As the Sensei continued to kneel and look forward, Kurt and I nodded to each other and indicated 'Backwards'.

"We simultaneously grabbed his wrists… and simultaneously experienced the first of a number of shocks that were about to happen in rapid succession. His wrists, rather than feeling like a small man's wrists, felt like a fire hose with water turned full on! Unsettled, we nevertheless carried on, and together gave an enormous yank to topple him (easily, we thought) backwards.

"The second shock – he didn't fall backwards! Instead, his fire hose arms moved slightly backwards and then returned to their original position. The truth was beginning to dawn…

"Turning to us he said 'Haawww, must glip lists harder! And so we did. Kurt and I communicating by eye and slight head nods, tried surprising him backwards again, then sideways, and finally forwards. The same thing happened – nothing! With a wry grin on his face, the Sensei said, 'Must slip harder, must tly harder!' and still nothing happened.

"Eventually as Kurt and I continued our futile efforts, the Sensei said, 'Haawww – not so stlong! Not so powerful', and as he said this, he gently gestured with his wrists and hands. The result of this minor movement was that both Kurt and I ended up in crumpled heaps on the floor beside him, as the watching beginners – and, eventually, us as well – all laughed.

"The lesson the Sensei had taught was a profound one. Physical Intelligence and power is not just muscular strength and general fitness. In addition to these necessary qualities, it is the mental power and fitness that can direct the otherwise physically fit body to even greater feats of strength, power and 'intelligence'."

Having suffered a slight setback on the physical front, young Tony was about to experience a corresponding shock in the arena of mental power performance.

The Professor

A student sat, frightened and enthralled. It was the first lesson of his first day at university. He, like the others in his class, had been forewarned that Professor Clark was not only the most brilliant graduate in English the university had ever had; he also looked down on his students from the height of his genius, and used his mental might to embarrass and confuse them. The Professor had deliberately come in late – to add to the tension!

Professor Clark strode nonchalantly into the room, and scanned the class with fiery eyes and a derisive smile.

Rather than going to his desk and ordering his papers in preparation, he stopped in front of his desk, clasped his hands firmly behind his back, and, with that same intent stare accompanied by a sneer, he said, 'First year English? I'll call the roll'. He then began to bark out, machine-gun fashion, the names of the petrified students:

'Abrahamson?' 'Here, sir!'
'Adams?'   'Here, sir!'
'Barlow?'   'Here, sir!'
'Bush?'   'Here, sir!'
'Buzan?'   'Here, sir!'

(all names - apart from one - have been changed here and in what follows, to protect the innocent)

When he came to the next name, he barked out, 'Cartland?', to which there was a deathly silence. Looking even more intently, the Professor, like some Grand Inquisitor, made soul-burning eye contact with each petrified student, as if expecting them to 'own up' to their already-identified name. Still receiving no response, he sighed deeply, and said, at twice the speed of normal speech: 'Cartland?... Jeremy Cartland, address 2761 West Third Avenue; phone number 794 6231; date of birth September 25th 1941; mother's name Sue, father's name Peter; ... Cartland?' Still no response! The silence became almost unbearable until, at exactly the right moment, he punctuated it with a shouted and terminal 'Absent!'

And so on and on the Professor continued, call the roll without hesitation. Whenever a student was absent he would go through the same. 'Cartland routine', presenting the entire database about the absentee even though he could have had no way of knowing, on this first day, who was going to be present and who was going to be absent, even though he had never seen any one of the students before. To everyone in the class it became increasingly apparent that he knew, in the same astounding detail, the same basic biographical information about each of them.

When he had completed the roll call with 'Zygotski?'... 'Here, Sir!' he looked at the students sardonically and said, with a droll smile, 'That means Cartland, Chapman, Harkstone, Hughes, Luxmore, Mears and Trovey are absent!' He paused again, and then said, 'I'll make a note of that...some time!'

So saying, he turned and left the room in stunned silence.

To the enthralled students, it was one of those moments where a life's 'Impossible Dream' became possible; the dream of training his memory so that it could, in a multitude of special situations, function properly.

To be able to remember the names and dates of birth and death and all the important facts about the major artists, composers, writers and other 'greats'!

To be able to remember languages!

To be able to remember the giant catalogues of data from biology and chemistry!

To be able to remember any list he wanted!

To be able to remember like the Professor!

The astonished student leapt out of his seat, charged out of the classroom and caught up with Professor Clark in the hallway. He blurted out his question: 'Sir, how did you do that?' With the same imperious manner, the Professor responded, 'Because, son, I'm a Genius!' And once again turned away, not hearing the student's mumbled response, 'Yes, sir, I know, but still, how did you do that?!'

For two months he pestered 'The Genius', who finally befriended him, and surreptitiously in class translated for him 'the magic formula' for constructing the memory system that had allowed him to so dazzle the students on that memorable first day.

For the next 20 years the student devoured every book he could find on memory, creativity and the nature of the human brain, with the vision constantly in mind of creating new Super Memory Systems that went beyond even what his Professor had been able to accomplish.

The first of these new systems was the Memory Mind Map, a 'Swiss army knife thinking tool for the brain', that allowed the user not only to remember with accuracy and flexibility but also to create, plan, think, learn and communicate on the basis of that memory.

After the Mind Map came the giant, enjoyable and easy-to-use Self Enhancing Master Memory Matrix (SEM3) that would act as a database, allowing people to have immediate access to whatever major information structures were important and necessary to them.

The enthralled student was Tony Buzan!

In 1959, Tony was elected Head Prefect of his school, and in that position had the responsibility of making many presentations, including those to parents, public bodies, the school's student body, and to disciplinary committees! At the end of his graduating year, he was elected Valedictorian.

From 1960-1964 his debating skills were honed in the debating society at the University of British Columbia Debating Society, after which, in a sabbatical year, he learned other necessary speaking and corporate skills, working on construction sites, in agriculture, and corporate training courses.

The academic year 1965-1966 was to have a major impact on, and a change of direction of, Tony's life. Let him tell this part of the story:

"In September of 1965, I was invited to graduate studies and to lecture, as well as to run for Inaugural Student President, of the newly completed Simon Fraser University. Simon Fraser had been designed on a neo-Grecian model, and to be the embodiment of a 'new Athens'. The university was perched on top of a small mountain, overlooking a river valley.

"The admissions policy for this new university was a simple and revolutionary one: if you could demonstrate that you could think, had thought, and had done something effective about what you had thought, you would be admitted to this extraordinary new campus.

"The mid-1960s were a time of global thinking revolutions, and the applications came from all corners of the globe, and from all political, ideological, sociological, and philosophical extremes. Simon Fraser University was a melting-pot of revolutionary thinkers!

"I ran for the post of Inaugural President of the University's Student Council and on the basis of the campaign that promised constant contact with the student body, a 'Speaker's Corner', a cultural programme, a new student newspaper to be called *The Peak*, the guarantee of the freedom of expression, and the defence of student rights, I was elected. The following months were riotous, unexpected in their content, and formative.

"Virtually every week there was a movement to have me impeached! One week it would come from the extreme right, accusing me of Communist leanings; the next week it would come from the far left, accusing me of being a Right wing extremist; the next week it was because I was not involved enough as President of the Council with student affairs; the next week it was because I was too involved with student affairs, and so on.

"Every week I had to stand at the top of the stairs of the Acropolis-like building, and defend my position against my attackers to the mass students below.

"I managed to complete my Presidency unimpeached!

The Acropolis and Parthenon in Athens Greece - inspiration for Simon Fraser University and later Tony Buzan's Renaissance Academy

"The Presidency also taught me many other life skills, as I presided over an annual operating budget of £1 million, had to deal with the press and the media, and also had to maintain good relations with the local community.

"I also learned many valuable lessons from the President of the University, Dr. Ian McTaggart-Cowan. One of my favourite examples being a time when I had confronted the local authorities over the towing away of students' cars, causing considerable disturbance to the local community.

"McTaggart-Cowan called me to his office and in a very severe tone said: 'Buzan, you've overstepped the boundaries'. Maintaining his stern posture, he then proceeded to tell me, with a growing twinkle in his eye, that I should have overstepped the boundaries. He then said, 'If you don't overstep the boundaries, you will never know where they are. Take the risk, Buzan, and every time you do overstep the boundaries, I'll push you back!' and so saying he patted me on the shoulder, and guided me out of his office..."

Tony's life work began to take form...

After graduating, Tony's first teaching post came in 1965/66, when he was a lecturer in psychology, English and creative writing. It was during this period that he began to realise that the standard method of lecturing from linear notes in a linear way was not only boring to his students, it was boring to him! He began to apply the information he had learnt about memory, creativity, neurophysiology and his other investigations, to teaching, presenting and communicating, as well as to note-taking. In 1966, Tony returned to England, where he worked for the Inner London Education Authority (ILEA) as a Special Projects teacher, dealing primarily with delinquent and disadvantaged children, and also the gifted and talented (this was also during his editorship of the MENSA International Journal *Intelligence*).

During this period, time and time again, his observation and assumption that there was more in there than was being realised, came true. Also during this period, Tony's educational thrust expressed itself through magazines and books, including his assistant editing of *Nursery World*, a magazine on how to bring up and educate babies and young children, and the authoring and presenting of the *Use Your Head* book and ten-part television series in 1974.

This led to him being asked to lecture around the world, and this he has done to the present day. On average, Tony visits over twenty countries per year and lectures at primary schools, secondary schools, leading universities and colleges, businesses and to government bodies.

In the early 1970s, Tony had developed the concept of Mental Literacy: the study of the alphabets of the brain's cognitive and physical skills, and the transferring of the knowledge of those alphabets into application in the fields of learning, learning how to learn, thinking, memory and creativity. In addition to his own teaching, he formed, in 1970, the first iteration of his Buzan Centres LMG, the Learning Methods Group, in which he taught teachers to teach students 'How to Learn How to Learn.'

In the late 1970s, having observed that in mass pop concerts children, after two hours, would leave having learnt many songs and dance movements, Tony developed the idea of the Super Class. This idea he demonstrated successfully in Jamaica, teaching a class of 200 senior teenagers in a small cricket stadium in Kingston, Jamaica. Tony had begun to set records for the largest classes ever and to open the boundaries concerning the number of children who could be taught at one time.

Hearing of the Jamaica 200, the Ministry of Education in South Africa asked Tony if he could do the same for 500 children in Soweto. If this was successful, an even larger number could be attempted. Soweto 500 was a success, and the decision was made to arrange a course for 2,000 students.

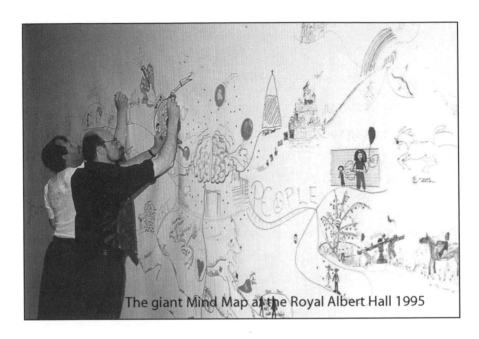
The giant Mind Map at the Royal Albert Hall 1995

In 1981, with the support of the South African Ministry of Education, Tony multiplied the Jamaican total by ten, teaching a full three-day Mental Literacy course to 2,000 Soweto school students in a stadium in Soweto. From that time on, Tony regularly taught classes of 1,000 or more.

In the late 1990s, on National Brain Day, the Chairman of Swindon Football Club, Rikki Hunt, sponsored the largest class yet: 4,000 children in the Swindon Town Football Stadium, an event that was televised nationally.

On New Year's Eve, as the 21st century began, Tony set the record for the largest ever single school class taught on television: 100,000 children taught in one day, in ten different groups of ten thousand simultaneously linked by satellite to ten locations in England and the United States of America.

He continued to extend the concept of the Super Class, in 2005 Teaching 9,000 school children, in two groups of 4,500, at the Royal Albert Hall in London. 2005 was a particularly eventful educational year. The BBC had challenged Tony to put his reputation on the line by taking six extremely disadvantaged and at-risk children, to see if training in Mind Maps and Mental Literacy could change their behaviours, attitudes and cognitive profiles.

To make the task even harder, he was given only seven sessions with the children. As Dr. Vivian Hill, Director of Professional Education Psychology Training at the Institute of Education, University of London, who was monitoring the process said, had she not known the process she would have assumed that the before and after cognitive profiles were those of completely different children. The BBC declared this to be a unique social experiment. Every one of the six children decided to stay in school, and successfully completed their year. As Tony concluded:

"Humans are hard-wired to learn. Everyone wants to be bright, to be loved, and to be successful. The *In Search of Genius Mind Mapping and Mental Literacy* module demonstrated that no child is ever a lost cause."

The following year, in March 2006, he took part in the Great Education Debate: Curriculum versus Creativity at the National Teachers Education Conference in England. Taking the side (obviously) of Creativity, his keynote speech emphasised the argument that Creativity is a vital ingredient for success on every level, and that our education systems need to pay attention to fanning the flames of generative thought, rather than stifling them with an overly prescriptive curriculum.

The concluding vote, after a lively discussion, was 198 votes to 2 in favour of Creativity! Other participants included Sir Ken Robinson (world renowned speaker on education and creativity) and Professor Chris Woodhead, former Chief Inspector of Schools who headed the Curriculum side of the debate. Tim Brighouse, Commissioner of London Schools, acted as a moderator.

In 2007, Tony completed and had published by the BBC, the then best-selling *Buzan Study Skills Handbook*, which has been described on www.ukparentslounge.com as "the perfect guide for any student who wants to get more from their studies, improve their brain power, consolidate their concentration and learn from the Master of Memory Tony Buzan."

In June 2009, at the 14th International Conference on Thinking, Tony, with Malaysia's Minister of Higher Education, and with the Vice Chancellor of the Graduate School of Management of the University of Putra Malaysia, officially launched the Age of Intelligence with the support of the 2,000 delegates, and with Professors Edward De Bono and Howard Gardner.

In a second keynote, Tony introduced and launched Buzan's Taxonomy for Reading, which extended Bloom's original Taxonomy. In the new Taxonomy, the guide for teachers around the world for teaching children how to read, now includes the vital steps, many not previously included, of: Recognition; Assimilation; Comprehension; Understanding; Retention; Recall; Communication; Use and Application.

In his educational life to date, Tony Buzan has physically taught hundreds of thousands of people, and has reached out through the media and electronic world to touch billions, who have read his articles and interviews in newspapers and magazines, who have seen his television programmes, and who have made his web presence in excess of 90 million pages.

He has worked with the Ministries of Educations in Singapore, Australia, England, Scotland, China, Malaysia, and Mexico, and has helped at every level of education, working especially for those with any form of learning difficulty, and also working ceaselessly to help raise the level of global intelligence. Regardless of the size, educational level, age, sex, or nationality of the audience, Tony's feedback from his audiences over the last 50 years has averaged over 94%, and as a result he has been given many awards to recognise both his excellence in education and specifically in teaching.

As Tony recently said in a communication to the Guild of Educators:

"I believe that teaching and education are the most important professions in the world...The problems the world is confronting today are not economic or financial; they are all problems based on an underlying bankruptcy, the Bankruptcy of Thought. This bankruptcy has been caused by inadequate resources and energy being devoted to the prime global need: enhanced and enlightened education systems."

Yvonne Burne OBE, former Master of the Guild of Educators

Yvonne Burne OBE was Master of the Guild of Educators when she invited Tony to deliver the prestigious annual Franklin Lecture. Yvonne writes:

"We met on a social occasion, and as a result I invited Tony to speak to an audience of City of London School pupils, who were enthralled. His work on Mind Maps has become an integral part of educational thinking and of children's revision and note taking. I think that it has become a key tool in education.

I love the way Tony is picked up by his wonderful and eye-catching 1930's style taxi! A glorious way to travel!

One of the loveliest things about him is his ability to listen, reflect and intuitively understand. He operates at a spiritual as well as intellectual and emotional level and is a joy to be with.

Having enjoyed a wonderful lunch with him, by chance we then bumped in to others in the same restaurant who knew him well – and hold him in high regard. He is clearly famous wherever he goes!

It was a joy and privilege to invite Tony to deliver the keynote Franklin Lecture for the Guild of Educators in the year in which I was Master. It was a great tribute to him that for the first time in the history of the Educators the Lecture and Dinner were attended by the Lord Mayor of London and Lady Mayoress as well as the Sheriff and his Lady. Tony's lecture was inspirational, stimulating and amusing. He gave us many insights into his development and thinking, and set my year in train as he 'unlocked the potential' of his audience.

It was a bonus to see the Lord Mayor and Lady Mayoress, as well as the Sheriff and his Lady, busily engaged in racking their brains, along with the rest of us, to consider the uses and non-uses of a paperclip, all eager to produce the longest and best lists to bring to Tony's attention.

Yvonne Burne OBE, past master of the Guild of Educators

Chapter 5

Unlocking Potential

Edited transcript of The Franklin Lecture, Draper's Hall, delivered by Tony Buzan, 11 December, 2009.

The Beginnings

My life has been and still is a life in the pursuit of answers to questions about: Creativity; the Brain and its Potential; the Revolutions of the Mind; Left and Right Cortical research; the Multiple Intelligences; the Pioneers; the Mind Map Thinking Tool; Modern Education Systems; and Teachers/New Definitions.

Creativity

In the creativity test on first the uses, second, the non-uses of a paperclip, the large majority have scored higher on the second test the non-use test. The reason you have posited for this higher score is that the second test is an easier test because there are theoretically an infinite number of non-uses for a paperclip, as opposed to the relatively small number of possible uses.

I would like you now to consider the best non-use ideas such as: you cannot in any way use a paperclip for carrying water, and see if there is any way in which you could use the paperclip for the purposes you have decided, initially, that you could not. When you discover those non-uses on which we can all unanimously agree, you will have a major insight into the function and potential of the human brain.

In fact, there is no unanimity on non-use and in my thousands of lectures over the decades there never has been.

Quelle horreur! Our survey shows that every single one of your best non-uses you now believe can be a use! Why this extraordinary and apparently contradictory result?

Let's explore creativity a little further, in order to shed light on the dilemma in which we currently find ourselves. Let me introduce this by using a metaphor to indicate the importance of the discussion in which we are becoming engaged. Imagine that you are an Olympian athlete, and that you get stuck in a swamp, and are beginning to sink. Imagine that you think that the correct way to get out of this swamp is to use your Olympian energy.

What will happen to you?

Correct, you will sink.

And sink how?

FAST!

And therein, as Shakespeare says, lies the rub. For what it indicates is that the more intelligent, focused, driven, educated, dedicated, kind, wonderful and loving you are, the faster you go down if you have the wrong formula. In education and in unlocking potential, we must find the correct formulae.

Let me shed some more light on this, by reviewing generic studies on creativity with age. Psychologists gave different age groups problem-solving tests, in which the students were given overall percentage scores for the creativity with which they solved the given problems. They were judged on speed of solution, originality, number of ideas, flexibility of thought, ability to imagine, ability to make associations especially new ones, and elegance of solution. The five age groups were Kindergarten, Primary School, Secondary School, University and Adult.

Predict the results! Kindergarten 95%+, Primary School 75%+, Secondary School 50%, University 25%, Adult 10%. The bad news, apart from the horrific results, is that globally these results are 'Normal'. To make this even worse, the average age of the average human is increasing, which means that the average per capita for creativity is decreasing. This explains the panicked front-page screamers on magazines such as the Harvard Business Review that there is a 'Looming Creativity Crisis'. (HBR, October, 2004)

The good news is that in this, as in many other instances in our cognitive practices, Normal is not Natural! Natural creativity is a creativity that flourishes and grows throughout life, as evidenced by most of the great writers, artists, poets and thinkers of all nations throughout history. We simply need to unlock the creative potential that we have unwittingly locked in.

Potential

In the fields of memory, learning and creativity, what percentage of our cognitive capabilities do you estimate we currently use? I note with interest that most quote figures of between 1% to 10%. It is interesting, isn't it, that in a body of Educators, we rate the use so low? I am pleased to inform you that your estimates are optimistic! The actual use is less than 1%. Is this good news or bad news?

Good news! Because it means that there is more than 99% remaining to access 99% of potential to unlock.

In Memory, we know this from the prediction in 1994 at the World Memory Championships in London, by the London University Psychology Department, that no one in the future history of the human race would be able to remember a spoken number of 30 digits or more.

To realise this for yourself, read the following numbers only once, and the instant you finish, look away and try to recall each number.

6, 1

3, 5, 9, 4, 2

3, 4, 7, 1, 6, 5, 8

2, 5, 6, 1, 9, 3, 7, 1, 4, 6, 8, 5, 2, 3

As you will see, the task increases in difficulty exponentially with each added digit. Thus, the psychologists' prediction of 30 being impossible becomes more understandable.

In the 17th World Memory Championships in Bahrain 2008, three competitors memorised a spoken number of 100 digits in length perfectly! The winner of the competition memorised a spoken number 202 digits in length. Ten hours later, at a celebratory dinner and after three subsequent competitions, he was asked if he could still remember it, and proceeded to repeat it without error. When he had finished his recitation, he asked would you like me to do it again, backwards?!

And he did!

Revolutions of the Mind

Since the recent dawn of civilisation, we have gone through a number of Revolutions of Mind. The first was the Agricultural Revolution in which we thought agriculturally, and in which the children were brought up as farm workers or labourers. This was superseded by the Industrial Revolution, in which we thought industrially, and in which the children were brought up to work in industry and the factories of industry. What revolution or age, are we in now?

I note with interest that almost unanimously we vote for the Information/Technological/Digital Age in which we learned to think informationally, technologically, and digitally, and in which our children were brought up to be information workers. You notice the past tense beginning to creep in here. This is because, as well as the wonders that this age brought us, it also brought us the global stress-producing syndrome of Information Overload and the delights of Death by PowerPoint!

Thus, the Information Age was recently superseded by the Knowledge Age, in which we learned to think knowledgeably, and in which the proponents of this age were stating that children of the future would no longer be simply information workers; they would become knowledge workers. The briefly-lived Knowledge Age gave rise to the concept of the Knowledge Manager, and the Director of Knowledge Management.

As recently as 2008, in Singapore, at a meeting of the Directors of Knowledge Management, they declared that Knowledge Management was not working. And why? Because there is something far more important that needs to be managed than knowledge.

And what is this? The answer is The Manager!

And, of course, the Manager of Knowledge is the human brain with its cargo of cognitive skills and intelligences. We are, therefore, now at the dawning of the Age of Intelligence, in which, finally, we will learn to think Intelligently!

I am proud to announce that on 25 June of 2009 in Kuala Lumpur, the Minister for Higher Education, Dr Dato Nordin, in conjunction with the 14th International Conference on Thinking, its 2000 delegates, Dr Edward De Bono, Dr Howard Gardner, and myself, formally declared that we have now entered the Age of Intelligence. It is in this age that the astonishing potential of the human brain will be increasingly unlocked and unleashed.

The Brain

The Left and Right Cortical Research

Professor Roger Sperry of the University of California won the 1981 Nobel Prize in Medicine for his ground-breaking research in the area of the cognitive skills possessed by the cerebral cortex. Professor Sperry's research showed that the left hemisphere was dominantly active in the areas of words, numbers, lines, lists, logic and analysis, whereas the right hemisphere was dominantly active in the areas of rhythm, colour, shapes, maps (gestalt), imagination and daydreaming.

This research has been transformative in terms of our thinking about education and potential, and has also been widely misinterpreted.

Which side of the brain is the business side?

Which the artistic side?

Which the academic?

Which musical?

Which the creative?

The vast majority of people answer that the academic and business side is the left, and the artistic, musical and creative the right. These assumptions are dangerous, and dangerously into-the-swamp wrong! If you examine the cortical skills carefully, you will realise that all areas of activity contain the whole range of cortical skills. Only by combining them in this way, can we experience the beneficial effect of the synergetic relationship between the two sides. Only in this way can we unlock an infinite potential that has so far been trapped in a self-destructive, either-or inappropriate method of thinking.

We have to synchronise the activities of the entire cerebral cortex and, thus, to benefit from the release of an infinite creative and cognitive potential.

The Multiple Intelligences

The Age of Intelligence will include, in addition to the unleashing of the extraordinary powers of the cerebral cortex, the discovery, nurturing and application of the Multiple Intelligences so excellently covered in the previous Franklin Lecture given by Dr Anthony Seldon, Master of Wellington College. It is important to emphasise at the outset that these intelligences initially and formally introduced to the world by Dr Howard Gardner of Harvard University, are all like muscles that can be trained and honed, and that everyone possesses the potential to develop every intelligence to a high degree.

The Intelligences include:

Verbal: the development of word power and the ability to juggle with the infinite manifestations of the alphabet.

Numerical: the development of number power and the ability to juggle with the infinite manifestations of numbers. The numerical also includes the ability to think logically.

Spatial: the ability to negotiate three-dimensional space and to handle objects in three dimensions. These three intelligences constitute the bulk of the traditional IQ test.

And there are more!

Personal Intelligence is your self-awareness and ability to love yourself to be your own best friend and best coach.

Social Intelligence is your ability to be successful in groups.

This intelligence also includes the ability to establish enduring relationships.

Physical Intelligence includes your general medical health as well as your muscular strength, bodily flexibility, and cardiovascular physical fitness.

Sensual Intelligence is your ability to use, as Leonardo da Vinci entreated us to, the Multiple Senses to the ultimate of their power and potential.

Creative Intelligence is the ability to think with the full range of the cortical skills, and to think abundantly, originally, imaginatively, flexibly, speedily, and connectively.

Ethical/Spiritual Intelligence concerns your compassion and love for other living things and the environment, your charitability, your understanding, your big-picture-thinking, your positivity and your generosity.

Ultimately, Intelligence is not just the ability to sit in a room answering IQ questions, but to face up to and surmount the second by second challenges which life and the planet hurl at you!

Envisioning a world in which every human being was educated to develop these vast resources has been the dream of educators and philosophers for millennia.

At the beginning of the 21st Century, and at the beginning of the dawn of The Age of Intelligence, we have the opportunity to make this dream, finally, come true!

Pioneers

Fortunately the first shoots of this Final Revolution are already with us. I have already mentioned Dr Seldon's Wellington College, where everything I have been discussing is now part of the curriculum for every student. In Singapore, the Ministry of Education has thinking, learning and intelligence as its major focus and communicates with its 28,000 teachers via Mind Maps. Malaysia has declared that by 2020, every citizen will be aware of the brain, learning how to learn, and all the benefits of a Mentally Literate society.

In the business world, most of the Fortune 500 companies are now incorporating forms of Brain Training in their Human Resource activities, and Bill Gates recently stated:

"... intelligence agents and Mind Mappers are taking our information democracy to the next stage... a new generation of Mind Mapping software can also be used as a digital blank slate to help connect and synthesise ideas and data and ultimately create new knowledge ..." (Newsweek, 19 December, 2005)

Universities are rapidly endeavouring to lead this trend. At the London School of Economics (LSE), a new course LSE 100 is specifically devoted to teaching the students in social sciences to think and learn. In Mexico, the Tec De Monterrey, a university with 33 campuses and 39,000 students, has made the 100-hour Mental Literacy, Mind Mapping and Learning How to Learn course mandatory for every student. Japan has recently had Mind Mapping software and books on the brain and learning at the top of its Amazon list and China has declared creativity and innovation to be a national priority. The revolution has begun. The brain's potential is beginning to be unlocked and unleashed!

The Mind Map an Egalitarian Thinking Tool

The Mind Map is the tool that uses each of the cognitive skills in synchrony, and which allows the individual to explore and develop each of the Multiple Intelligences. Placed in perspective, the current debate in England over the class system and privilege is inappropriate, out of place and irrelevant. What education needs for its present and its future are tools that allow each brain to mine its own potential and then to manifest it. The Mind Map is such an Egalitarian Thinking Tool.

Education Systems and Teachers

Our current education systems are becoming dangerously akin to factory farming, producing Conveyor Belt Kids who are still being designed for the industrial and information ages. What the world needs now are schools and universities that focus not from the outside in (agriculture, industry, information, technology and knowledge); we need education systems that focus from the inside outwards (the cognitive skills and the Multiple Intelligence), allowing us finally to think intelligently and creatively about knowledge, technology, information, industry, and agriculture. And who is going to lead this final educational revolution?

The Teacher - a new position of priority with new definitions. If we look at the original root of education, it is the word Educere. This word from which Duke also arises, means not, as it has been primarily interpreted, to draw out. It means to Guide; to Head; and to Lead.

As such, the teacher (and I include here all parents) must become the most important individual in the world. The teacher of the future will no longer be simply a specialist in a given subject area. The teacher of the future will be a leader, a mentor, a custodian of intelligence, a facilitator, an advisor, a guide, a coach, a guardian, and a beacon for all those incredibly beautiful and potential-filled minds of the future.

Chapter 6
Close Encounters With Michael Jackson

Education is important for all children, young and old, rich and poor, famous and infamous. Tony loyally waited until after Michael Jackson's untimely demise before revealing hitherto confidential details about their relationship. I have spent a great deal of time discussing with Tony his experiences with one of the most stupendous and charismatic personalities of all time, and with his three children.

Selected by Jackson personally as the world's most eminent tutor in Mental Literacy, Tony, before the storm broke, had been invited to teach those children on a private and exclusive basis.

Tony was lecturing in Singapore in 2006 when he received a call from his long standing friend, supporter and sponsor-to-be of two World Memory Championships, Sheikh Hamad, of the Bahraini royal family. The Sheikh said: 'A fan of yours would like to speak to you.' An unfamiliar voice came on the line. 'Hi, it's Michael', and over the next 45 minutes Jackson raved with enthusiasm to Tony about his books. He wanted Tony to explain his ideas to his children and to "teach them how to think".

I can bear personal witness to the fact that Tony attracts this sort of out-of-the-blue approach from superstars. I was with him once at his home in Marlow when Benny Andersson of ABBA suddenly rang for some advice about how to improve his brainpower!

Tony promptly flew to Bahrain, checked into his favourite hotel and for the following week commuted to the Jackson family's palace in the desert. He was met at the gate by Jackson in person and Tony was immediately struck by how deeply attached the children were to their father.

"I would watch them coming and going from the international school every day. They left happy, and came back happy. On their return, those three kids could not run any faster from the car to get to hug their daddy. The house itself resembled the Sistine Chapel, filled with Renaissance art. There were giant prints of paintings by Michelangelo, Leonardo and Raphael on every wall."

Indeed, the first thing Jackson did on Tony's arrival was to ask him all about Leonardo da Vinci.

"He was fascinated by the idea of geniuses, from Alexander the Great to Charlie Chaplin and Muhammad Ali, but he didn't consider himself as one of them. He was very humble. He saw himself as a student."

Tony was also taken aback to discover that Jackson "was an indulgent father, not one of those hot-housing parents, forever forcing the children to study extra maths, take dance classes or learn musical instruments."

In the evenings the family snuggled up on the sofa to watch DVDs. Tony observed that alongside the old masters, Jackson had hung larger-than-life-sized photographs of his own children, which greatly amused them. "Michael had a massive printing machine." Tony later acquired one himself, which he christened Robocop, to create imaginative variations, prints and replicas of the work of his favourite artist and Muse, Lorraine Gill.

"The children were fast learners like their father, who was probably the best pupil I've had." Tony witnessed no tantrums or raised voices.

"The kids seemed to enjoy each other's company. It's unusual in groups of three, where tensions can often arise. They were very different personalities. Prince was a very bright, witty but serious little boy. In a class, he would be the child the teachers noticed. He was confident and very quick on repartee.

"Paris, by contrast, was a sedate princess. Very independent, contemplative and self-contained. She was quiet but kind, always offering things. She had great poise and presence and she was very good with the boys.

"Four-year-old Blanket was just wild, a little dynamo, always on the move, tumbling, hanging off the furniture. He was like a mini-Michael. I saw Blanket do lots of dance routines."

Tony was sure that Jackson was Blanket's biological father.

"He had the same eyes and his skin was much darker than that of the other children - his complexion made him look Mediterranean."

At mealtimes, there would be served precisely the sort of food approved by Tony and his brain nutrition advisers, Dr Andrew Strigner and Professor Michael Crawford: "beautiful vegetables, fresh seafood, hummus, fruit juices, and no alcohol. The children were respectful but would push the boundaries.

"Michael talked a lot about creativity and the process of being a star and about the naysayers in his past who had said you can't do this or that- before he did it. He loved a challenge. The album *Thriller* had been his ultimate achievement and now people were saying that he couldn't repeat it. He felt he could comfortably outdo *Thriller*."

Jackson also opened up to Tony about his own upbringing:

"He talked about how wonderful it was to have Elizabeth Taylor as an aunt figure and Fred Astaire showing him dance moves. How he loved singing and dancing with his family, travelling the world with the Jackson Five."

"Michael would talk to them about many great figures from the past, but I never heard him refer to Jesus. The children and their father were hermetically cut off from the outside world, doubtless reflecting Jackson's determination to isolate himself and his kids."

Only once did Jackson mention scandals to Tony and he was evidently still smarting at media accusations that he was a "mad, bad dad" after he had dangled Blanket, then just nine months old, out of the window of a Berlin hotel.

"Michael was indignant about that," said Tony. "Jackson was adamant: 'I'm a dancer, one of the fittest, strongest people in the theatre. I lift and carry adults with no difficulty.'"

As Tony noted, "Children will adapt to whatever situation they come into, as long as a parent is there for them; and Michael was always there."

• • • •

"Learning how to learn is life's most important skill."

Tony Buzan

World MEMORY Championships

Left: The Athenaeum Club in London - Venue of the first World Memory Championship in 1991. Right: Dominic O'Brien, Creighton Carvello, Tony Buzan and Andi Bell in Simpson's-in-the-Strand

Tony Buzan outside Simpson's-in-the-Strand, which has hosted the World Memory Championships more times than any other venue.

Since 1991, the World Memory Championships have been held annually and the Mind Sport of Memory is now practiced in thirty countries using a system of ten memory disciplines developed by Tony Buzan and Raymond Keene OBE.

Chapter 7

Master Of Memory

> "I never thought much about whether I could improve my memory across a wider set of domains, but now I think I could, after reading *Moonwalking with Einstein: The Art and Science of Remembering Everything*, by a young science writer, Joshua Foer. It's absolutely phenomenal, one of the most interesting books I've read this summer." *Bill Gates*
>
> (*Moonwalking with Einstein* recounts Josh Foer's successes in Memory Championships founded by Tony Buzan)

"Tony Buzan – the Biggest Name in Memory."

The New Yorker Magazine

Memory has become one of the main fascinations, focuses, and passions of Tony's life. He describes in *The Memory Book* (BBC/Pearson) the story which transformed his understanding and appreciation of the power and potential of memory and that he assures us 'you will remember for the rest of your life'.

Let Tony tell you the story:

"Like most people I, as a student, thought that you were either born with a good memory or a poor one. I was perplexed by the fact that I could understand something in class or from a book, assume that I would remember it, and yet when trying to do so could not.

At the 2010 World Memory Championships in China, competitors were greeted to the sight of a Mind Map about the competition, draped over a hill beside the venue.

"Under the pressure of exams, when asked questions that I knew I knew, my mind would go totally blank. I thought that my memory was OK-ish, though certainly not spectacular or ever capable of being so. Like others I 'knew' that as far as my age was concerned, my memory would soon be reaching its peak, after which there would be a long and steady decline for the rest of my life – a most encouraging prospect! Again, like everyone else, I thought that the best way to commit things to memory was to take neat notes written in blue or black ink, and consisting mainly of words written on straight lines."

We have already read about Tony's life-changing encounter with Professor Clark. That 'enthralled' student (Tony) now applied himself vigorously to the development of the Major System that he had been taught by the Professor. He found that within a few weeks he was able to double the amount of data and information he could remember in any given time, and that within a few months he could memorise, five to ten times the amount he had been able to remember in his previous 'best-ever' memory performances.

Within a year he had fallen in love with Memory, and begun to approach this enticing, relatively unexplored, and globally misunderstood subject, from as many different perspectives as possible.

From 1960s, he studied neurophysiology, mnemonic systems, the great brains, global note-taking systems, the psychology of memory, his own brain, his own notes, and the opinions and experiences of the general population during his lectures and social experiments. He discovered that the essential 'operating principles' of mnemonics were the ability to create multi-sensual images, combined with the ability to create vigorous associations between those images, while at the same time 'stabilising' them for the brain by giving them a specific location.

Neurophysiology gave him an understanding of the biochemical and electromagnetic processes by which networks of brain cells 'lay down' our memories.

The neuro-physiological findings were beginning to demonstrate that the brain cells formed networks of associations between themselves, and that these formed 'traces' of memory. The more these networks were repeated, the stronger and more long term a memory became.

The mnemonics systems of the Greeks, Romans and other tribes regardless of century, colour, location, race, or religion, were all based on the same identical principles. These principles were the same as those that he was applying in Professor Clark's major system.

The great brains, when they spoke about memory, discussed and described it in virtually identical ways. They always discussed their memories in vividly expressive terms, marvelling at how a specific smell, sight, sound or touch could trigger streams of associations; 'remembrances of things past'. The note-taking systems of history's best minds, regardless of their 'native language', were all fundamentally similar, and they were, we observe with a certain irony, what currently would be called 'messy'! These 'messy notes', regardless of the local spoken/written language, were always laced with doodles, drawings, codes, symbols, images and connective/associative techniques such as lines and arrows. Tony had begun to realise that his own notes were not the memory aids that he had thought they were; indeed he had the uneasy and growing feeling that they were perhaps the reason that his memory did, when it did, fail him.

While studying the psychology of memory, he focused developing a deeper understanding and application of Recall During Learning, and Recall After Learning. The Recall After Learning graph he now calls 'the Most Important Graph in the World'.

He was astounded that it was presented as 'stuff to learn and memorise'; not 'priceless information to apply!' Over the coming years and decades, he was to develop the Recall During Learning Principles into multiple new learning techniques, tools and systems.

The two 'Pillar Principles' of Recall During Learning were Imagination and Association. These were supplemented by the Von Restorff effect (you will remember something if it is outstanding) and by the interest effect (the greater your interest the better your memory), the Primacy Effect (you will remember 'first things' better) and the Recency Effect (you will remember 'last things' better). They rounded off a neat picture that gave a complete and comprehensive understanding of how our recall works while we are assimilating information.

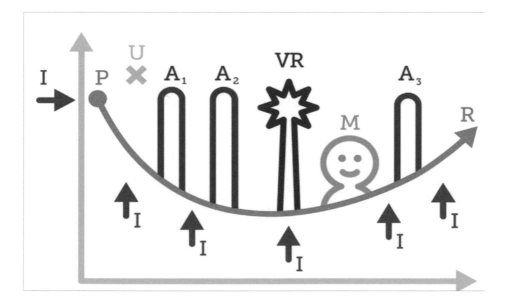

The Recall After Learning graph gave some profound insights:

1. that, contrary to 'common sense' expectations, Recall actual rises immediately after learning stops;

2. that as much as 80% of detail learnt is lost after 24 hours;

3. that if no corrective action is taken, the result is negative Recall, i.e. misremembering what one had learnt;

4. that a few simple and appropriately spaced reviews can transfer information comfortably from short term through mid-term into long term memory.

These findings coincided immaculately with the findings of the neuro-physiological studies. When examining the way in which his own brain functioned, and those of his friends by their own reports, it became apparent that the findings outlined above applied to both himself and everyone else, and explained both the successes, failures and misunderstandings about memory on a global basis.

By his fourth and graduating year at university in 1964, Tony had mastered the Major System, and applied it to the complete and perfect memorisation of an entire year-long psychology course, memorising the names of all the psychologists covered, all their experiments and the details and results of those experiments, all dates of significance, specific quotes by the lecturer, summaries and conclusions of recommended papers and books, as well as additional ones, and even quotes from the professor himself including the year, month, day and often the time!

The final exam was a 'breeze'. The memory system allowed him to remember everything perfectly, while simultaneously allowing him to make connections and associations between each of the elements in his memory banks. It was a combination of total recall and total creativity. Tony expected a 'summa cum laude' (highest honours) with special distinction and the first '100%' paper in the history of the department. Sure enough, a few weeks after the examination, he was called to a special meeting with the three heads of the department.

Thus begins another story which, in a different way, transformed his life: a threatening encounter with the enemies of Mental Literacy, and, sadly, enemies in positions of great authority.

Striding into the room full of great expectations, Tony was met, rather than with open smiles and congratulations, with grim faces and an ominous atmosphere. The head professor explained that, although they knew he was an excellent student, they had the very unpleasant task of accusing him of cheating in an exam. Stunned at this reversal of his high expectations, knowing he had not cheated, and already beginning to relish the prospect of a debate in which he knew he had all the evidence as well as the moral high ground, he asked them what evidence they had.

The answer? That his paper was too perfect, and that such perfection could only be achieved by cheating! Taking the initiative, Tony asked them to explain how he could have cheated in the examination room in which he took the exam. After fumbling around with such ideas as notes on shirt cuffs, smuggled papers and even the suggestion that Tony had employed a friend to hire a ladder and hold up significant information at one of the high windows in the examination hall, their case began to disintegrate.

Tony pressed his initiative. Because the memory system had allowed him to lodge the entire year's course in his long term memory, he was able to challenge them to ask any question from the exam again, as well as any other question that they could make up on the spur of the moment, and stated that he would be able to respond as well and as comprehensively as he had in the exam itself.

This they did, and he did!

Eventually one of the professors paused, and in a very detective-like, imperious tone, asked, 'Buzan, are you using some kind of memory system?'

'Well done, professor!' said Tony.

The response?

'That's cheating!'

'What!' said the accused. 'Do you mean to tell me that a methodology that allows me to have perfect short term memory, to have perfect mid-term memory, to have perfect long term memory, to be able to relate any aspect of my knowledge to any other aspect, and in addition to that to reproduce it, again perfectly and in a creative way some weeks after the exam and under the pressure of both accusation and authority; do you mean to tell me that that's cheating?!'

Their answer? 'Yes.'

Without knowing it, they had helped Tony increasingly realise his direction in life. He had no doubt, from the experience just described, that the universe of memory was still comprehensively misunderstood, and that the opportunities for new investigations into it and of its potential and applications were similarly infinite.

In congruence with his experience with the professors he increasingly realised that much of the material in the texts being distributed was either out of date, inaccurate, or, as with the Recall During Learning and Recall After Learning curves, presented solely for the purpose of memorisation rather than application.

At the end of 1966, he returned to the UK and worked as a Special Assignment teacher, primarily teaching the art and science of memory and its techniques to disadvantaged children. He was continuingly amazed by the transformation in performance, confidence and character that teaching the real art and science of memory produced. During this time he expanded his knowledge of mnemonic techniques, and began seriously to apply the many perspectives of his memory studies to the development of a new system for note taking.

Also during this time he worked on the first of his now over 120 published books. In 1971, *Speed Memory* was published by Anthony Cheetham's Sphere Press, and became an instant success. This success led for many requests from schools, universities, businesses and government bodies, for courses on the enhancement of memory.

So passionate about memory was he, that in those years he would visit the major universities, carrying giant placards inviting students to come and discuss, debate, and learn about memory. As a result he was invited to run courses at Oxford and Cambridge Universities, London University, Manchester and Liverpool, among many others.

By now, the new note-taking/making technique combining all the elements of Tony's memory studies had evolved: Mind Maps were born!

Originally, Tony's Mind Maps were invented entirely on the basis of memory, for memory. His brother Barry expanded the application to note-making.

In 1973, the BBC discovered Tony's work, and immediately requested a ten-programme series featuring memory, *Memory Mind Maps*, the brain, and speed reading and study skills in the context of memory. With the programme they wanted a comprehensive book.

The programme was filmed and the book written in 1973. In April of 1974, when Tony was 32, the *Use Your Head* television series was screened and the classic book *Use Your Head*, was published. The programmes were screened on BBC 1 and 2 on average two times a year for 17 years! The *Use Your Head* book rapidly became an international best-seller, and was published in 2010, in its seventh edition, 36 years after its first publication in 1974.

Also in 1973, Tony travelled the world as a special consultant on the memory, brain and learning for a feature Thames Television one-hour documentary entitled *The Enchanted Loom*.

Of special interest is the fact that of the many 'Brain Stars' with whom Tony worked, were Professor Robert Ornstein, the author of the *Psychology of Consciousness*, and his assistant, Dr. Michael Block, who had been applying the findings of Professor Roger Sperry and his research on the left and right brain, to the development of memory and cognitive skills. Tony worked with Dr. Block on a number of papers that pursued these topics and the applications of the findings to life.

Another event of extreme significance in Tony's 'memory life' was his visit to Moscow in 1973, for the purpose of meeting Professor Alexander Luria. Professor Luria was one of Russia's and the world's greatest neuroscientists. He was the author of the seminal *The Mind of a Mnemonist*, a book that was the result of Luria's decades-long study of 'S', a man with an ostensibly perfect memory. Tony spent hours with Luria discussing memory, its ramifications, manifestations, and the positive implications of teaching it as a special and distinctive subject applicable to the assimilation, understanding and recall of all other subjects. Parts of their discussion were included in *The Enchanted Loom* when it was screened in 1974.

During this time, Tony also began the training of memory BLIs (Buzan Licensed Instructors), people who were qualified by Tony to teach Mind Maps as a memory and learning tool, as well as to teach the special memory systems and techniques he had developed. There are already over 300 worldwide, and their number is growing.

In 1985, the fruit of his researches was published in his next major book on memory: *Master Your Memory*. In this book, the BBC stated "there have been only two major advances in memory technique since the mid-seventeenth century. The first major advance was the origination of Mind Maps. The second major advance was the Self Enhancing Master Memory Matrix (SEM^3). SEM^3 allows you to memorise up to 50,000 pieces of information perfectly, while at the same time improving your creativity and other mental skills."

During his continuing development of memory systems, SEM^3, and Mind Maps, Tony explored, using Mind Maps for the exploration, the fundamental structures, principles and themes underlying memory and its functions. As he built his giant Memory Mind Map, the Mind Map revealed through its structure and content, a paradigm-shifting realisation that contradicted everything he had been taught: Tony's Mind Map on Memory, its principles and functions, was identical to a Mind Map on Creativity!

The Mind Map revealed that, in order to recall something 'A' from the past using Memory Systems, you had to link that item 'A', to a located image from your Memory System 'B', to create a new image C. When you triggered B, it would immediately 'hook out' C, an image which contained and with which you could now re-create the item you wanted to remember, 'A'.

Thus you will be using your memory to bring the past into the present (the present being the 'future' of the past!). The act of creation was identical. The great creative geniuses linked item 'A' (for example apple or rock strata) with item 'B' (moon; time) and Newton and da Vinci created new item 'C': gravity, and geological stratas as the 'clock' of the earth's life. In creativity, item 'A' was being linked to item 'B' to produce new item 'C' in the present, and projecting it into the future where it became a reality.

This realisation explained why Tony had felt more creative while studying the Memory Systems, and why the Mind Map, developed as a memory tool, was identically powerful as a creative thinking and brainstorming tool.

It also explained why, in Classical Greek Myth, Zeus, the all-powerful God of Energy, chose Mnemosyne, the Goddess of Memory, for a nine-days-and-nights tryst. The product of their joining?

The muses – the Gods and Goddesses of Creativity!

Thus it became clear that if you put energy into your memory, you will generate a potentially infinite creativity. The result of this was Tony's Memory/Creativity equation:

Energy plus and into Memory yields infinite Creativity – Creativity mathematically raised to the power of infinity. When taught properly, memory results in an Enhanced Creativity, and, similarly, correctly learned creativity generates a better memory.

Memory Roller Coaster

As a sportsman and Mind Sportsman, Tony had noticed, on his world-travels in the '70s and '80s, that there were world championships for virtually everything: tiddlywinks; beard-growing; chess; cricket; boxing; crosswords; martial arts; piano playing; rope-climbing; wood-cutting; swimming; running; spelling; oyster-eating; dancing; pigeon-racing; golf; sky-diving and so on and on and on…

Yet there was no world championship for that most important cognitive function of all, and without which none of the others could exist – MEMORY!

Throughout the 1980s and '90s, Tony had been incubating the idea of a World Memory Championships. In 1991, in partnership with myself, he founded the first World Memory Championships, which have grown into an international phenomenon, now involving over forty countries worldwide establishing a major new Mind Sport on the global stage.

The purposes for the World Memory Championship were and are the following:-

1) To promote Memory as a new Mind Sport, and in so doing to expand opportunities for Mentathletes in all countries.

2) To redefine the art and the science of Memory by establishing new norms, benchmarks and records, and to provide certifications and rankings for these.

3) To reintroduce Memory as a fundamental skill for early childhood education, thereby reinvigorating faith in and enjoyment of memory skills.

4) To demonstrate that Memory is the basis of creativity.

5) To recover and validate the mnemonic systems of earlier human cultures and to revive the traditions of oral memory.

6) To create a global community of like-minded individuals fascinated by exploring the power and potential of Memory and the human mind.

These insights grew to become the Magna Memoria, The Great Memory Charter (see Appendix C).

This new sport rapidly grew.

In 1995, Prince Philip of Liechtenstein gave Royal patronage to the Grand Master of Memory title, for those prodigious memorisers who were at the top of the ranking systems created by Tony and myself. In the 1990's and into the new century, the Mind Sport of Memory grew exponentially. By 2010, 28 new National Mind Sport organisations had been established.

During this hyper-energetic period in the growth of Memory, Tony wrote, in 2002, a new book: *Memory and Concentration (Mind Maps for Kids)*. In 2005, he was named "the biggest name in memory" by *The New Yorker* magazine. In 2006, he starred in a one hour prime-time TV feature show on Memory for Chinese television, which was reportedly watched by 350 million viewers.

In 2007, he participated in a special BBC prime-time programme on Memory with Professor Robert Winston at Longleat. In 2010, BBC/Pearson published an updated full-colour version of his previous Memory books (*Use Your Memory* and *Master Your Memory*) as *The Memory Book*. His work in this tantalising new field has filled his life with new friends, wonderful creativity, new realisations, new awareness about the limitless potential of the human brain, and millions of wonderful memories. Here, for example, is what the outstanding Buzan promoter in Australia, Bill Jarrard, has to say about *The Most Important Graph in the World* - Recall after Learning:

"I recall as a young teenager my father telling me things like 'you only get one chance to make a first impression, so make it a good one', and later as I did part time work during school holidays he said 'figure out what works and keep doing it' and 'don't be afraid to stand out'.

I won my first speech competition with the Optimist Club when I was fourteen, and even then the old adage 'tell them what you're going to tell them, tell them, and then tell them what you told them' was strongly imprinted in the approach I learnt from my Toastmaster teachers.

As I worked in various countries and industries, eventually becoming a senior executive, I had the privilege to work with a range of mentors who shared their strategies for success, including 'try to see the big picture, but remember the devil's in the detail', 'deliver a great service, then leave them wanting more', and 'make it about them, and they'll always invite you back'.

All these lessons have served me well over the last 45 years, but what I didn't realise until just a few years ago, was that each of these lessons touched on one or more of the powerful principles embodied and consolidated in *The Most Important Graph In The World*.

I remember the exact day it happened. Jennifer and I had organised for Tony Buzan to speak to a group of about 120 professional speakers at a National Speakers Association of Australia meeting. It was the second time we had invited Tony to tour Australia with us as the Buzan Centre Australia/NZ and he and I didn't know each other as well as we do now.

Tony had started his presentation well, but it was apparent about 5 minutes in that the audience was looking for something extra special and, spotting this himself, Tony turned to me and quietly said 'I'll do *The Most Important Graph in the World*'. He started with his word memory test, and then debriefed it using The Graph to explain Primacy, Recency, Von Restorff and all the memory principles embodied there.

It was soon clear these professional speakers were now getting the something special they wanted. They hung on every word, easily relating as to how the memory and memorability principles Tony was sharing could make them even more successful presenters. I watched in delight as he proved again that he is one of the best speakers in the world, but I was even more delighted because the full power of The Graph of Recall after Learning was now firmly planted in my own understanding – so I could also share it with others."

So, for Tony, who has become known as 'Mr. Memory' and the 'Memory Man', it has already been a Memorable Life!

The first World Memory Champion, Dominic O'Brien

China is recognised at the 2009 World Memory in London as the winner of the bid to host the 2010 World Memory Championships

Students taking part in the 2009 UK Schools Memory Championships

Eva Ball, the 2009 UK Schools Memory Champion,
with Dominic O'Brien and Tony Buzan

For more information on the Mind Sport of Memory and the
World Memory Championships,
visit www.worldmemorychampionships.com

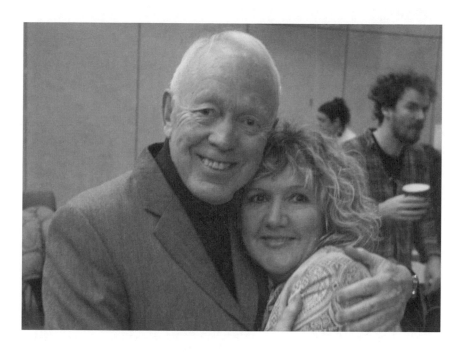

Jennifer Goddard, Master Trainer, ThinkBuzan

How I went from 15 year old high school dropout to collaborating on two books with the most prolific BRAIN author of our time...

As you have gathered so far in reading this book, Tony preaches what he practises and has a wealth of knowledge, unique insight and a passion for helping others. This passion is at both the Macro level (his ongoing vision of Global Mental Literacy) and at the Micro level (mentoring many people, including myself).

I first came across Tony's work in 1996 when I was lamenting to a business colleague that I was considering quitting my undergraduate university studies. Frustrated with my difficulties in coping with studying part time, working full time and being a single mum, I had given up on myself and my ability to learn new things. 'Who did I think I was, trying to do a degree?'

Having left school at 15 and finding out I was dyslexic at 21 was one thing, becoming a teenage mum and having to support myself and my daughter after my first husband drowned when she was little was something else altogether. That colleague gave me a copy of *The Mind Map Book* by Tony and Barry Buzan on what turned out to be our very first date. He told me that Mind Maps were a way to take notes and make notes that were in tune with my brain. I decided to give it a go!

That very next semester, I received a Distinction and a High Distinction, simply through applying Tony's techniques and the paradigm shift it caused in my self confidence and ability to learn. I went on to do my Masters degree in Entrepreneurship and Innovation with eight out of eleven High Distinctions, two top student awards, in under two years while still working full time.

How? By simply applying new knowledge about how my brain works in relation to reading, memory, studying and thinking - not from medical journals – but through Tony's work. It wasn't just Mind Maps that helped. I soon discovered that Tony Buzan had written nearly 100 books on Memory, Speed Reading, Creativity, Multiple Intelligences and, of course, Mind Mapping. I read every book he wrote and attended his workshops in England and Australia. I developed such a passion about learning how my brain works that I wanted to immerse myself in this area to help my brain and help others with the insights I gained.

The game changing ah-ha moment was in 2001 when I read *Head First* – based on Tony's new research and insights into our 10 multiple intelligences. Most so called self-help books approach things from only one or two perspectives – procrastination, dieting, depression etc.

When I discovered that we all have 10 different intelligences (not just the three traditional IQ elements of Numerical, Verbal and Spatial Intelligence) that interrelated and encompass all elements, a big weight lifted from my shoulders. Many of us are strong in one or two intelligences (such as Social Intelligence and Physical Intelligence) – it is like playing chopsticks on the piano with two fingers. Once you learn to use all 10 fingers/intelligences – imagine the infinite melodies of life you can play!

Towards the end that year, I was working in England for a major corporation and heard on the grapevine about the World Memory Championships. I rang Vanda North, one of the key organisers and asked if I could come and watch – she said that I should come and help!

In the next couple of weeks I read and really studied *Use Your Memory* so I could hone my skills and not embarrass myself by forgetting someone's name etc. It is amazing what you can achieve with a bit of motivation and application!

It was such a wonderful experience working with Tony, Raymond Keene OBE, Phil Chambers, Chris Day and Dominic O'Brien (8 times World Memory Champion) that I continue to volunteer at the World Memory Championships and convene the Australian Memory Championships.

Why have an annual sporting event on memory? Just like the Olympics, which calls the world's best sportspeople to compete together in a friendly environment, the Memory Championships invites people around the world to test their skills and strategies against themselves and each other.

Just like all other sports, millions of people around the world engage in that sport with no aspirations to compete at the world level. Every day to day occurrence has its foundations in memory –

remembering someone's name, an anniversary, a project deadline, a phone number etc. Memory is such a fundamental part of who we are yet we don't study it and learn how simple it is to improve our memory. Often it is not until we start to experience so called 'senior' moments that we get interested in how to keep our precious memory in shape.

We have also not understood the true nature of memory and its link to creativity and innovation. Even though I have a Masters degree in Innovation it wasn't until I was listening to Tony speak at a prestigious conference, where he first revealed a radically new formula for creativity. $E +> M = C\infty$ that I developed a much deeper concrete insight into a somewhat nebulous term 'creativity'.

Energy plus and into Memory yields infinite Creativity

Essentially, if you can remember something that you read, saw or discussed 6 days, 6 weeks, 6 months or even 6 years ago and, through the brain's natural ability to associate and synthesise, to the current situation, you will be much more creative and innovative.

At another conference in front of some of Australia's most prominent professional speakers, Tony revealed the strategic importance of the Recall During Learning Graph to all elements of personal and business success - not just the standard classroom scenario.

This fascinated me (and the rest of the audience) and I started to see long established principles in a new light, such as the Von Restorff effect. Named after psychiatrist Hedwig Von Restorff, this effect shows that we remember, other things being equal, anything which is outstanding, different or unique.

In November 2011, while Tony was speaking at a major conference in Sydney, I asked him what he would like to do during his two days R&R before leaving Australia to speak at another major event. He instantly said that he was energised by a new book he was writing and would love to make even more progress on it. I said that I would be happy to assist any way I could. Tony knew that I could touch type and that I had a strong interest in the Recall During Learning Graph, so over the next two days we cloistered ourselves in his hotel room with the occasional brisk walk to get some fresh air and a brain break.

Tony had a very clear direction in his head through the Mind Maps he had prepared on the chapter outlines and fluently and coherently verbalised his thoughts while I maniacally typed them on my computer (which was connected to a large TV screen so he could see the manuscript progressing).

At the end of each section he stopped and asked for my opinion and if I had anything to add. It was an amazing working environment – highly energizing and collaborative. At the end of the two days we had produced over 16,000 words and completed a good third of the book.

The synergy worked so well that we continued to work on the book remotely until it was finished. I would Skype Tony for an hour each week to focus on a chapter, clarify any key points, offer suggestions and debate different ideas. Each session was recorded so I could go back and capture his thinking in detail and revise key discussion points. He would then review the manuscript and we continued writing this way for 8 weeks.

Being part of the writing process was an amazing gift and a master class in Writing. The ability to draw back the curtain and see behind the scenes as well as the challenge to add real value in the applications of what is now called *The Most Important Graph in the World* - The 7.5 principles memory principles that lead to business and personal success, has significantly transformed my ability to convey ideas to others. Tony and I then collaborated on the new series "Brain Training for Kids" but that is a whole different story.

P.S. that business colleague who first lent me *The Mind Map Book*… his name is Bill Jarrard and we have just celebrated our 10th Wedding anniversary. As many other people have experienced, Mind Maps really did bring true love.

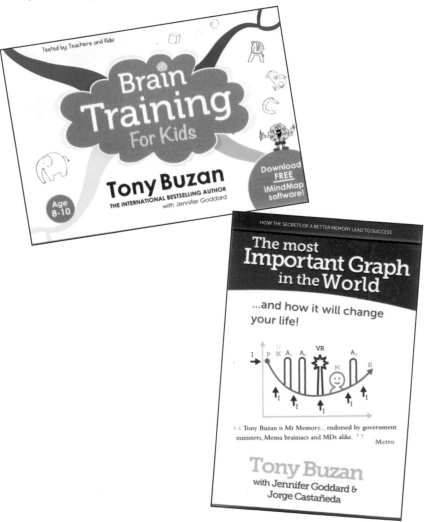

Chapter 8

Mens Sana - Mind Sports
(A Healthy Mind)

Tony's interest in Mind Sports, although he didn't recognise it at the time, started when he was a very little boy playing board games at Christmas. He was especially entranced by Monopoly, and this led to an early interest in draughts/checkers.

When he was eight years old, and helping in his parents' restaurant, The Lantern, in Whitstable, Kent, one of the regular customers, an elderly spinster who used to come for lunch, and who was known as a bit of an eccentric, said to Tony's mother, 'I think it's about time your young boy learnt to play chess. I'll teach him.' His mother thought this was a good idea, and so Tony began learning a game that was to engage and entrance him for the rest of his life.

Tony's parents supported him greatly by inviting the local Whitstable Chess Club to have its weekly meetings and competitions in the second room of the restaurant. He was thus 'blooded' in a chess club where he was regularly taught chess tactics and strategy by the members, and where he could also play with players from weak to fairly high strength.

As the years progressed, he joined his school chess team, eventually, in his senior years, becoming captain of the team. When he was 17, in his final year at school, he and his team were due to play in the provincial schools' team championships, and were among the favourites.

The tournament was to take place in a city that required water ferry travel to get there.

At this particular stage in his career, although he was both captain of the chess team and Head Boy's Prefect, his relationship with his Headmaster was not the best. As a result, the Headmaster banned the team from travelling, saying that the trip was 'too dangerous' and that in view of this the school could in no way support either Tony or his team.

Not to be denied, the team worked hard for a few weeks to raise, successfully, the funds they would need to transport them to the championship. They paid, travelled, played, and won! Upon return the school embraced them as the Provincial Chess Champions.

By a strange coincidence, mirroring, as we shall observe in the next section - In Corpore Sano - Tony's cricket-playing powers and my own, an identical situation arose at my Public School, Dulwich College. The Master in charge of chess, for reasons which remain unclear to me to this day, forbade the team from travelling to Oxford University for what we in the team considered to be an important event. We went anyway, and upon returning with the Trophy, not a word was uttered against our trip!

Postal Chess

During his university years, from 1960-1966, Tony played correspondence chess. In these tournaments the players are divided into groups of seven, and to move into the next round you have to win at least four games. In his first big tournament, Tony easily qualified for the second round, where the level was obviously much higher. Fairly quickly he won his first three games, and had good positions in the remaining three. His progression to the advanced round looked secure. One game ended in a draw (half a point) and in another he made an over-confident move, and lost to a sharp counterattack.

Not to worry, for in his final game he was playing a man called William Windom, and in the last few moves Tony had taken, in succession, his opponent's rook, bishop, and knight, and had a threatened checkmate within the next six moves. The victory was assured. Tony sent off his next devastating move, and waited excitedly for William's response and resignation.

He received in the post a postcard filled with microscopic lettering of chess moves, each of which was a different possible progression of the game, and each of which led to checkmate, not for Tony, but for William Windom.

'Impossible!' thought Tony – William must have lost his mind.

Tony went to his chess board and played through the first variation, the basic format of which was 'your move X; if you do this then I do this, if you then do this then I do this, if you then do this I do this, you then have to do this and I do this, checkmate!'

And it was correct.

With growing amazement and disbelief Tony played through each of the variations, and each one was a different variation of an inevitable checkmate - of himself!

He slowly began to realise that all the pieces that he had previously been taking so confidently, were in fact a string of brilliant sacrifices by William Windham that had drawn him in unsuspectingly to one of the most sophisticated and 'devilish' entrapments that he had ever imagined.

His reaction, rather than of fury and despair, was of total exhilaration. He had participated in a brilliant game, had played his best, had been confident that he had won, and had been outwitted and outsmarted by a player many levels beyond his.

A rare and educational privilege.

He found out later that this particular William Windom was the famous actor who starred in *Murder, She Wrote* co-starring with Angela Lansbury.

GO

Let Tony explain to you his introduction to Go:

"In the late 1970s, a friend of mine introduced me, against my protestations, to the Chinese/Japanese game of Go. I was convinced, being the total acolyte of chess, that no game could entice me in the same way.

"Within ten minutes of being introduced to the game, I knew I was wrong. I had found another truly major Mind Sport."

Tony followed Go, had lessons from the British Go champion and Grandmaster Matthew Macfadyen, played the game in both Japan and Korea, and in Korea was named an honorary Dan for his understanding of the theory, and the applications of that theory, to life in general.

Draughts and Chess Championships

In London, at the Park Lane Hotel in 1992, Tony and I organised the first ever man-versus-machine world championships in any thinking sport. This was the historic Professor Marion Tinsley versus the

Chinook Computer Programme Draughts World Championship. Professor Tinsley was a towering giant in the world of draughts, no Grandmaster in the game having come even close to defeating him in competition in thirty years. The Chinook computer had reached Grandmaster status in the field, and had comfortably demolished a number of the world's other top players.

The championship was a gargantuan battle in which, in the final game, in a position in which it appeared that the computer was winning, Dr. Tinsley, who was 63 years old at the time, made a move to which the computer would not respond. It had a 'nervous breakdown'! The subsequent analysis revealed that the move was unanswerable, and that no matter what the computer did, it would have lost both the game and the championship.

Dr. Tinsley, at the moment of triumph, rose from his table, hands above his head, and said "a victory for human beings!"

When Grandmasters in draughts who had not seen the match were given the games without knowing which colour was the computers and which was Dr. Tinsley's, the extraordinary conclusion that most came to was that Dr. Tinsley was the computer. Immaculate conceptions of the human mind...

In 1993, Tony supported the World Chess Championship in London, between Garry Kasparov and Nigel Short, and on behalf of the Brain Trust Charity was one of the finalist bidders for the Championship.

Once the championship was under way, Tony made regular appearances on Channel 4 TV coverage with myself and Carol Vorderman. He also submitted a special article on the championships for the Duncan Lawrie Review.

In 1994, Tony and I co-organised the return match between Dr. Marion Tinsley and the Chinook computer in Boston, Massachusetts.

This match was sadly halted early, because it was discovered that Dr. Tinsley was suffering from a terminal illness. His previous victory still stands out in the history of Mind Sports as one of the greatest ever accomplishments.

In 1995, in England's Hanbury Manor, Tony's World Memory Championships were honoured by the establishment, by Royal Decree, of the title of 'Grandmaster of Memory' under the Royal patronage and command of Prince Philip of Liechtenstein.

At the same time the title of International Arbiter for Mental World Records was also established by royal decree, with Tony and myself being the inaugural recipients.

In the same year, Tony established, with Prince Philip of Liechtenstein, the Liechtenstein Global Trust (LGT) Academy, a six week residential course teaching a Renaissance Curriculum which featured, as one of its main thrusts, the teaching of Mind Sports and the transference of all the skills learned in Mind Sports – concentration, memory, tactical thinking, strategic thinking, creativity, the art of winning, the art of losing – to all other aspects of personal and professional life.

The Mind Sports Faculty became a key feature of the Academy when Tony introduced Chess, Bridge, Shogi, Go and Xiangqi, with a special feature starring Dama Lectures by Sheikh Hamad Bin Ibrahim Al Khalifa, accompanied by distribution of specially-made Dama (Turkish Draughts) sets to LGT executives.

In 1996, Tony and I co-authored IBM Deep Blue Versus Kasparov and in 1997 the return match, IBM Deep Blue II Versus Kasparov.

In 1997, Tony and I founded the Mind Sports Olympiad, which starred as its centrepiece, the World Memory Championships.

During this time, Tony also founded World Championships in Creativity, Speed Reading, and Mind Mapping.

Tony explains, "In 1997, I had one of the highlight experiences of my Mind Sports career in Paris.

"In the Jules Verne restaurant one third of the way up the Eiffel Tower, Raymond Keene and I met with Garry Kasparov, the reigning world champion and highest rated player of all time, to discuss the coming world championship against Vladimir Kramnik and to discuss the world of chess in general. After a superb lunch, Raymond and Garry got into a discussion of the ten-part television programmes that each of them had separately done on the world's ten greatest games. The discussion was intense and immense.

"After this discussion, they began to discuss all of Garry's championship games throughout his career.

"Each of them remembered every game and could identify it by saying things such as, "Ah yes, that was the game twenty-four Rh6..." The energy, enthusiasm, perfection of memory, and machine-gun speed with which they held this conversation was miraculous to behold."

Also during this time, Tony attended a number of major chess tournaments, and met and conversed with many of the world's leading Grandmasters and champions, including Vladimir Kramnik, Nigel Short, Michael Adams, Boris Gelfand, Jan Timman, Victor Korchnoi, Yasser Seirawan, and the recently departed President of Fide (The International Chess Federation), Florencio Campomanes.

In 1999, the first edition of a new global concept – *The Book of Mental World Records*, that Tony and I co-authored, was published. This book came out in its second edition in 2005.

In 2000, Tony was invited to become, and accepted, the position of, Chairman of the Appeals Committee for the Kasparov versus Kramnik

World Championship match held in London. He was also a commentator on this match on the web and on global television and media.

In 2002, he helped to establish, with the King of Bahrain, and with Sheikh Hamad bin Ibrahim Al Khalifa, the brother-in-law and uncle of the King, the Mind Sports Centre in Bahrain – a million-dollar building designed especially for Mind Sports, featuring the Arabic/Indian game of Dama.

During the 1990s, Tony was a member first of the Athenaeum Club's Chess Club and team, and secondly of the Royal Automobile Club's Chess Circle and team, playing in interclub competitions whenever he had returned to England from his travels.

The medal awarded for International Grandmaster of Memory is highly symbolic. The sea horse indicates the Hippocampus, the seat of Memory in the brain, as well as the chess knight. Chess, of course, was the template for royal endorsement of the Grandmaster title, when Czar Nicholas II conferred the original chess Grandmaster titles on Lasker, Capablanca, Alekhine Tarrasch and Marshall at St Petersburg in 1914.

Finally, the central image also refers to that stupendous astronomical phenomenon, The Horsehead Nebula, honouring the vastness of universal memory, which modern science continues to unearth retrospectively, by virtue of the insights revealed through the speed at which light travels from distant galaxies, a trace of events aeons ago, which still reach us in the here and now.

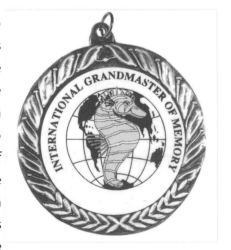

In 2007, Tony starred in a major Channel 5 primetime television documentary on the World Memory Championships, which had been held in Bahrain.

Also in 2007, Tony and I established World Councils for Speed Reading, Mind Mapping, Creativity, Memory and Intelligence, and formed The World Memory Sports Council. He had also become Chairman of the World Council for Mind Sports.

In 2008, Tony realised another dream, and founded, with eight-times World Memory Champion Dominic O'Brien and myself, the first ever Schools Memory Championship. In the short space of only two years, the Championship has attracted participation from over 300 schools, the training of over eleven thousand children in the art and science of memory, regional championships, a national championship, and support from the Government Body, Aim Higher.

For over forty years, Tony Buzan has been a pioneer across the breadth and depth of the Mind Sports field. His many pioneering projects blossomed early, and have grown stronger and more widespread with the years.

Mind Sports

He has initiated tectonic shifts in the field of Mind Sports, which continue to evolve, and which continue to have increasing positive impact on the fields of education, business, Government, and, most importantly, the individual.

The evolution of Mind Sports is a significant aspect of the evolution of Mankind.

In identifying the match between world chess champion Garry Kasparov and IBM's Deep Blue computer as one of the most significant moments in his BBC TV History of the World, Andrew Marr said: "Chess has always been seen as the ultimate test of human memory, planning and intuition."

• • • •

"The world's biggest-selling book" is the proud boast of Guinness World Records . Nevertheless, a mere 7 pages even have entries on mental achievements or Mind Sports. Although poker has five entries , draughts and bridge receive no treatment at all. Meanwhile it documents such vital attainments as: "most heads shaved in 24 hours", "fastest time to drink a 500-ml milkshake", "longest tandem bungee jump", "fastest carrot chopping", "largest underpants" and "most socks worn on one foot" .

And that is it. Not one world-class chess Grandmaster is mentioned by name and there is no indication that any Mind Sports championship titles have ever existed. Indeed, the total space devoted to Mental World Records in the entire book is less than that accorded to one exploit by Kathryn Ratcliffe (UK), who, on 25 October 2003, and with a tally of 138, broke her own record "for the most Smarties eaten in three minutes using chopsticks".

"Tony Buzan is one of the very few people I have met

who really understands so

completely how important the brain is to any sportsman or sportswoman – a breakthrough for anyone who wants to go out there and win and for anyone wanting a fitter, healthier and more successful life."

Sir Steven Redgrave, CBE

Chapter 9

In Corpore Sano – Sportsman (A Healthy Body)

Tony is a recognised figure and significant author and contributor to the field of sports. His own sporting career, though, got off to a particularly inauspicious start. As a child aged two, it was thought that his legs were becoming slightly 'bowed', and so for two years he was in leg splints to make sure his legs developed in alignment. He had to sleep, during the last two years of the war, every night with his splints on, underneath the staircase, which was the safest place in the house to protect him from the possible negative impact of the 'doodle-bugs' and bombs.

A few years later, in his first 'at bat' in cricket, he was bowled out 'HBW' – hand before wicket. The fast ball hit him square on his right thumb and forefinger and led to immediate bruising and swelling.

He was mocked for 'overreacting' until it was later discovered, as the swelling and bruising continued, that his hand had been seriously damaged, and required three weeks of medical attention.

From that time on (by an amazing coincidence - just like the author at his school Dulwich College) he preferred to play as a fielder, positioning himself as far away from the wickets as the grounds would allow. The only highlight of his early, and very short, cricketing career was in the field. He was on the boundary of the pitch, and having observed that there was hardly any action, lay down on a hot summer day, on the cool and newly mown grass, raising his right arm and hand to protect his eyes from the sun. Tony was looking up into the limitless blue of the sky, drifting and daydreaming, when miraculously something landed perfectly in his open hand. It was a cricket ball! With the probability of tens of trillions to one, he had 'caught out' the batsman who would otherwise have scored 'a six'!

His venture into soccer was similarly unprepossessing.

Having never kicked a ball before, he floundered around the soccer field and before the first half was over had been both spiked and kicked heavily in the shin.

This diminishing experience was followed by his introduction to rugby, where, whilst standing on the sidelines waiting for his first 'play', one of the better athletes in the school was laid down on a stretcher near where Tony was standing, with a suspected broken back. Tony elected not to participate! With these experiences to guide him, he decided that any activity involving any kind of ball, was not for him.

At the age of ten, inspired by the film *Scaramouche* with Stewart Granger and Janet Leigh (1952) and its astonishingly refined sword fighting sequences, Tony took up fencing, which he both did and enjoyed, until unfortunately the club closed a few months later.

Through fencing he began to realise the importance of perception, alertness, balance and speed as factors in physical ability that were equally important to strength and muscle bulk.

The only activity in which he took any pleasure was the 'punishment' of having to go on cross-country runs. These he enjoyed, because the longer he went and the slower he ran, the more time he had to spend in the woods and with nature, and the more time he had to chat with those of his friends who had worked out the same strategy: longer and slower meant more time away from school!

His poor impression of sports was compounded when at the age of nine, on a cold and windy day on the seaside of Whitstable in Kent, the physical education teacher took the boys to a concrete swimming pool filled with very chilly seawater, and made those boys who could not swim, including Tony, 'jump in at the deep end' because then you'll have no choice but to swim'.

There was a choice – drowning! A choice which Tony nearly took...

Sports had become associated in his young brain with punishment, pain, damage to hands and legs, broken spines, freezing, and death by drowning! Here is the expanded version of how, at the age of thirteen, Tony's life and attitudes were transformed.

"I had vaguely begun to realise that a fit body was attractive to girls! An athletic friend of mine introduced me to push-ups and sit-ups. In the cooperative/competitive nature of friends, we began to compare notes, and I tried to match him. At first my performances were pathetic.

"Gradually, though, as I persisted, my results improved. Then came the 'WOW!' When checking in the mirror I could see, for the first time in my life, the faint outline of my abdominal muscles (the 'six-pack') and the first definition of the muscles in my chest, shoulders and arms. I began to realise that the body with which I had been blessed was not simply 'there' - it was a flexible 'machine' which would respond to the way I treated it. It was mine to abuse, lose, or use.

"Suddenly a whole new world opened up to me, and I embraced it with gusto. Physical training was not the pain, agony and torture that I had imagined it to be in my earlier years. It was energizing, stress-reducing, and had made me both look and feel good.

"During my senior years at school I managed a 'paper shack' for the morning paper The Province. The paper shack was a little hut where a gaggle of teenage boys gathered at 5.00 a.m. to collect the 'rounds' of newspapers which they then delivered. My 'round' was to the houses along the seafront. It was over two miles long, and I used it as training by cycling it hands free as much as possible, and by folding the newspapers into missiles that I would aim at the distant porches. In the middle of the route, on the seaside, was a double Olympic-sized natural seawater swimming pool, which at that time in the morning was unpopulated, and which was not a particular attraction for the boy who had nearly drowned in a smaller version of it!

"One morning of a particularly hot June, it entered my mind that swimming could obviously be a pleasurable activity, that it would expand my physical and social range of opportunities, and that the only reason I wasn't doing it, and was actually consciously avoiding it, was because I was terrified of drowning.

"The following morning, after finishing my paper rounds, I was in the pool, standing chest-deep in the water holding on to the bar at the side of the pool with white knuckles, shivering, not from the cold (the water was quite warm) but from fear, and commencing the process of taking in a deep breath and forcing myself to exhale it under water – a terrifying and body-tightening experience that should have held no terror at all.

"Morning after morning I repeated the routine, eventually becoming relaxed as my face broke the surface, diminishing the spluttering and hypochondriacal coughing that had featured in my earliest tries, and actually beginning to relax in the water. From this I progressed, day-after-day, to jumping from the edge from one feet away, two feet away, three feet away, until I could glide some distance while exhaling, and successfully reach the bar at the edge of the pool. From there I progressed to rudimentary dog paddling (the dogs did it better than I did!) and eventually to formal swimming lessons. Within two years I had qualified as a bronze-level lifeguard, and swimming had become a way of life. To this day, long-distance ocean swimming is one of my greatest joys."

As we shall see, later in this book, ocean swimming also led to one of Tony's most spiritual experiences.

"One day, while cycling over a bridge that spanned an ocean inlet, something emerged from under the bridge that grabbed my peripheral vision, and on which I immediately focused. It was the first time I had ever seen an Olympic sculler rowing in a racing shell. It looked like a spear on the water, using oars that recalled the fine legs of a water skimmer, with muscles that were those of the ideal athlete, with a rhythm that was mesmeric, and in a setting that could only be described as paradise. Instantaneously I braked, wheeled around, sped down to the rowing club, and asked how I could be trained to do that.

"Within an hour I was being trained. Within a month I had saved up enough money to buy my own racing shell and blades. During my first outing in that most beautiful and graceful of machines, I had become addicted, and had found one of my life's main pleasures and passions.

"Sculling in a single shell exercised every one of my major muscle groups, taught me balance, taught me the appropriate (and inappropriate!) use of strength and power, allowed me to experience rhythm as I had never known it before, taught me to breathe, and was like a moving yoga. The fact that I was on a mirror-like surface, reflecting the swans who glided majestically by, that I was surrounded with nature and birdsong as the sun rose, and that I was inhaling the most fresh and ion-filled air, were added bonuses. Rowing had become an integral part of my life."

Dance

At the beginning of his dance career, Tony was one of those people who thought he had 'two left feet'. Good teachers quickly taught him that he actually had a left and a right foot, and that if he could walk, he could dance! In 1959, when he was 17, Tony took up competitive Viennese Waltzing, and was quickly disabused of his previous assumptions that dancing was a 'weakling's activity'. He reached the finals of the schools championships.

His interest in dance stayed with him and grew during his university years, during which he learned and competed in ballroom, Latin American, jive and free dancing. In 1965, at the Pedersen's professional dance exhibition award competition, he won first prize.

When he returned to England in 1966, he taught, part-time, ballroom and modern dances. Dancing has remained a passion throughout his life, and to this day you will see him 'mixing it up' in discos and dance clubs around the world!

Fitness and Martial Arts

"So spoke the master of the Martial Art,
and touch'd, with transport great, Atrides' heart."

Alexander Pope, in his translation of Homer's Iliad, 1715

This was the first mention of Martial Art in English.

While at university, and to earn money towards his tuition fees, Tony became, a physical fitness instructor for private health clubs and gyms. During this time he also began his explorations of the martial arts, expertise in which, he had long held as a distant dream. He began first with judo, a form in which, for three reasons, he spent comparatively little time.

Firstly, the instructor (Sensei), a 1st Dan black belt, was arrogant and egocentric, and was more interested in demonstrating his own powers than teaching students.

Secondly, Tony was spending most of his time with his arms twisted into various particularly uncomfortable positions, while his face was pressed into a rough and not particularly clean mat.

Thirdly, because one day a new student came to the club, and the Sensei who made a point of humiliating newcomers, tried unsuccessfully for ten minutes to throw the new recruit.

When the newcomer came back to the excited gaggle of students waiting at the edge of the mat, he was deluged with questions about how he had managed to stay upright against the Sensei, when none of us had been able to. He explained that he had studied karate, and how he therefore knew how to balance in opposite directions to those forces being applied by the judo player.

The whole class then insisted on a karate versus judo combat, to which the Sensei unwisely agreed. It took the karate student less than three minutes to corner and trap the totally frustrated judo bully. The students, including Tony, assumed that the Karateka must have been an advanced student. Wrong. He was a relative beginner. Within five minutes, the entire class had decided to switch their allegiance to karate, and thus, as he was about to leave for England in 1966, Tony's karate career began.

Tony arrived in London with the intention to go to Japan to study karate in a land of its origins. He was then told that the world's number one karate teacher, Tatsuo Suzuki, had just been sent by the Japanese Karate Federation to London to help promote karate as a major new sport in Europe. Tony decided to stay!

For over a year he studied under the leadership of Sensei Suzuki. As Tony was already working in the literary and publishing worlds, and as Suzuki wanted to get his basic lessons for each level of karate published, the two worked on the project together, and Tony published them in 1969.

Tony loved karate, especially the dance-forms or 'katas'. The only thing that concerned him were the injuries that this contact sport were inflicting on him and his friends.

During these early karate years, Suzuki was to teach Tony a life-long lesson that came out of the blue and was spontaneous.

Tony explains: "Japan regularly sent its national and world karate champions for continuing study with the ultimate master – Suzuki. Part of their studying was to teach. One particular young world champion was obviously influenced by Bruce Lee, and was very flashy in his movements, and slightly arrogant in his bearing and his attitude towards Suzuki's students. He was consistently showing off, which was not Suzuki's style or manner.

"One day, after a particularly ostentatious display, in which he had done flying kicks, roundhouse kicks, rapid-fire, multiple punches to all parts of the body, and all kinds of acrobatic leaping about, Suzuki beckoned to us students, indicated that we should go to the edge of the dojo, and said: 'demonstlation'.

"He then beckoned the world champion on to the dojo floor and said 'flee fighting'. This means that all techniques can be used, contacts can be made, the one restriction being that there must be no permanent damage or injury to the opponent. We were all agape with amazement, for here was a real world championship, in the privacy of our own dojo, with the world's greatest (and undefeated!) 45-year-old Sensei of the art, and the new remarkably good and younger world karate champion.

"The fight started, with the world champion, his honour on the line, throwing everything at Suzuki in blurs of multi-limbed movement. Throughout these storms of attack, Suzuki, who was only about five feet tall, stood like a little oak tree, hardly moving at all, eyes fixed on the forehead of his opponent, and very casually, with the slightest of arm movements, deflecting everything the world champion threw at him.

"As he was doing this, his feet were not stepping forward, they were moving him forward like slow caterpillars, his toes, with the sensitivity of fingers, reaching out and then drawing the remainder of his foot behind them. It was almost as if he were slowly gliding across the floor towards the opponent. After about seven minutes, during which the world champion had not landed a single blow, Suzuki's left foot shot out like a cobra, the ball of his foot landing powerfully in the middle of the champion's right shin. The champion, through his world championship preparations and combats, was trained not to express any reaction of pain, but the way in which he quickly withdrew his right leg indicated that he had really felt the blow.

"For roughly the next seven minutes, the fight continued as it had done for the first seven minutes, ending in exactly the same way: the cobra strike was repeated, the blow landing in exactly the same place as the previous one. This time the champion's reaction to what must have been incredible pain was more apparent.

"For half an hour the master class continued, until the world champion, his right shin now swollen and massively bruised, and still not having landed a single blow on Suzuki, stood before him, bedraggled, dishevelled, pouring with sweat, slouched, and gasping for air. Suzuki stood in front of him in exactly the same pose and with exactly the same calm and poise, as he had at the beginning of the demonstration.

"He looked down at the defeated champion, and said with deep irony and sarcasm in his voice: 'Haawww, world champion??! No power! No strength! No technique!' after which he paused, and then, in a much more loud and violent voice, said:

"'NO STAMINA!!'

"In that half hour, and in that final statement and second, I and my fellow students had been taught two seminal lessons: firstly that real mastery produces a great calmness and serenity, whereas incomplete mastery will tend to generate desperation and arrogance; the second lesson, and one that has stayed with me throughout my life, was that flashiness, unnecessary 'decoration', and even style and championships were not what greatness was all about – as Suzuki had said, it was about the ability to continue in the pursuit of your art regardless of the circumstances.

"To combine training, skill, focus, persistence and commitment, with a warrior-like long-term series of initiations by testing, by which, and only by which, one will arrive, by experience, at true transcendence – the becoming of the true adept, on a spiritual plain, in which these accumulated powers are used wisely and correctly with the grace required of one's art."

The lesson the Sensei taught Tony was a profound one and there can be detected an important and significant intersection between Mind Sports and Martial Arts; the ability of the one to defeat the many. Who has not admired the Samurai feats of Toshiro Mifune in the films of Kurosawa, an early inspiration for Steven Spielberg? In these films physical intelligence and power are not just muscular strengths and general fitness but transcend this and permit the true Master to overcome simultaneously numerous less skilled opponents.

Similarly in chess I have taken on 107 opponents at one and the same time and achieved a 97% success rate. Such performances are also to be seen in related Mind Sports, such as Shogi and Xiangqi respectively the Japanese and Chinese national variants of chess; it is mental power that can direct to even greater feats of strength, power and 'intelligence'. The single Grandmaster or 9th Dan can easily overpower huge numbers of untrained practitioners.

Tony, as we shall soon see, was not primarily disturbed by the pain inflicted by judo and karate, but he was concerned by long term physical damage. Hence Aikido became Tony's main martial art, and he even went to Tokyo to experience lessons in the Dojo of the founder, O Sensei Morihei Ueshiba. Here Tony was thrown around like a limp octopus by a 78-year-old man who did nothing but smile and laugh, used all of Tony's 'strength' and energy, and did not hurt him once in a half-hour session.

Tony continued to study Aikido for many years, incorporated it as part of the Renaissance Academy for Prince Philip of Liechtenstein, and in 1997, was given an honorary black belt in Aikido awarded for his services to and knowledge of the art.

Partly through shared love of Martial Arts, Tony was to meet Michael J. Gelb, the author of Body Learning, an illustrated book on the use of the Alexander Technique (of which more later) who was also a professional juggler. Tony quickly learned that another thing that he 'could never do' he could do - juggle! In 1994, Tony and Michael published Lessons from the Art of Juggling, the book that transferred the approaches and skills learned in juggling, to all other forms and subjects of learning.

Tony's Friend...Pain!

During the early and particularly vigorous stages of his physical and athletic career, like all other athletes Tony regularly suffered injuries, including back injury and a number of others. These he found extremely frustrating, annoying and aggravating, and at first he resented them!

"When running, in particular, I would regularly sprain my left knee, and began to hate that part of my body for its constant interference with and interruptions of my 'best laid plans'. Then one day the universe sent me a flash of realisation and inspiration.

"I suddenly became aware that my knee, an incredible work of engineering genius, was one of my lifetime companions. It had been travelling with me from before the moment I was born, and had devoted its life, exclusively, willingly, and selflessly, to me and all my demands of it. Having supported (literally!) me and my activities and dreams for some 30 years, it was now trying to communicate with me in order to help.

It was saying something like: 'Hey Tony! Help!... I've been willingly helping you walk, run, swim, and dance for 30 years, and now your off-poise-balance is doing something that is hurting me! If you keep on this way, I won't be able to help you anymore. Tony!... I'm your friend!... Please help me! I am trying to give you feedback here...'

From that moment on I looked upon all injuries, pain and illnesses as communications from that vast army of friends and companions called by body and brain, whose sole purpose and pleasure in life was to please and support me. If they were any way in pain or disease, then it was my responsibility and commitment to adjust the behaviour that was causing them pain, and to care for them as they cared for me."

In 1977, having increasingly come to realise the importance of diet as a factor in overall health, Tony enrolled in a thirty-years-plus study of the subject with England's leading Nutritional Doctor, Dr. Andrew Strigner, FRCM, author of *The Food Fallacy*.

Under Dr. Strigner's tutelage, Tony studied, and continues to study the full range of dietary factors in human nutrition, including: the role of vitamins; calories and their true nature and effect; fat and its negative and positive attributes; ancestral habits and their effects and signposts for modern diets; the human body, its design and how this design directs us to an appropriate diet; the meta-studies of the studies on nutrition, and what the consistent and general conclusions are; the brain and its needs for correct diet; blood types and their indications for behaviour and diet, and the truly balanced diet. In 2013, Tony switched to drinking non-alcoholic wine and has even convinced the oenophile author of this book of its charms!

In addition, Tony has also worked with and studied under Professor Michael Crawford, Director of the Institute for Brain Chemistry and Human Nutrition, and the World's leading expert on the advantages of using a predominantly fish-based diet to promote brain development and growth.

In the late 1970s, during a romance with his Scandinavian girlfriend, Tony learned briefly downhill skiing, and for weeks on end the delights of ski du fond (cross-country skiing). The exhilaration of the rhythmic and aerobic nature of the sport, and the incredible beauty of the vast expanse of white, the snow clad trees, and the penetrating light blue of the sunny winter skies, made this one of his favourite sports.

In the early 1980s, Tony ventured into horse riding, one of his first experiences being taken on an unscheduled gallop through the Jamaican underbrush, with the horse only stopping because it came to the edge of a high cliff, overlooking the ocean! Deciding to take more instruction, Tony, when he visited South Africa, took three days of personalised residential instruction from Major General George Iwanovski, master of the Lipizzaner stallions. He also supplemented this training with two exceptional lessons from the head equerry of the Swedish/Stockholm police force.

Then, in 1982, Tony moved to Marlow-on-Thames in order to re-ignite his early love of rowing. As part of his charitable work, Tony coached members of Marlow's rowing squads and in 1988, was asked by Mike Spracklen, head coach of the English national rowing squad, to help the squad in general, and particularly the eight, prepare for the Korean Olympics.

In 2001, Tony published his major work on the mind and body, *Head Strong*. In 2003, this was followed up with *The Power of Physical Intelligence*.

In these books, Tony introduced the new concepts of Meta-Positive Thinking, the TEFCAS (Trial, Event, Feedback, Check, Adjust, Success) model for learning how to learn, thinking, and the new science of Holanthropy – the study of the inter-relationship between the brain and the body; the body and the brain.

In the early part of the 21st century, Tony coached with Jezz Moore, one of the national rowing coaches, three junior quads in three consecutive years to silver and gold medals at the Royal Henley Regatta.

Wherever you are in the world with Tony, you will find him, five days a week, at dawn or dusk, in the gym, in the swimming pool, or in the dance studio. Whenever he returns from his global travels, you will find him between 6.00 and 7.00 a.m. at the rowing club, either working out on the ergometer (rowing) machines, or on the River Thames rowing amidst the swans in a single, double, or quadruple scull.

During the next two years Tony was to participate at various levels, in helping with England's preparation for the 2012 Olympic Games. The key messages in transforming the rowing crew's mental toughness abilities were Tony's formulae of Meta-Positive thinking and TEFCAS. I will now explain in detail what they are:

Meta-Positive Thinking:

THE POWER TO CHANGE YOURSELF FOR THE BETTER

A BBH is a Big Bad Habit, one that is counterproductive to your survival. It's one you are aware of and have decided to change. Let's imagine this habit is eating two boxes of chocolates per day, that you weigh 400 lb (181 kg) and have been doing this for 20 years. It could equally be a BBH that is going to take 12 years off your life, such as smoking 40 cigarettes a day; or 8 years off such as an Olympic gold-medal winning level of alcohol intake; and so on... but let's stay with the chocolate analogy for the moment.

What's the first thing that comes into your mind when you say: 'I am not going to eat chocolates'? Notice the first thing that occurs to you when you even read that phrase - was it not the chocolates themselves? Did you see the packaging of your favourite ones?

So, a thought is whizzing through the circuits of your brain. It has run through many times before, for it is a habit, something you don't even think about - it is paraconscious and now you are trying to change it, consciously. The good news is that even thinking 'I am going to change' actually does change the brain on a physiological level, causing different traces to activate through your brain cells.

But - and it's a big 'but' - a habit is something you have been doing for years, and along comes a birthday and someone gives you –

chocolates. What are you thinking now, as you look at the box? Possibly, 'I'll just have one!'

This is a BBH, a Big Bad Habit; it took years to install it in your mental software, so is it logical to think that you can change it all at once? But, bit by bit, every time you re-commit to your goal you can install new thought patterns and make new positive thoughts the GNH (Good New Habit).

META-POSITIVE THINKING: THE KEY STEPS

How do you do this? The best way is by deciding what to focus on and then by re-committing to it regularly. In the chocolate example, where was your focus? It was on the chocolates, wasn't it? So a more appropriate way of getting a handle on the subject would be to think about what you might gain by not eating chocolates. Your ultimate goal in conquering your Big Bad Habit and establishing a Good New Habit is to become fitter and healthier. How could we actually describe this goal? To be really effective, an affirmation has to fulfil the following criteria:

- It must be personal - I ...
- It must be stated in the present - I am ...
- It must cover the process of what you are doing. This is important, because if you say to yourself, 'I am healthy', you aren't, you are actually lying to yourself, so - I am becoming... -.
- It must contain the goal within it - I am becoming healthy.

Re-committing to this goal regularly will help your brain re-wire its BBH into a GNH. This is called meta-positive thinking or - thinking for a change for the better.

THE NEXT META-POSITIVE STEP: TEFCAS

TEFCAS is a mnemonic devised by Tony to reflect how the brain learns and to help you remember this easily. To understand how TEFCAS works, let's take a concrete example. We teach 'Go', chess, Mind Sports and juggling at The Renaissance Academy, as a metaphor for learning. Juggling often strikes particular terror into the audience!

When first confronted by the balls, many a stout- hearted individual has been seen to back away - even physically. The first throw may be successful or not - but how do you judge if it was successful if you have nothing to compare it with? You might look around and see how others are doing. If you were having limited success you might give up quickly.

So, how do you learn? Over the years Tony has have been collecting people's views from around the world and they are generally the same, that everyone learns and acquires new or changed habits in a smooth curve.

How completely wrong this illusion is! Yet it is extremely powerful and pervasive, in all cultures and all languages.

The brain has a very specific procedure for learning and the integration of new skills, and I will use Tony's TEFCAS mnemonic to spell it out:

T is for Trial. You try something new: juggling, eating more healthily, cutting back on drinking, stop smoking, starting aerobic exercise, etc.

Keeping interested and challenging your brain is part of trying something.

E is for Event. Something happens. You catch the ball, or you don't. These are just events, not success or failure on their own. Divorcing the emotion from an event means that you can continue, when others have 'failed'. It also means that you can apply clear criteria as to what has happened, be it a 'good' event, or a 'bad' one. You can learn from the data, without the labels of judgment.

F is for Feedback. How did you do? Did you feel you failed? There is no failure, only feedback that "This is what happened when you did…" Getting appropriate feedback means that you will be able to assess accurately and plan your next stage …

C is for Check. Check against a professional, or teacher, Check against your own goals. Check the feedback of yourself and others – is it accurate?…

A is for Adjust. It was once said that the definition of madness was to carry on doing something, while expecting a different result. So if what you are doing doesn't work, opt for a changed approach - a different teacher, different type of equipment.

S is for SUCCESS. Time for celebration, giving the brain something to look forward to when it succeeds, which it will when it follows the correct formulae.

"Es irrt der Mensch so lang er strebt"

"Whilst striving to achieve, mistakes are inevitable"

Johan Wolfgang Von Goethe

Do not be discouraged if you sometimes receive negative feedback. This is normal and natural in the learning or changing process.

Rowing

In his role as Mental Toughness Instructor, Tony had been helping to coach a rowing squad for the Olympics, who were so poor that they regularly did not appear on any of the international ranking lists. When he checked their thoughts and feelings about themselves, they identified their two main weaknesses as lack of physical strength and lack of mental strength – a wonderful combination!

This conclusion had come about because of their regular poor placings, no matter what mental self-improvement techniques they had tried. One main technique when facing crews who had beaten them in earlier races, was to repeat to themselves the affirmation, 'We are not going to let them beat us again; we are not going to let them beat us again…'

What image had they been placing in their collective brains? 'Beat us again' And, sure enough, all the other crews did!

159

As soon as they learned more appropriate Meta-Positive Thinking techniques, both their mental and physical demeanours changed, and in a period of just three months they rose from being commonly regarded as 'the dregs' to fourth place in the Olympic final. A perfect example of Meta-Positive Thinking applied to real sporting life occurred on the crew's way to the Olympic Final. Just two months before the Olympics in Seoul, they were racing in a final of a Regatta on the River Thames against the undefeated Australian Eight.

All bets were on the Australians (except the crew's and Tony's!) Right from the start, the Australians pulled into the lead of two-thirds of a length, which they maintained until there were only a few hundred meters to go. It is 'rowing lore' on this stretch of the Thames that any crew significantly behind at this stage of the race is doomed to defeat.

The Meta-Positive Thinking British squad did not accept this. Their Cox yelled at them that anything was possible, and with a sudden leap, the British boat took nearly a quarter of a length out of the Australian's lead. The Australians, already relaxing into their 'assured victory' were taken by surprise, and the British boat maintained its impetus, creeping up inch by inch as they approached the finishing line. It appeared as if it were a dead heat. The crowd waited in suspense for over three minutes before the announcer proclaimed:

'In the final of the Grand Challenge Cup between the Australian Olympic Squad and the Olympic Designate Squad from Great Britain, the winners, by a foot were Great Britain'.

When Tony debriefed the Cox afterwards, he said, mischievously, and with a smile on his face, "What, Tony, do you think that foot was?"

"A thought!" he beamed

He was right!

The crew's mental and physical demeanours had changed, and in the period of three months, they rose from being commonly regarded as 'the dregs' to fourth place in the Olympic final! In 1990, Tony was made Mental Toughness Coach of the Marlow Rowing Club, and continued to help the national squads in both the 1992 Barcelona Olympics and for the 2000 Sydney Olympics.

On 3 August 2011, a fire badly damaged the 140-year-old boathouse at Marlow Rowing Club (Tony Buzan's home away from home). Almost twelve months later the community gathered together to raise money to rebuild and return the club to its former glory, as well as for the Macmillan Cancer Support charity. The main event was 'Row with Redgrave' – an exclusive opportunity for guests to row with the five times Olympic rowing gold medallist, Sir Steve Redgrave. Six of the guests rose to the challenge, one of which being our very own Tony Buzan.

• • • •

Two times World Memory Champion Wang Feng with eight time
World Memory Champion Dominic O'Brien and Tony Buzan.

Chapter 10
Loving Humanity

Tony distributing books to eager youngsters in Sierra Leone on behalf of the Brain Trust Charity

Tony is devoting increasing amounts of his time to charities, especially where they focus on the welfare of the earth and its cargo of intelligence. He has already committed years of his life to charitable initiatives as wide-ranging as general support for the Worldwide Fund for Nature, research into animal communication, providing ongoing help in the investigation of perception and the role of the artist in society, and has similarly provided support for investigation of the mother's nutrition of the developing brain of the embryo.

Throughout his life he has consistently provided global support for under-privileged children and schools, to help them with the development of their thinking skills, and to assist students with any learning difficulties. In this respect the sitting of the 21st World Memory Championship in the London inner city Lilian Baylis School is both typical and indicative. Above all, Tony is the founder of the Brain Trust Charity, created to promote the worldwide development of the growth and nurturing of intelligence.

Tony's charity work began at the age of seven, when, because of his love for animals, he joined the RSPCA (the Royal Society for the Prevention of Cruelty to Animals), and the PDSA (the People's Dispensary for Sick Animals). At that time he was not fully cognisant of the words 'charity' or 'philanthropy'. He volunteered his time and energy for a number of years to those Societies, simply because he wanted to help animals.

This continued as part of his normal behaviour through his teens and early twenties, where he would donate, as a matter of principle, ten per cent or more of his time/income to helping both animals and the disadvantaged. He both contributed to, and lectured for, the World Wide Fund for Nature during these times.

During the 1980s, he had become aware that an alarming number of people around the world had negative impressions about the brain, associating it with forgetting, Alzheimer's, mental illness, stress and depression, etc.

In addition, most of the highly worthy charities devoted to the brain were set up to deal with the malfunctioning of the brain: Age Concern, Help The Aged, The Spastics Society, and many other organisations connected with mental health problems.

The Brain Trust Charity

Helping to unlock and deploy the vast capacity of the human brain

The Brain Trust Charity

He struck upon the idea of a charity devoted to the positive side of the brain, and in 1990 founded the Brain Trust Charity (Charity Number 1001012) with the following Charter:

"To promote research into study of thought processes, the investigation of the mechanics of thinking, manifested in learning, understanding, communication, problem solving, creativity and decision making; to disseminate the results of such research and study and to promote generally education and training in cognitive processes and techniques and to develop and exploit new techniques in cognitive processes."

A main focus of the Brain Trust is to provide resources to disadvantaged children who wish to learn about and enhance their mental capabilities. On a global scale, the objective of the Brain Trust is to maximise the ability of each and every individual to unlock and deploy the vast capacity of his or her brain. In this capacity, the Brain Trust also provides financial encouragement for mental awareness and practical cognitive activities of all kinds.

Brain Trust Areas Of Activity

Tony established the Brain Trust to bring about greater 'Trust in the Brain' and to involve itself in the following areas:

- research, investigation into and support for initiatives connected with mental performance;
- the advancement of education;
- the advancement of health - in particular mental health;
- support of the intelligent advancement of the arts, culture and science;
- the advancement of amateur sport - especially mind sports such as chess and draughts, as well as competitive memory and speed reading events;
- the relief of those in need - especially where declining mental performance may have adversely affected welfare, well-being and circumstances;
- research into animal intelligence and thus the advancement of animal welfare and other areas connected with mental performance and brain research.

Raymond Keene, Tony Buzan and Dominic O'Brien in Regents Park Zoo adopting the Malaysian elephant Layang Layang for the Brain Trust in September 1993.

Brain Trust Accomplishments

In its young life the Brain Trust has - by means of specific fundraising events - helped to publicise the following worthy public causes both nationally and internationally:

- intensive work in deprived inner-city schools to help raise the level of Mental Literacy, pupils' concentration on academic work and thus behaviour and overall scholastic performance;
- the World Wide Fund for Nature (research into animal intelligence);
- London Zoo - research into the memory power of elephants and its applications;

Major Initiatives

The Brain Club

In the late 1980s, Tony formed the International Brain Clubs, for which he wrote The Brain Club Manifesto. The Manifesto laid out the ways in which schools, universities and independent bodies could form clubs devoted to the brain and its nurturing and development.

The Brain Club University

Tony initiated and majorly sponsored the idea of a Brain Club Floating University. The university was a one week academy held on those giant Turkish yachts called a gullet. Each morning began with swimming and swimming lessons in the Aegean Sea. This was followed by a breakfast of fresh fruits, yoghurts, and honey.

The remainder of the morning was spent studying a choice from memory, creativity, art, poetry, speed reading and study skills, Mind Mapping, and communication and presentation skills.

This was followed by a lunch consisting mainly of fruits, salads and vegetables, followed by a one hour siesta and then an afternoon spent either continuing the studies of the morning, or exploring the surrounding bays, villages and mountains.

After an evening dinner of 'the fruits of the sea' and for those who wished local wines, free time was given for playing chess and the Bahraini board game Dama, for reading, and for discussion and friendship.

Each day followed the same Renaissance Academy formula, the differences being that the boats had moved to new bays, the menus were varied, and the specific topics studied during the day rotated.

The Brain Clubs and Brain Trust represent a growing presence in the charity universe, and have as goal the reaching of every brain on the planet.

The Brain Of The Year Award

Observing, as he had done with the absence of Memory Championships, that there were no awards or recognition for all round use of the brain, Tony established, in 1991, on behalf of the Brain Trust Charity, the Brain of the Year Award. This award, unlike the Nobel prizes, is given not for one specific area of excellence; it is given for overall 'Brain Excellence' incorporating the multiple intelligences.

To qualify for consideration for this award an individual will need to satisfy the Awards Committee that they comfortably meet the following criteria. The candidates must:

1. be pre-eminent in their field;

2. have made a major new contribution to their field in the preceding year;

3. have contributed major new creative developments to their field of endeavour;

4. have made a notable effort to educate others in their chosen discipline;

5. have integrated the principle of Mens sana in corpore sano (a healthy mind in a healthy body) in their lives;

6. have exhibited persistence and stamina over time;

7. have demonstrated a general cultural awareness;

8. have demonstrably contributed to society;

9. have demonstrated a concern for humanity;

10. be active and known on a global level;

11. be an outstanding role model for those in their field and for youth in general.

Brain Of The Year Award Winners

Chionofuji - Sumo Grand Champion who used brain rather than brawn to triumph and to transform his sport - Japan;

Professor Leif Edvinsson - Global Educator and author of the book 'Intellectual Capital' – Sweden;

Michael Gelb - 5th Dan black belt in Aikido, author of bestselling books on the body, the brain and thinking including *How to Think Like Leonardo da Vinci and Thomas Edison*, Vice Dean of the Academy, Pioneer in the fields of creative thinking and innovative leadership, Brain of the Year 1999 – USA;

John Glenn - Pioneering astronaut, US Senator, athlete and fighter pilot;

Professor Stephen Hawking - Astro Physicist Extraordinaire, holder of Sir Isaac Newton's Professorship at Cambridge, and author of *A Brief History of Time* – UK;

Ted Hughes - Polymath, Sportsman, Educational Pioneer, Playwright, Author and England's Poet Laureate – UK;

Dr. Lana Israel - Rhodes Scholar, teenage polymath and world promoter of the ideal of Mental Literacy - South Africa/USA;

Garry Kasparov - World Chess Champion (highest rated player of all time for the longest period), linguist, athlete and campaigner for improved global education –USSR/ Russia;

Dominic O'Brien - Memory Grand Master, Eight times World Memory Champion, bestselling author, educational visionary – UK;

Sir Steve Redgrave - Five Olympic Gold Medals in rowing, and proponent and living example of the belief that brain power can be the determinant for success in an ostensibly physical activity – UK;

Gene Roddenberry - Engineer, philanthropist, the originator of and mastermind behind Star Trek – US;

Dr. Marion Tinsley - Legendary mind sports champion, and the first human ever to win an official thinking sport world championship against a computer – USA.

Wang Feng - Two times World Memory Champion with highest ever ranking at the time - China.

Prince Mohsin Ali Khan of Hyderabad - for his services to world peace, his tireless work for tolerance and understanding and his support of charities, particularly children's charities.

Professor Michael Crawford   -   for his pioneering work on the biology of the brain.

Brain Of The Year 2012 - *Prince Mohsin Ali Khan of Hyderabad (India), Chairman World Peace and Prosperity Foundation*

Living Brain Of The 20th Century

In 2009, the Brain Trust gave a special award for the 'living brain of the 20th century'. This award was given to Baroness Susan Greenfield - British Scientist, writer, broadcaster and member of the House of Lords. Her specialty is the physiology of the brain and she has worked to research and bring attention to Parkinson's disease and Alzheimer's disease. Baroness Greenfield is Professor of Synaptic Pharmacology at Lincoln College, Oxford and former Director of the Royal Institution. She is noted for her endeavours to bring scientific understanding to the public.

Further awardees were Dr. Edward De Bono, Malta, elected by the Brain Trust Charity as Brain of the Year 2010. The citation reads:

'Edward de Bono is one of the leading authorities in the world in the field of creative thinking and the direct teaching of thinking as a skill. He has written 62 books with translations into 37 languages and has been invited to lecture in 54 countries. He is the originator of lateral thinking which treats creativity as the behaviour of information in a self-organising information system - such as the neural networks in the brain. From such a consideration arise the deliberate and formal tools of lateral thinking and parallel thinking. Dr. de Bono is a Rhodes scholar, a scholarship given to him for academic excellence, achievement in sport, and demonstration of his positive contribution to society.'

Tony is continuing to expand his global charity work on behalf of the brain and intelligence, and invites everyone to visit the Brain Trust Website (www.braintrust.org.uk) and to assist in this vital and global initiative for the freeing and nurturing of Intelligence.

Part Two

Mind Mapping

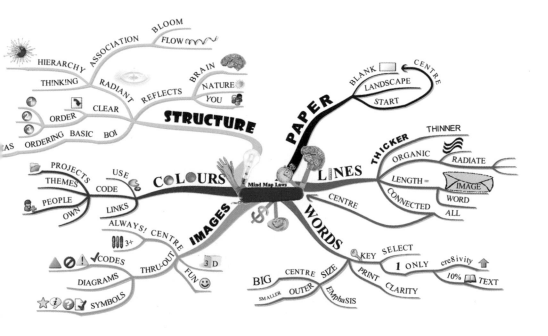

The Brain's Big Bang:

Mind Maps – The Definition

A Mind Map is a thinking tool based on architecture of thought, the three balustrades of the Cathedral of Thinking : Imagination; Association; and Location .

The three balustrades support the natural process and structure of thinking: **Radiant Thinking.** In Radiant Thinking , each thought radiates from its centre and extends from that centre in 360 degrees . Furthermore, Radiant Thinking extends *spherically* on an infinite number of spherical points, each radiating, potentially, infinitely.

A Mind Map is therefore a manifestation of the infinite number of infinitely radiating thoughts. A Mind Map incorporates the internal universe of an infinity of infinite thoughts.

The Mind Map is globally known as 'the Swiss Army knife of the brain'; the tool that can be applied to every aspect of cognition, learning, and thinking.

Chapter 11

A Man so various

"A man so various, that he seemed to be, not one, but all mankind's epitome." Poet Laureate John Dryden (1631-1700)

I n the late 1980s, Craig Collins, the Director for the Development of Asia for Management Centre Europe, organised Tony's first visit to Singapore. Craig had arranged for Tony to speak to hundreds of Singapore teachers and senior civil servants under the auspices of the Singapore Government's Ministry of Manpower.

Craig had developed a unique, never-seen-before way of introducing the speaker:

He started by telling the audience that there were a number of famous, interesting, and globally successful individuals in the auditorium on this particular day, and that before handing over to Tony, he wanted to introduce the individuals to the audience, and to have the audience copy the Mind Map that Craig was going to build up, and which would feature these individuals.

Using a projector and a giant screen, Craig drew an image of Singapore and the brain in the centre of the Mind Map, and then proceeded to introduce the individuals one-by-one and branch-by-branch, building up the Mind Map as he progressed.

The 'famous and successful' individuals included a best-selling author, a media personality, a government and corporate keynote speaker presenter and consultant, a prize-winning poet, a creator and inventor. When Craig had finished the Mind Map, and everyone (including Tony!) was waiting to see them, Craig increased the volume of his voice, and said to the packed auditorium:

"By an extraordinary coincidence, all of these globally successful individuals share the same name; and by an even more extraordinary coincidence, they all inhabit the same body and mind!

The name they share is Tony Buzan, and the body and mind they inhabit is that of the singularly remarkable individual you are about to meet!"

· · · ·

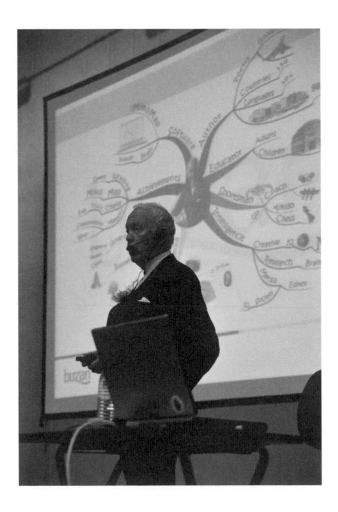

Chapter 12

Professor Barry Buzan On the Invention of Mind Maps

....which are known increasingly as the Swiss army knife of the mind or the flowers of intelligence.

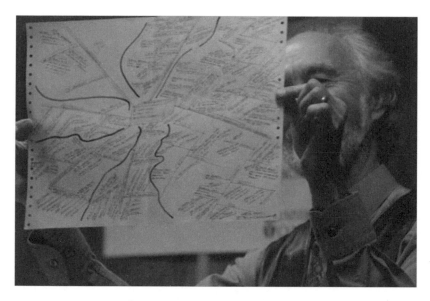

Professor Barry Buzan with Mind Map

I intersected with Tony's idea of Mind Maps in 1970, shortly after I had also settled in London. At that time, the idea was in its formative stages, only just beginning to take on an identity of its own, as distinct from mere keyword note-taking. I was just one part of Tony's broader agenda of learning methods and understanding of the human brain. As a sometime participant in Tony's work, I was on the fringes of this developmental process. My own serious engagement with the technique began when I started to apply it to the business of writing a doctoral thesis.

What attracted me to Mind Mapping was not the note-taking application that had captivated Tony, but the note-making one. I needed not only to organise a growing mass of research data, I needed also to clarify my thoughts on the convoluted political question of why peace movements almost always fail to achieve their stated objectives. My experience was that Mind Maps were a more powerful tool for thinking because they enabled me to sketch out the main ideas and to see quickly and clearly how they related to each other. They provided me with an exceptionally useful intermediate stage between the thinking process and actually committing words to paper.

I soon realised that the problem of bridging the gap between thinking and writing was a major deciding factor in success or failure for my fellow post-graduate students. Many failed to bridge this gap. They became more and more knowledgeable about their research subject but less and less able to pull all the details together in order to write about it.

Mind Mapping gave me a tremendous competitive advantage. It enabled me to assemble and refine my ideas, without going through the time-consuming process of drafting and re-drafting. By separating thinking from writing, I was able to think more clearly and extensively. When it was time to start writing, I already had a clear structure and a firm sense of direction, and this made the writing easier, faster and more enjoyable.

I completed my doctorate in under the prescribed three years, and also had time to write a chapter for another book, help to found, and then edit, a new quarterly journal of international relations, be associate editor of the student newspaper, take up motorcycling, and get married (doing a Mind Map with my wife-to-be to compose our wedding vows). Because of these experiences, my enthusiasm for the creative thinking side of the technique grew.

Mind Mapping remains a central element in my whole approach to academic work. It has made it possible for me to sustain an unusually high output of books, articles and conference papers. It has helped me to remain a generalist in a field where the weight of information forces most people to become specialists. I also credit it with enabling me to write clearly about theoretical matters whose complexity all too often inspires incomprehensible prose.

Thunderbolt

Meanwhile, back to the early 1960s and a young university lecturer is addressing first-year philosophy students on the power of memory.

Just like countless lecturers before him, he prepares his presentation with a few pages of notes made up of linear sentences. Announcing his subject, he says, 'Today, the topic is memory'. He stands behind the podium of the front of the lecture hall and starts to read, expecting his diligent students to take 'proper notes', just as he did when he was in their shoes.

He presents information specifically about the requirements for memory to work. There are two main elements: imagination – incorporating images and sensual feedback – and associations or connections. As well as these two main elements, he says, memory works more efficiently when things stand out. Here, the lecturer remembers that very day over 40 years ago:

"As I droned monotonously on, going slowly enough so that the students could copy my words, I realised that I was boring myself to distraction. As I looked at the drooping shoulders, heavy heads and clenched hands as they tried to scribble my rubbish, I realised that I wasn't doing much for my students either.

In addition, although I was telling them that in order to remember something, it has to have images, associations and things that stand out, I was lecturing in a monotone voice, asking them to write page upon page of rigid single-colour notes, with no images, associations or anything that stood out. In other words I was presenting to them the entire essence of memory in a manner that could have been designed to make them forget everything I said."

That lecturer was Tony Buzan, and that lecture with the ironic contrast between subject matter and presentation came like a thunderbolt from the skies. Looking back on it, that lecture represented a watershed in how he presented information.

It became clear that he needed to convey information in a way that would assist the audience in understanding and remembering it.

"I needed to impart information in a form that was easily digested by the human brain – not in linear lumps, which would remain unabsorbed. I realised that from now on my lectures should no longer use just sentences, but also include key words and images, alongside connections and associations, as well as elements such as colour, shape and size to help significant points stand out.

It was also clear that this insight should apply not only to my presentations as a verbal speaker, but also to the presentation of my own thoughts on paper. It was as relevant to me in a personal sense, as much as it was to the use of a blackboard, an overhead projector or a whiteboard.

So I went back to the drawing board – started with a 'blank slate', an imaginary white page – and asked myself two simple questions:

New Ways with Note Taking

Q: What do I need, on this note page, to help trigger my imagination?

A:

Q: What do I need on this note page to help me associate those things that have triggered my imagination?

A:

The answers to the first question included:

- Images
- Colours
- Codes
- Key image words
- Symbols
- Visual rhythms

The answers to the second question included:

- Lines
- Arrows
- Connection in space
- Numbers
- Colours
- Codes

Put these together on a page, and what do you get? A Mind Map.

In transforming myself as a presenter, this was the only 'training' I gave myself, and it led to all the other attributes of being a good presenter. These days, my presentation skills get plenty of practice. In an average year, I give up to 120 presentations. The audiences could not be more different. I might be presenting to 1,000 educationally disadvantaged children or 7,000 university students in a football stadium, and I could be in any of a number of different countries around the world, from Australia to Mexico, Scotland to Singapore, addressing, perhaps educational or government authorities.

The presentations can vary hugely in length - anything from one hour to six weeks. In the business world, I present to organisations such as Oracle, HSBC, IBM, the Singapore Institute of Management, Barclays International, BP and Boeing, helping them plan major events or their long-term business strategy, or one-to-ones with company presidents or CEOs.

But whoever it is that I am addressing and whatever the subject, the preparation and planning has been exactly the same from the first day I came to Mind Maps. Ever since then, the feedback I have received has been incredible. Audiences are asked to rank my presentations out of 100 and my average is 94.6. Saying this may seem immodest, but I am very proud of it. If I had to score myself as that young lecturer speaking about the power of my memory, I would give myself 20 - and that would be for my desire to help the students and for my love of the subject. For my ability to convey that passion, I would give myself 0 because, if anything, I helped them to forget."

Chapter 13

Mind Mapping Explained

There now follows a complete guide to get you started on this revolutionary concept.

What is a Mind Map?

A Mind Map is a powerful graphic technique that provides a universal key to unlocking the potential of the brain. It harnesses the full range of cortical skills - word, image, number, logic, rhythm, colour and spatial awareness - in a single, uniquely powerful manner. In so doing, it gives you the freedom to roam the infinite expanses of your brain. The Mind Map can be applied to every aspect of life where improved learning and clearer thinking will enhance human performance.

Originated in the late 1960s by Tony, Mind Maps have now been adopted by millions of people around the world - from the ages of 5 to 105 - whenever they wish to maximise the efficient use of their brainpower.

The Laws of Mind Mapping

- Start to draw in the centre of a blank, unlined page of paper, with an image of the desired topic, using at least three colours.
- Use images, symbols, codes and dimension throughout your Mind Map.
- Select key words and print - using capital letters.
- Each word/image must stand alone, on its own line.
- The lines must be connected, starting from the central image. In the centre, the lines are thicker, organic and flowing, becoming thinner as they radiate outwards.
- Make the lines the same length as the word/image.

- Use colours - as your own code - throughout the Mind Map.
- Develop your own personal style of Mind Mapping.
- Use emphasis and show associations between different related topics in your Mind Map.
- Keep the Mind Map clear by using numerical order or outlines to surround your branches.

How to Mind Map

- Place a large white sheet of paper horizontally, or use a Mind Map pad.
- Gather a selection of coloured pens, ranging from thin nib to highlighter.
- Select the topic, problem or subject to be Mind Mapped. This will be the basis of your central image.
- Gather any materials, research or additional information that is needed, so that you have all the facts at your fingertips. Now start to draw in the centre of your page.
- Start in the centre with an unframed image - approximately 1½ inches (3cm) high and wide for A4 and 4 inches (10 cm) for A3.
- Use dimension, expression and at least three colours in the central image in order to attract attention and aid memory.
- Make the branches closest to the centre thick, attached to the image, and 'wavy' (organic). Place the Basic Ordering Ideas (BOIs) or chapter headings on those branches.
- Branch thinner lines off the end of the appropriate BOI in order to hold supporting data.
- Use images wherever you find it is possible.
- The image or word should always sit on a line of the same length.
- Use different colours as your own special code to show people, places, topics, themes, dates and to make the Mind Map more attractive visually.
- Capture all your ideas, or those that others have contributed, then edit, reorganise, make more beautiful, elaborate, or clarify as a second and yet further advanced stage of thinking.

Similarly to a road map, a Mind Map will:

- Give you an overview of a large subject/area.
- Enable you to plan routes/make choices.
- Let you know where you are going, and where you have been.
- Gather and hold large amounts of data.
- Encourage daydreaming and problem-solving by looking for creative pathways.
- Be enjoyable to look at, read, muse over and remember.

Uses and Benefits of Mind Mapping

1. Learning - Reduce those 'tons of work'. Feel good about study, review and exams. Develop confidence in your learning abilities.

2. Overviewing - See the whole picture, the global overview, at once. Understand the links and connections.

3. Concentrating - Focus on the task for better results.

4. Memorising - Easy recall. 'See' the information in your mind's eye.

5. Organising - Parties, holidays, projects, etc. Make it make sense to you.

6. Presenting - Speeches become clear, relaxed and alive. You can be at your best.

7. Communicating - Communicate in all forms with clarity and conciseness.

8. Planning - Orchestrate all aspects, from beginning to end, on one piece of paper.

9. Meetings - From planning to agenda, chairing, taking the minutes ... these jobs can be completed with speed and efficiency.

10. Training - From preparation to presentation, make the job easier.

11. Thinking - The Mind Map will become a concrete record of your thoughts at any stage of the process.

12. Negotiating - All the issues, your position and manoeuvrability on one sheet.

13. Creativity - It is often assumed that the greater the quantity of ideas generated, the more the quality declines. In fact, the reverse is true. The more you generate ideas and the greater the quantity, the more the potential quality increases. This is a key lesson in understanding the nature of your own creativity.

14. Lectures - When you attend a lecture, use a Mind Map to keep a vivid visual memento of it.

As a young child, Tony loved the idea of taking notes and of learning. By the time he was a teenager his thinking was already getting into a mess, and he began to hate anything to do with study, especially note -taking. He began to notice the extraordinary paradox that the more notes he took, the worse his studies and memory became. In an effort to improve matters he began to underline key words and ideas in red and to put important things in boxes. Magically, his memory began to improve.

In his first year of university, he was still struggling. It was then that he became fascinated by the Greeks, for he learned that they had developed memory Systems that enabled them to recall perfectly hundreds and thousands of facts. The Greek memory systems were based on Imagination and Association, which he noticed to his amusement and concern were absent from his own notes! He then began to notice that everyone around him was taking the same kind of crowded, one-colour and monotonous notes as he was.

As Tony says, "None of us was using the principles of Imagination and Association - we were all in the same sinking boat! I suddenly realised that in my head and the collective 'global brain', there was a gigantic log -jam that needed a new note-taking and thinking tool to unblock it. I set out in search of a thinking tool that would give us the freedom to think in the way we were designed to think.

"I began to study every subject I could, especially psychology. In psychology I discovered that there were two main things important to the brain during learning: Association and Imagination. Similar to the Greeks! By now I was becoming fascinated by my brain and what I realised were its power and potential. The power and potential were both much greater than I had thought. I began to focus on memory, note-taking and creativity, as it seemed that the answer to my quest would lie with them.

"I quickly discovered that most of the great thinkers, especially Leonardo da Vinci, used pictures, codes and connecting lines in their notes. They 'doodled' and thus made their notes come alive. During all these explorations, I would often wander in nature, where I found it much easier to think, imagine and dream. It began to dawn on me that, as we are part of nature, our thinking and note-taking must relate to nature and must reflect nature; we must mirror the universal laws of nature in our own functioning!

"There was only one possible solution to my dilemma. The thinking tool had to apply to the full range of human daily activities, and had to be based on the way the brain naturally wants to work. I needed something that reflected the processes of nature and how our brains naturally work rather than something that put us in a mental strait-jacket by forcing us to work against our natural design. What emerged was a star-like, simple, and beautiful tool that did reflect the natural creativity and radiance of our thinking processes. 'The first Mind Map was born!' . . . ."

188

Chapter 14

Jeremy (Jezz) Moore BSc, MBA, friend, colleague and fellow rowing coach with Tony.

"Buzan Diagrams" Aka Mind Maps

Based on my experience as a former Director of KPMG Private Equity and ABN AMRO amongst others, and the expertise I have gained through coaching British oarsmen to successfully take on the world, my current aim is to secure a senior role in a business which wants to develop a high performance management team and drive operational performance to exceptional levels.

I went to school from age of five and hated it. I went to Priory Road School in High Wycombe and was so unhappy, I used to run away. I hated school and I don't think they liked me much either. I was a bit of a problem kid, always daydreaming and unable to concentrate in class.

Eventually my parents 'bailed' me out and I was the only one of their children to get a private education, I was sent to Davenies School in Beaconsfield approximately age 10, and I remember failing 11 plus then and sitting common entrance at 13. I actually enjoyed Davenies, mainly because of the sport, but again I would daydream and had various private tutors to help me keep up with school work. I wasn't disruptive but I was a bit of a 'problem'.

Dad wanted me to go to Barnard Castle school where he went so I sat their entrance exam and, as you guessed, failed. Eventually, I went to Clayesmore school in Dorset (a boarding school). Same theme, loved sport but rubbish academically. It gets a bit more interesting now. I failed all my O levels on first sitting and managed 4 grade C's in the following term on my re-sits. This meant having just turned 17 I didn't qualify for 6th Form so had to leave school, and ended up working in a factory in Saunderton High Wycombe. I briefly flirted with a term at agricultural college (Rycotewood in Thame), but hated it and lasted one term. Fate led me to become a computer operator for Wilkinson Sword in High Wycombe and that's where I stayed for a couple of years.

I then had a 'shift experience', I got scared that suddenly my life had passed me by and I hadn't so much as even read a book. I enrolled on an A level course at Wycombe College in Computers and I actually completed the first year and got a grade B in my first year work, so I was now the proud owner of what was then called an A/O Level… still not an A level!

However, I noticed a prospectus for Newland Park College in Chalfont St Giles, an annex of Wycombe College and saw that you could get onto an HND (Higher National Diploma) in Business Studies with either one A level or even no A levels if you were over 21 and had three years work experience. I was 20 but explained I would be 21 in the first term so I managed to persuade them to take me a little bit early.

It's worth pointing out that when I had been at college some time one of the lecturers disclosed to me that they had accepted me before they had received my school reference. Apparently, I hold the record for the worst school reference ever given!

Anyway back to the story. This is the key bit!

I was only two weeks into my first term when we had a lecture by a Dr Bastic (I still remember his name) and he introduced us to this method of learning he called BUZAN DIAGRAMS … He explained that you put the topic in the centre of a page and you populate the area surrounding it with all the 'key words' or 'prompts' that are relevant. You didn't need to keep re-reading your notes, simply find the key words and numbers, dates etc that relate to the content, and you string it all together with lines.

I watched this closely and then a massive penny dropped! This Buzan diagram that I was looking at was so simple and it meant that even I could learn a single page!!

So that is how I discovered Buzan diagrams, and I went on to get a distinction on my HND, which led me to go on to The University of Bristol to read Joint Honours Economics and Politics. Also a Post Graduate certificate in Corporate Finance from London Business School and an MBA from Henley Business School in 1999.

At this stage, I had never met Tony Buzan.

A friend of mine, Roger Hatfield and I rowed at Marlow Rowing Club, where Tony had started to be involved. I have known Roger since I was 17 and he had seen me go from 'uneducated dropout' to someone suddenly motivated to study. I can't remember the precise date but it would have been either in my second year of my HND or my first at University. Roger said ... "Come to the annual club supper; there is a guy you have to meet!" So I did and I sat on the top table with Tony sitting just one person away. I had no idea who he was!!!

As the supper progressed and we were coming to the latter part of the evening, so people were beginning to get up and move around, I got a chance to sit next to Tony. The subject of learning and education quickly started and fuelled by a massive amount of passion for how I had come to realise 'being clever was easy' and probably a decent amount of wine, I began to lecture Tony on how I had discovered Buzan diagrams. I would not let him get a word in edgeways and I even asked him to slow me down if I was going too fast as I explained their workings and the power of the method of learning and memory recall. I got a serviette out and drew away, head down, intent that my new disciple Tony would understand the brilliance that I was folding out before him. When I eventually finished and drew breath I put my pen down and announced… 'there you have it… Buzan diagrams'.

A moment lapsed and then in the silence of that brief moment he quietly asked, did I realise he WAS Tony Buzan, of course placing the emphasis on Buzan so that this thick dinner guest would 'get it'….. It is probably the only time in my life where 'wishing the world would swallow me up' would have been insufficient. Of course it was all in good humour…

And so the rest is history. We have become friends and Tony has helped me with several of my rowing crews and athletes that have gone on to row for Great Britain. The most notable being in 2003 when coached the Fawley Cup Junior quad that won at Henley Royal Regatta and contained Zac Purchase who went on to win an Olympic Gold medal in China 2008 and Silver in London 2012…

• • • •

Chapter 15

The Mind Map Which Beat The Federation

Ray Keene shares how Mind Mapping underpinned negotiations in the creation of The Times World Chess Championship.

Early in 1992 I approached Rupert Murdoch, head of Newscorp (owner of *The Times*) and briefed him on momentous changes that were afoot in the world of chess. Ever since the famous match of the Century between Bobby Fischer and Boris Spassky in 1972 this Mind Sport had commanded the largest multi-million dollar prize purses.

The Strategy of Central Control

I sought to enlist Mr. Murdoch's corporate sponsorship and this advance strategic meeting represented my first branch on the MIND MAP: the centre and focus of which was to bring the World Chess Championship to the UK, preferably with a British challenger to the dominant Garry Kasparov. In warfare it is considered generally favourable to occupy the central high ground, a policy endorsed by military strategists from Sun Tzu via Julius Caesar to Napoleon and beyond. In chess, strategy dictates that one should strive for central control, and by analogy, all Mind Maps should start with the central focus, not with any particular branch or offshoot.

On Saturday January 30th 1993, the game plan took off when Britain's strongest ever chess player, Nigel Short, concluded a series of spectacular wins to gain the right to challenge the supreme champion, Garry Kasparov, for his world crown. Next day I created a Mind Map for the P.R. campaign and issued a press release, co-signed by Adam Black, at that time the Publicity Director of the British Chess Federation. It called on any UK sponsor interested in chess to back a bid for Nigel Short to take on Kasparov in the UK. Initial interest was shown both by The Times and the City of Manchester, the latter anxious to bolster its flagging aspirations to hold the 2000 Olympic Games.

The Governing Body Decrees

FIDE, the World Chess Federation, and its president Florencio Campomanes had other plans. Allowing an impossibly short bid time onlytwo contenders had emerged: one, from Santiago de Compostella in Spain, offered a one million Swiss Francs prize fund, while the other from Jezdimir Vasilievic of Belgrade (the backer of the Fischer – Spassky rematch of 1992) proposed a repeat of his earlier bid. This bid quickly dissipated. Two new bids emerged, one from the City of

Manchester for slightly in excess of a million pounds, and the other, a somewhat larger one from Channel 4 television.

Again a flurry of furious negotiations took place but Campomanes seemed determined that Manchester would win and announced Manchester the winner with unseemly haste. (Conventionally, with rival bids for a world championship match, both contenders had been given plenty of time to inspect the venue facilities in person, before making the ultimate decision.) Now, it appeared, the governing body had issued its decree and there was no going back.

It's Not Over Till It's Over...

Recalling Tony Buzan's comment that 'it's not over till it's over - and even then it's not over!' I was inspired to produce a Master Mind Map which would dictate our strategy for gaining the rights to the match, whilst operating in a tricky, volatile and indeed treacherous situation, where friends and allies might turn into foes and rivals with almost no notice.

The chief obstacle was the autocratic Campomanes, regarded by many as a dictatorial brake on the development of global chess. Campomanes' organisation, FIDE, was deeply modelled on, and sustained by, the USSR state and the KGB, so no friend of Kasparov. Nor of Nigel Short, who had not even been informed as to the number and substance of the bidding offers, before Campomanes had unilaterally taken the decision.

Short telephoned his friend and editor of *The Spectator*, Dominic Lawson (soon to become editor of the influential *The Sunday Telegraph*): Could there be a rapprochement with Kasparov with a view to taking the match into their own hands?

In view of FIDE's violation of its own rules over the years, the time was ripe for such a revolution. As the popular saying went at that time: Britannia rules the waves, but Campo waives the rules! Lawson rang me, and I rang Kasparov. A series of international calls resulted in a Mind Map draft of a press release announcing a new world championship breakaway from FIDE and seeking bids from new sponsors.

The Mind Map Emerges

The centre of the MIND MAP was now in place, the relative strengths and weaknesses of the opposition - such as FIDE itself and rival bidders, in particular Manchester, were identified by the branches, so the time had come to strike.

The international media picked up on the story. In Madrid, for example, the first editions were cancelled and the newspaper presses rolled again with a new front page story. This was partly because of the explosive personalities of the leading protagonists, voluble rebels against any system, such as Short and Kasparov, partly because there is a vast audience around the world for intellectual battles, as exemplified by chess, and not least the millions of fans and dollars involved

The Mind Map brutally exposed the weaknesses of the opposition, crucially the need for Manchester and FIDE to avoid any conflict with the International Olympic Committee, which was due to inspect Manchester's bid for the Olympics. Any congress with a breakaway group would damage Manchester's Olympic standing. This constraint forced both FIDE and Manchester to operate within inflexible parameters, as the Mind Map had predicted would be the case. The confluence of tactics, strategy and stratagems from warfare, Mind Sports and business, also comes clearly to the fore when the Mind Map is plumbed for its deeper significance.

'The Times' Succeeds

The Times became the successful bidder for the inaugural match when the bids were opened, while Channel 4, the original highest bidder from the UK obtained the exclusive TV rights. Channel 4 broke fresh ground by transmitting a total of 80 programmes, hosted by Tony, Carol Vorderman, Daniel King, Jon Speelman and Cathy Forbes, with myself as senior commentator in the permanent team of presenters.

It should be observed that I had carefully selected the date for the presentation and opening of the fresh bids in a media frenzy at Simpsons in the Strand. Strategic reconnaissance had revealed that the City of Manchester would be entertaining a delegation from the IOC in support of its 2000 Olympic bid at the selfsame time of the bid offers and the last thing Manchester could be seen doing was submitting a bid for a chess championship going ahead in defiance of an existing world governing body! With Manchester effectively neutralised the way was clear for our bid from *The Times*, backed by Channel 4 TV to sweep the board.

In The Style of Sun Tzu

By Mind Mapping our strategy, we had clearly identified the prime weakness of Manchester's position, which, in the style of Sun Tzu, we then proceeded to batten on and exploit.

Campomanes and FIDE reacted by announcing that they would stage an alternative "FIDE World Championship" to rival *The Times* match. But who wants to watch the chorus when the irresistible alternative is to see the tragic heroes in action instead?

As the World Chess Federation, hide-bound national chess bodies and chess traditionalists fumed impotently at the bold breakaway by Kasparov and Short, the stage was set in London by *The Times* for the most gigantic chess extravaganza the world had ever seen: a £1.5 m prize, massive amounts of live television on both Channel 4 and the BBC, two million copies of a free chess pull-out in *The Times*, a special Checkmate game with £1000 given away every day to *The* *Times* readers, and chess promotions involving the British Museum, the Happy Eater restaurant chain, *Classic FM* radio and virtually every chess outlet across the nation.

This would lead to an increase of up to 500% in the sale of chess books, chess sets and membership of chess associations. Nothing like this had ever been seen before in the chess community.

By Mind Mapping our campaign at every stage, we were able to detect weaknesses in the opponents' armoury, manage the disparate and often confusing strands of who stood where, at any particular moment, and by marshalling our intellectual forces, we were empowered to deliver decisive blows at the most devastating moments.

• • • •

Part Three

Global Mental Literacy

16. Tributes From Friends And Colleagues

Isobel Abulhoul
Professor Michael Crawford
Sally Farmiloe
Angela Folley
Sjoerd Gehrels
Michael Gelb
Chris Griffiths
Bill Jarrard
Maneesh Johari
Jock Lowe
Neil Massa
Vanda North
Dominic O'Brien
Julian Simpole
Dr. Kirpal Singh
Jane Stephenson
Dr. Henry Toi
His Serene Highness Prince Philipp Von Und Zu Liechtenstein
Dr. Sue Whiting
Sutanto Windura
Ben Zephaniah
David Zhang
Joe D Adams
Chris Day
Phil Chambers

17. As Nestor To Agamemnon

18. Tony In Turkey

19. The Banner Of Mental Literacy

Isobel Abulhoul

Director of Programmes at the Dubai Poetry and Literature Festival

The Emirates Airline Festival of Literature held annually in Dubai provided my first opportunity to meet Tony face to face. I had invited him to attend as a well known writer and very popular in the region, to talk about Mind Mapping. I think Mind Mapping really helps all of us to recall a large number of facts and information. It is so useful for students to learn this skill.

Tony is a unique human being who has helped countless people globally use more of their potential through his books and his work. The opportunity for audiences in Dubai to meet Tony and listen to him: witty, humorous engaging, was so welcome.

Tony is a human dynamo, always energetic and ready for the next challenge. He is an example to us all.

Mind Mapping, his invention, has revolutionised how we understand and use our brains.

• • • •

Professor Michael Crawford

Imperial College London, Director of The Institute Of Brain Chemistry and Human Nutrition

Tony, chess and the threat to global mental health

I first worked with Tony in 1989-90 during the formation of the Little Foundation by the late Ian Dawson-Shepherd. The Little Foundation is a Charity for research on the cause and prevention of Cerebral Palsy and Allied Neurodevelopmental Disorders. It was then that Tony introduced me to his creation, the Mind Map, a beautiful illustration of the way the mind makes connections with a massive variety of things often unconnected - except in the mind. That raises lateral and cohesive thinking into a higher plane of creativity, imagination and intellectual enjoyment.

Later I recall sitting together at a table in a flat over looking Hyde Park with a full bottle of whisky and two chess boards with a Grand Master by the name of Ray Keene opposite.

We played chess. We had a good game (two of them side by side). Tony had some very groovy moves. Ray kept on telling us things about chess. I am not ashamed to admit that after a great struggle somehow Ray won both. Needless to say the bottle was emptied as check mate was declared. I had never realised that chess could be quite so entertaining. Tony and I then said our farewells and communed with the stars for a bit before finding our way to our respective homes. I had learnt a good lesson.

Not long afterwards, I was visiting a 42nd cousin in the USA where I was destined to stay for a few days. Her husband was a really great and jovial fellow a much bigger than life sort of bloke. He liked to go fishing off Mexico and send flowers to my 42nd cousin whilst he was away. Not just flowers that would go in a vase you understand but huge bunches of them! He had a lovely, open, antique MG which he adored. He later bought an Aston Martin Vanquish which I applauded as my first motor car was a 1930 Gran Prix 2 litre job with overhead cams, twin carbs and twin external exhausts the noise from which was music.

Tony, by the way, also had a wonderful car that used to come and pick him after dinners in town. A lovely taxi looking yellow job with someone at the driving wheel which helps on such occasions. Hugely comfortable and reminiscent of a bygone age when people made cars of beauty. I guess Tony has an eye for beauty.

To cut a long story short, after dinner in the house of my 42nd cousin and her husband, with some fine Californian wine, he brought out a chess board. A surprise as I had no idea before that he played chess. As it happened, I had brought a bottle of duty free whisky with me. So remembering how Ray managed to beat both Tony and myself, I suggested he opened the whisky. He clearly enjoyed the whisky and I enjoyed winning!

"Tony has an ever present positive mind, even when dark clouds are behind. He will not run off because there are still some vultures in the air."

Prof Crawford also does not pull his punches, writing: a rising level of mental illness poses a massive threat to mankind; increasing cases of brain disorders and depression need to be addressed to avoid a doomsday scenario.

Someone once said that we could become a nation of morons and that prediction is coming true. It is very scary. If this rise continues it will threaten the sustainability of medical health and the peace and happiness of mankind. It is the most severe threat we have ever faced. Brain disorders have overtaken every other group of ill-health and we are facing a mental health epidemic. This is a danger to humanity itself if we do not change.

Treating mental health conditions currently costs the UK £77billion a year.

Research has shown a daily intake of omega-3 fatty acids, found in oily fish such as salmon and mackerel, helps combat various mental health problems as well as heart disease. The evidence that fresh oily fish can benefit the brain is overwhelming. The only side effect is better health.

Professor Michael Crawford was recognised by
The Brain Trust Charity as the
Brain of the Year 2013

Sally Farmiloe

Actress, Former Mensa High IQ Society Businesswoman of the Year

Tony Buzan is a superstar! He is also quite simply the brainiest chap I have ever met.

I first met him at a MENSA event in 1997. I had been given an Award but only knew one person at the gathering (old pal Sir Clive Sinclair) so I was delighted when a very elegant gentleman dressed in pure white approached me and introduced himself. That was Tony and we've been friends ever since, although I don't see enough of him as he is always flitting all over the world doing lecture tours and intelligent stuff.

My daughter Jade benefited hugely from Tony's Mind Mapping for her school work and fell in love with his 'cool car' which he kindly took her out in from time to time.

In fact, Tony is pretty cool himself. Beauty and Brains don't always go together but Tony has the package. He is always immaculate from top to toe and, if we are attending a 'do' together, will always check what I am wearing so that he can match or tone (excuse the pun) his suit or tux to my dress. Such sartorial splendour!

Tony is one of the UK's most brilliant and fascinating personalities and I am proud to call myself his friend.

Angela Folley

Harleyford Manor Estate

Having lived at Harleyford for 57 years, and loved it as much as Tony, I was delighted in 1982 to see arriving at the cottage a charming, attractive and elegant young man. Immaculate house full of mirrors, gym equipment, marble bathroom, conservatory filled with rowing machines and weights etc. He enjoyed enormously the country life including eating as many pheasants that he could get hold of.

Always generous, he gave my grandson Tim a wonderful book and

chessboard, all signed by Raymond Keene, and then went to play chess with Tim in his home.

Every Christmas he would give us all beautiful holly leaves for our front doors. Always with a teddy bear in the centre.

Then he persuaded my son Nick to build him a double holiday lodge, the only one allowed on the estate. He has been there ever since!

Sjoerd Gehrels

Director of Programmes, Stenden University, The Netherlands

I very much wanted to meet Tony at the ICOT Conference in Kuala Lumpur on 22nd June 2009 and I had to put in a great effort to get to speak to Tony because the attendees of the conference worshipped Tony as a film star and were crowding around him to get his autograph. After a brief talk, he asked to call him at his office in Marlow the week after.

With Rhian, I then agreed to call him exactly at 16:00 UK time while I was still travelling in Asia (23:00 local time). I guess that my following up on the commitment to call Tony at the moment while being on the other side of the world created trust.

For us as higher education professionals, Mind Maps have provided enormous opportunities to stimulate students.

Mind Maps are one of the most powerful tools in the world to connect people of different backgrounds in learning and using their brains. Since then I have had the pleasure and the honour of taking Tony to any location when he is visiting The Netherlands, we had many interesting and nice conversations for hours in the voluntary confinement of the car.

Tony is a man who, besides being one-of-a-kind in terms of his knowledge about learning and the brain, also loves the essential values of enjoying life. On the latter topic we have spent hours talking and we came to the conclusion that we will write a book together about adventures in life with the work title *Searching the Light*. It has been of the greatest pleasure to discuss 'life issues' with Tony and to see the way he brings matters down to their appropriate context.

Tony is one of the very rare people who has combined life and academic intelligence with 'down-to-earth' reasoning. He is unique in this world and the only official Visiting Professor at our Stenden University of Applied Sciences in Leeuwarden, The Netherlands, who can address all school and programmes in the university.

• • • •

Michael Gelb

Vice Dean of the Renaissance Academy; Head of the Martial Arts Faculty

Author of: *How to Think Like Leonardo da Vinci*; Brain Trust Brain of the Year, 1999, and a Pioneer in the fields of Creative Thinking and Innovative Leadership.

I first met Tony in 1975 when I was training to be a teacher of the Alexander Technique at the School for Alexander Studies in London. Tony was taking private lessons in the Technique with Paul Collins, the Director of the school. At Paul's request, Tony addressed our class on the subject of his bestselling book *Use Your Head*. I was very inspired by Tony's talk and afterwards I approached Paul Collins and said, "Tony Buzan is brilliant! He has figured out the essential elements of mind development and made them accessible. I want to learn more." Paul responded that Tony had approached him similarly:

"Who was that brilliant, young American fellow who asked such incisive questions?"

Thus began a collaboration and friendship that continues to this day. It began when Tony invited me to attend the meetings of what he called The Learning Methods Group. The group included artists, physicists, psychologists and philosophers and was convened to explore the nature of the human mind and how to cultivate it. We met for intense discussions, debates and dialogue either at Tony's home in Hampstead Way or at a local pub or curry palace. Members included future thought leaders such as Peter Russell and Mark Brown.

After receiving my certification as an Alexander Technique teacher in 1978 I was honoured to have Tony as one of my first Alexander pupils. I also taught him how to juggle and coached him in the art of aikido. Tony taught me speed-reading, memory development and Mind Mapping. (I used what I learned from Tony to complete my Master's Thesis, which then became my first book).

Beginning in 1979, Tony and I travelled the world together-we went to South Africa, Japan, Australia and many other places- leading five-day Mind and Body seminars for senior managers.

Among the many highlights and precious memories of our travels and teaching together I particularly cherish:

Our time together in South Africa (1980) where we worked with a business group devoted to helping end Apartheid by the year 2000. (Miraculously, this actually happened!). Among many highlights, we taught a 3-day seminar for 500 Junior High School students in Soweto. Tony is always enthusiastic, but his special energy and love for children and his devotion to the development of their full potential has been consistently evident in the 37 years I've known him.

In 1981, Tony and I taught a 5-day seminar for managers in Japan. We both love Japanese culture and on this trip we played many games of Go, and enjoyed fabulous kaseki meals. Our seminar was held in a mountain resort. On the day we arrived we went for a run up a mountain despite a raging typhoon, thus we initiated "The Typhoon Running Club." (That was our only official meeting!) At the end of the seminar the managers used a Mind Map with Japanese Kanji characters to summarise everything they had learned. We then had a memorable party featuring Karaoke performances including Tony's rendition of *God Save the Queen*!

In 1984 Tony and I spent 4 months in Stockholm, Sweden leading a series of 3-day seminars for a major shipping company. We lived at the Grand Hotel and dined there most nights. I still remember the look on the waiter's face when Tony insisted that his freshly killed game birds be served "very rare… bleu". Even better, Tony relished picking up the recently breathing, almost raw meat and eating it with his fingers as though it was the only way to dine!

In the mid-90s Tony and I worked together on a series of 3 week residential seminars for the Liechtenstein Global Trust in Switzerland. Tony assembled a dream team of creative resources including the author, chess Grand Master Raymond Keene, Poet Laureate Ted Hughes, conductor Benjamin Zander, and painter Lorraine Gill. We drank wonderful wines, shared poetry and played many games of chess!

In 2004 we both happened to be presenting at the same conference in Istanbul. We had a delicious Turkish meal in a restaurant overlooking the Bosphorus and discussed our continuing research into the nature of the human mind and how to cultivate it. This conversation continued when I met Tony in London during his 70th birthday year, primed with Chekov's pre-revolutionary piece, Uncle Vanya, and fortified by oysters and roast grouse at Simpsons in the Strand.

This lifelong curiosity and passion for understanding, combined with elegant living, is the through-line of our lives and the integrating force of our friendship.

Chris Griffiths
CEO, ThinkBuzan Ltd.

It is rare that you come across an individual who can make a profound difference to the way you live your life. It is rarer still that you meet an individual who can make a profound difference to the way millions of people live their lives. Tony Buzan, my mentor, colleague and friend, is such a man. His Mind Mapping technique is now used by hundreds of millions of people to help them create better lives. It is fair to say that his exceptional genius, wisdom and techniques have been an inspiration for my own creative journey.

We are what we think, and what we think is based on our memories. The more memories we have, the more that we become. Most people do not realise that Tony's work on Mind Mapping originated from his ongoing exploration of memory. His work on *The Most Important Graph in the World*, an insight into how to have a better memory, allows people to store more of these moments and have a fuller more meaningful life.

My fondest time spent with Tony is when we were invited to the Petra Nobel conference arranged by Elie Wiesel and King Abullah II of Jordan. A two day conference attended by over 30 Nobel Laureates to discuss way of ending child poverty and starvation. The conclusion of which was a better education for all which fits perfectly with Tony's overriding ambition of helping the children of the world achieve

Global Mental Literacy. His love and focus of helping children were never more evident than when he held an event in the Royal Albert Hall in London, where over 9000 children were invited to attend free of charge to learn how to learn.

Once, when I was having a conversation with him, right at the beginning of our friendship, he started staring over my shoulder, seemingly totally ignoring my words. In the end I felt I had to say something so I said, "Tony, am I boring you?" to which he replied, "No, not at all." However, he still continued to look vacantly behind me. Finally, I could take no more and asked him more firmly why he was ignoring me. He said calmly and quietly, "Chris, when I first get to know someone with whom I am planning to invest much of my time, I imagine the billions of children in the world standing behind them and ask myself how will this person help me reach those children. This is how I decide how much time to spend with that individual…" The response was the measure of the man.

Finally, I would like to share how lucky I have been in my position of CEO of ThinkBuzan, to see more than almost anyone the positive impact Tony's techniques have had on individuals from every corner of the planet. Long may it continue.

Bill Jarrard

Mindwerx International and the Buzan Centre Australia/NZ

Meeting Tony Buzan

I first met Tony in July 2001, at his office on the Harleyford Manor Estate, Marlow - but of course I 'knew' Tony long before this, which I'll talk about shortly. On the occasion of our first meeting in Marlow, I was with my partner, now wife, Jennifer Goddard who already knew Tony pretty well having spent time writing with him and others in Turkey, which I am sure she'll tell you about. Also with us was my then 16 year old son Will, who was on holiday with me in the UK, as Jennifer was living there on a six month corporate contract.

Upon meeting, Tony welcomed us warmly, having heard about me from Jennifer and also from then Buzan Centres CEO Vanda North, who joined us that day. He gave us a tour of his studio and explained how he wrote his books, and we could see about six books in varying stages of development. It was a fascinating insight into how he is such a prolific and successful author, and he showed me a process I have tried to emulate with much less success - so far.

Following our studio tour it was time for lunch, which was what we had arranged to do. It was a beautiful summer day, so we all walked over to the converted Thames Canal Boat, now a restaurant, docked on the estate, for lunch. It was interesting to see Tony and my son Will walking ahead together having a lively conversation, and it was clear they were becoming friends – a relationship that has endured, despite rare meetings of the two since then.

Jennifer, Vanda and I followed not far behind, but on the way Jennifer tripped in a 'mole hole' which was interesting, because one topic Will and Tony were talking about was that Harleyford Manor was the Manor House used to model Toad Hall, from the classic *The Wind in the Willows.*

So of course Jennifer tripping in a mole hole, instantly brought up images of the character of Mole (Moley).

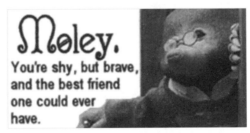

Will was fascinated to be on the Estate and see the Manor house with the giant Willow tree out front, because my father, his Grandfather had many times read or told *The Wind in the Willows* story to him and his sister, with Mr. Toad, Badger, Moley, and all the other characters. My dad loves the story and has shared it with all his children and grandchildren, and even today he has a framed picture of the Willows characters hanging in his home. So being with Tony in this situation was truly memorable.

During lunch the conversation was varied and fascinating, and I believe Tony and I became friends immediately, and that friendship has built significantly over the ensuing years, during which we have had many occasions to work (and play) together.

I said earlier that I 'knew' Tony long before I met him at Marlow. This was due to his most significant contribution to thinking and learning – the Mind Map®. I had first heard of Mind Mapping in 1988, but unfortunately, as I learnt later, it had been a very poor introduction by someone who really wasn't Mind Mapping properly. In fact it was several years later that I saw *The Mind Map Book* and heard of Tony Buzan. I bought the book and could not put it down until I had read it completely – after which I was annoyed, even angry that years earlier I had been given such a bad introduction to Mind Mapping.

What I read in *The Mind Map Book* was clear, concise, colourful, engaging – and simply brilliant. I probably read the book three or four times in the first few weeks (and many times since), and started Mind Mapping more and more to capture my thinking on so many topics. However it was a few years later in January 1997 that I met Jennifer, and Mind Mapping became truly important. Jennifer will tell you her own story, but in short she had returned to University to do a business degree, and was struggling. In working together we found that we also had personal feelings, and so a few weeks after meeting, on our first date, I actually gave her a copy of *The Mind Map Book* and recommended she adapt her study methods. Which she did, and in that semester she went from struggling to High Distinctions. Our shared commitment to Mind Maps was now set!

In mid-1998 Jennifer and I were now in a committed relationship, having even trekked to Mount Everest, and were considering how we might work together even more. It was in July 1998 that I captured in a Mind Map, all our thinking about creating a new kind of business – a business that focused on creative thinking as a skill that can be developed by anyone.

That Mind Map became the Vision for Mindwerx International which we formally launched in early 1999. In that Mind Map you see a branch about Associates with the name Buzan and Brain Club clearly shown. At that time the only thing I knew about Tony Buzan was *The Mind Map Book,* but I knew even then that we would be associated with him in some way, at some time.

As soon as we formed Mindwerx, people quickly started asking us about Mind Mapping – probably because for every presentation I did in those days I gave out a Mind Map summary of the talk. At the same time Jennifer was developing her own passion for Mind Mapping, as she completed her university study with Distinctions in all subjects. At that time there were no official Mind Mapping courses in Australia, but people were asking me to teach them. So I converted *The Mind Map Book* into a very successful one-day workshop, following Tony and Barry's process exactly. As part of the workshop I would give every participant a copy of *The Mind Map Book*, the large colour version of the time. This was the only way I knew to acknowledge and repay Tony for his work.

In 2000, I was engaged to teach a Masters subject for an Australian University that had licensed the course to an executive school in Israel, and I was due to go to Tel Aviv in June 2000 to teach a Creativity and Innovation subject over about 12 days. On that trip, which I repeated annually for seven more years, I was returning via London, so I arranged to meet Jennifer there with the intention of meeting as many people in the creative thinking community as we could. One of the people we were lucky to meet was Vanda North, then CEO of Buzan Centres Worldwide.

When we met in her offices in Poole, our discussion ranged over a number of things, and she and Jennifer were both Mind Mapping the conversation. What was evident immediately was that we three shared a passion and commitment to Mind Mapping, and in the conversation I invited Vanda to come to Australia to run an Instructor Licensing Program, and even suggested that Jennifer and I form a Buzan Centre in Australia. Vanda smiled politely and invited us to send her a plan and proposal – I found out later that she received verbal requests like this almost every week from people all over the world, none of whom would ever send her a plan or proposal – but we were different.

On the train back to London Jennifer and I Mind Mapped our plan to bring her and Buzan training to Australia, and to start a Buzan Centre. Two days later on the plane home we turned the Mind Map into a proposal with a business plan, including financials. Eight days after meeting, I emailed Vanda our proposal, plan and Mind Map and in response got just three words: Love it, go!

And that was how we started. About 6 months later, in early 2001, Vanda arrived in Australia and we trained out first 21 Licensed Instructors. She came again later in that year and one or two times each year for about 3 years.

The reason I mention Vanda here in a biography about Tony, is that it was from her that we learnt so much about Tony. Of course she had a personal message from Tony thanking us for our support and wishing us every success with our Buzan Centre, but we had not yet met him. Fortunately Vanda was his ultimate champion and inspired everyone she spoke to by sharing Tony's story, his work, his passion, and his vision of Global Mental Literacy.

She was his voice, and through her we started to know him – I said to her once that even after spending so much time with her, I knew more about Tony than I did her. She wasn't interested in talking about herself; her mission was to promote Tony and his work. My view is that many, many Mind Mappers and Tony Buzan followers were inspired directly and indirectly by Vanda, as it was through her that we and hundreds of other licensed instructors, and then all the people they taught, heard about Tony and Mind Mapping.

Shortly after that first instructor program, Jennifer was engaged to go to the UK for six months, and while she was away I and a young BLI started building the Buzan Centre – my vision was to have hundreds of properly trained Mind Map instructors influencing and helping people in every field, particularly education – and our course participants included many teachers. Over 10 years we trained and licensed about 150 instructors, who in turn have taught Mind Mapping to an estimated 50,000 others. We alone would have introduced Mind Maps to 15,000 plus people in over 25 countries, either directly or through our online programs.

In the UK in about April 2001, Jennifer caught up with Vanda and met Tony for the first time. Not long after that she joined them on a 'floating university' in Turkey with about a dozen others including Tony's mother, Jean, where the group talked, wrote and formed great friendships. It was a couple of months after that when my son and I were in the UK and met Tony for the first time. And not long after that Jennifer assisted at her first World Memory Championship (2001) in London, before returning to Australia a day before September 11.

As it turned out, just a couple of weeks after she returned to Australia, Tony was due to be in Australia, but only up on Lizard Island writing – something he loved to do. But with him so close, our intention was to bring him closer and so we invited him to come to Sydney to run the first Australian Memory Championships, which he and Jennifer did. At that event was my daughter Kylie, who had earlier that year participated in the BLI program, and at 17 years old became the youngest BLI in the world. Then at the Memory Championship, where she had simply been asked to help out, Tony surprised her and asked her to compete. She came second, with no preparation, although she had been trained in study skills by one of our BLIs and of course Vanda.

So Tony was now a friend and mentor to Jennifer, me, and my two children, and would on a future visit also influence Jennifer's daughter Jasmine, and become friends with my parents as well.

Over the years since then we have organised several Tony visits to Australia, running public workshops, conference presentations, client work, and when possible to run an Australian Memory Championship. Each time he has been here, we have had the great fortune to get lots of personal time together, to hear his stories, to talk about fascinating events, and to share ideas and visions – usually over long relaxing dinners and a glass or two of fine wine. From all that what is clear to me is that the vision and passion I had when creating Mindwerx, is the same sort of passion and mission Tony has – we share the same goal.

Tony Buzan – much more than just Mind Maps

I said that Tony's most significant contribution has been the Mind Map, and that is true. But his body of work, both as an individual and in cooperation with other great brains, is hugely impressive. His work in the whole field of memory is of great importance – not just the books, but the memory competitions which demonstrate the power of the amazing human brain to exceed all predictions.

His work in the area of Multiple Intelligences has perhaps been overlooked somewhat by that of Gardner and Goleman, but in my view Tony's approach made the development of multiple intelligences something anyone and everyone can do. I enjoy facilitating the programs I have developed based on this work.

The collaborative work Tony has done with people like Richard and Lana Israel, Tony Dottino and of course Jennifer has shown how his ideas and Mind Maps can be used in so many different ways. And then there are the people he has influenced to produce significant works of their own – Michael Gelb, Steve Lundin, Lana Israel and many more.

In short Tony Buzan, Mind Maps, and much of his other work has changed the world, and continues to do so, and it is my great pleasure to call him friend.

• • • •

"To date, leaders have always been
taught basic management skills
in the cauldron of business
and their own life experience.

But no one has taught
them how to think"

Tony Buzan

Maneesh Johari

CEO, Buzan Centre Pune, India

USE YOUR HEAD!! When Maneesh heard his wife, Jas, say these words to him, paying no heed to the consequences, he retorted, "Yeah! How 'bout you doing the same too, sometime."

But, then when he turned to face her what he saw stopped him in his tracks.

Jas was holding up a book titled *Use your Head*, and had 3 other books in the pile next to her.

Intrigued, Maneesh gingerly extended his arm and first apologised for 'shooting before thinking' and then reached out towards the pile of books.

Next morning, along with his lunch basket, he carried the book, written by Tony Buzan, went to his office and, for the first time in over a decade – did not enter the shop-floor of his manufacturing unit! He was totally engrossed in the book!

Next day – the activities were repeated – only this time, the book which did not permit him to do what he normally would do – was titled *Embracing Change* written by Tony Buzan.

During the next week, Maneesh tried his hand at creating 'Mind Maps' as explained by Tony in his books – actually, he created a few – on his 'strengths'; on what really excites him; on how he could increase his present business activities, etc.

The one, which made him actually 'sit-up' was the 'Mind Map' he created on his perception of the future. What stared at him were actually his thoughts on the situation he found himself in at that point of time.

Maneesh and Jas have two wonderful daughters on whom they dote.

Jas runs a "Children's Enrichment Centre" in Aundh, Pune, India – which included a Library – exclusively for Children (she herself is a voracious reader and that's how she came across Tony Buzan's work!).

Maneesh is the Managing Director of a precision turning component manufacturing industry and catered to the needs of the local industries in the well-developed industrial areas in and around Pune, India.

The 'Mind Map' he made, which actually changed the course of the lives of the Johari family, was an 'eye-opener'.

Typically, the industry which one sets up is treated as the 'first child'! You are emotionally attached to it and would like to see it grow and prosper.

The Mind Map helped Maneesh realise that he probably did not want to visualise his daughters coming in and running his industry, a few years later, especially when they would have access to expand the activities of 'Jungle Book' – the Activity centre for Children! Jungle Book is a 'child-friendly' place, the interactions with the people coming there were of a very different level, mentally stimulating and satisfying, as compared to the Industrial environment – where you were dependent on factors beyond your control, at times, on the whims and fancies of officers, on the government rules, the competition and more importantly – the interaction with the workers, officers etc. was of a very different nature.

He shared his 'Mind Map' with Jas, and a week later – after the consequences of taking the action proposed, sank in and were internalised, took concrete steps to implement the vision of the future.

The workers were asked to find other opportunities, the clients were requested not to supply any more raw materials, the existing work orders were completed within a month and the stage was set to start disposing of the assets – acquired over a period of time, investing a huge amount of sweat and toil!

Simultaneously, Jas enrolled for the 'Licensed Instructor Certification' from the Buzan organization and was the first person in India to acquire this License – to teach 'Mind Mapping'. There was nothing available at that point in India – so she had to travel to Hong Kong for the course and then to Singapore for her evaluation – investing a lot of resources to do so.

Since October 2005, when she got her License – there's been no looking back!

In 2007, Jas acquired her 'Buzan Advanced Licensed Instructor' certificate – which permitted her to train in 'Speed Reading' and 'Knowledge Management' too.

Maneesh and Jas work as a team and started spreading the awareness of this simple, yet extremely powerful technique, in India. They then set up the 'Buzan Centre Pune, India' in September 2007 and have trained thousands of people from all walks of life – including CEOs, MDs, EDs, VPs of well known corporate houses, faculty members of schools, International schools, Business schools and colleges and also students.

Their older daughter Laksheeta, scored an impressive 96.2% in the ICSE examination – without enrolling for any extra coaching class (which is the norm, otherwise). This was achieved in spite of pursuing her hobbies of dancing, playing the drums etc.! This was possible only because she applied the techniques of 'Speed Reading' (gave her a lot of time to pursue the extra-curricular activities) + "Mind Mapping" (which gave her all the information of 20+ pages on a single sheet, helped her comprehension etc.) + 'Power Recall' (helped her recall facts and figures at will – even months after studying).

This prompted her to enrol for the 'Licensing Program' being conducted by the Buzan Centre Pune, India and presently she is the youngest Asian to have acquired the Buzan Licensed Instructor certificate!

Maneesh and Jas were instrumental in inviting Tony (with whom they interact a number of times every year) to India in Sept. 2007. What a great way to celebrate the Second Anniversary of the centre – by being honoured by the presence of the 'inspiration' for them – Tony Buzan. He himself cut the cake on 17th Sept. 2007 in Mumbai during his first ever public programme in India.

Maneesh and Jas are extremely satisfied today by the turn of events in their life.

They have been able to make an impact on the lives of many people – by exposing them to the 'Operations Manual for the Brain' and have seen scores of individuals improve their productivity, efficiency, creativity and have a much better 'work-life balance'.

Jock Lowe

First Concorde Test Pilot

We first met on Concorde in the eighties and found that not only did Tony and I both admire Concorde but we lived near each other. So we met for the occasional lunch or dinner (sometimes at the Compleat Angler) and of course saw each other at the Henley Regatta and Festival and at Christmas time. On ALL occasions he was enthusiastic and thought provoking and I felt privileged to be talking to him. Tony once gave a presentation at British Airways (I think it was for the launch of one of his books).

Those attending comprised a mixture of aircraft engineers and marketing/commercial people. Towards the end of the talk he persuaded the audience to admit if they were left brain dominant i.e. logical, organised-typical engineer or if they were right brained, creative individuals. The audience split roughly in half and at that point he asked them to raise their hand if they thought that Concorde appealed mostly to their "brain" group. Everyone raised their hand. And that Tony said was the secret of the appeal of Concorde.

Tony then asked if anyone could think of something else which achieved this dual level of appeal. No-one could think up an alternative. For the last 25 years I have repeated this cameo (always giving credit to Tony) during lectures around the world.

No-one from many thousands of people has given a sensible answer to "give another example".

Mind Maps - irreplaceable in business life and of great value in one's personal life.

Tony exudes so much knowledge and enthusiasm and is such a warm welcoming person that any conversation with him is invigorating and motivational - it is a pleasure and privilege to know him and I forgive him for making me feel so lazy in the mornings when I tumble out of bed and occasionally catch sight of him rowing past my house on the Thames where he has obviously been for some time.

• • • •

Neil Massa

Businessman, Teacher, Science Graduate

Lorraine Gill, Neil Massa and Tony

Positivity Personified

I first met Tony personally on 6th April 2011. It was an IOD (Institute of Directors) meeting to discuss how business in Buckinghamshire can be promoted. It was very much a meeting of chance. Tony was one of the high profile guests and I was first reserve (fortunately someone dropped out last minute!). I had encountered Tony 15 years before in Manchester at one of his seminars (and had religiously used Mind Maps ever since). Mind Maps – simply brilliant, brilliantly simple.

I constantly use Mind Maps and have introduced them to thousands of people (family, friends, colleagues and clients) over the last 15 years. It was me telling Tony the story of how I tested the effectiveness of Mind Maps at the IOD dinner that got us talking. We talked for several hours after the meeting and Tony said that we should stay in touch, something people often say but never do. Not Tony. When he returned from China he got back in touch and has remained in close contact ever since.

I've spent most of my time with Tony in his 70th year. I imagine most other contributors have known him for far longer. I would like to share one thing about Tony. He is without a shadow of a doubt the most positive person I have ever met – bar none. Positive in a number of different ways. Positive in his encouragement of others, Positive about the excitement of each day, Positive about life and its vast potential, Positive about new ideas and the yet undiscovered territory they unlock, He's positive about the future and what can be achieved. And positive about situations or circumstances, regardless of the significant downside. He is the glass half full. He is a great tonic and at 70 years old to be that way is inspiring. A lot of old, wise people could take a leaf out of his book.

I am currently working with Tony on The Art Project (TAP) in which we are supporting the promotion of Lorraine Gill, an outstanding Australian artist who is yet to receive the worldwide recognition she so thoroughly deserves.

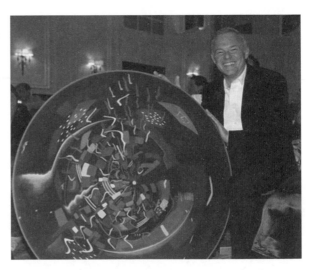

Vanda North

Former President, the International Society for Accelerated Learning & Teaching

I first met Tony in the summer of 1984 at the Education Explosion Conference in Tarrytown, New York.

We were both presenters and as I had used his maps for several years, I was interested to see if he was congruent with his material (he was!)

As it happens, I had the draft of the first book I had written called *From Oak Trees to Acorns* and had determined that I would show it to one of the published authors at that conference, the one who most earned my respect.

My choice was Tony, but he was very popular and although we had met and chatted briefly, he was never alone.

It was the morning when everyone was leaving and I had walked to a small garden to reflect on the amazing movement that was being launched in education, when Tony appeared – alone! Grabbing all my courage, I asked him if he might look at my manuscript. In his usual enthusiastic manner, he not only looked at it, but gave one of the most thoroughly motivating major re-write suggestions I have ever received.

A year later we met at another conference and a year after that, I brought Tony in to speak at the Quantum Mind conference I was organising in Palm Beach, Florida.

One of the early projects that Tony and I worked on was the revising of *Use Your Head* and so we had many very detailed discussions about this corner stone work of his. This lead to my being involved as a sounding board and master mapper for all of his books, tapes and videos from 1987 until 2005, I felt privileged and delighted to be able to offer many suggestions and ideas that were incorporated.

Maps are such a simple, yet profound way to have a conversation with your brain. Whether to put information in, remember it, contemplate it or pull it out. I have used them to communicate with non-literate people and to solve complex problems. It was because I felt that the basis of Tony's work needed to be spread all over the world and that it enabled me to also achieve my purpose on this planet – to share easy, practical ways for people to enhance their joy of life - that I founded and was CEO of the Buzan Centres for 22 years.

We created a global network of dedicated people helping others to see that their brains did work, if you knew how to use them. One trainer from the Far East said that we had reached the stage where every hour, someone, somewhere was becoming mentally literate from our teaching. I am thrilled that many of that loyal team are still enlightening and delighting people to their true abilities.

Tony's dream is of a mentally literate planet. When we first started on this endeavour I was hard pressed to see how we would be able to achieve it. However, in this electronic day, I see that it is an achievable goal. To this end, Tony would stop and teach anyone – a waitress, taxi driver or workman – who he was able to chat to for a few minutes.

Training as many thousands of people with the Mental Literacy skills as I have, it never ceased to amaze me how many people have carried scars from a throwaway line that diminished their abilities. I would see the expressions of mixed delight and anger – delight that they could indeed have a brain that worked and anger that they had suffered and been held back for so long.

For people who are dyslexic (such as me) mapping is particularly powerful as a brain unleashing process. To find a way to organise thoughts and convey information that mirrors how the 'big picture' brain functions is a real gift.

Tony is one of the most constantly positive people I have met. Over the years that I have known him I saw him deal with near financial ruin, sickness, people betraying him, people lying, being envious and jealous, or trying to cut him down, and he would always keep steadfastly and resolutely working towards global mental literacy.

One of the lessons I learned from him was after a very close friend had cut a deal behind his back, badly betraying him. For a while they didn't speak (I think because the person was embarrassed) and then Tony said he wanted to spend time with him again. I could not believe this after what had occurred. Tony said that he enjoyed his company and he trusted him! He explained he trusted him to be lead astray in certain financial matters and betray the friendship – this broadened my understanding of 'trust' greatly!

Others may have already said about his total delight in and involvement with such a broad range of aspects of life: sports; food; nature; sci-fi and music to name a few. He also had the title of Mr. Indefatigable as he appeared to never tire, always being the last to leave any gathering.

I am on this planet to be a 'Joy enhancer'.

I accepted this 'job' at seven-years-old when the thought first came.

This is my passion and purpose and everything I have done (and AM doing) is within this context.

From running the NASA canteen in Grand Canary to being President of the International Society for Accelerated Learning and Teaching; from the Education Unit of Unilever, UK - teaching students all over Great Britain about the latest fabrics to Florida Power & Light, USA – running live cooking schools for thousands; from initiating a 5000 strong school volunteer programme to a 'Happiness & Wellness' TV show and from teaching people how to use their brains effectively to helping them develop their resilience - all done so people may enhance their joy quotient in simple yet highly effective, practical ways.

Building resilience is my most recent way of increasing people's enJOYment of life. After experiencing the pandemic of stress and the lack of coping strategies (and the perceived lack of time do any of them), I created a unique (yet based on proven psychological and brain research) 8 steps in 8 minutes routine. This very simple, yet powerfully effective routine is now assisting people all over the world to hold the reins of control and build their resilience.

Tony and I shared parallel purposes, by that I mean Tony's purpose of a mentally literate planet and mine of enhancing peoples' joy fitted together perfectly. So I was able to work on achieving my purpose, while helping him achieve his and his work helped people to become more joyous – perfect!

We worked very intensely, frequently long hours with tight turn-around time frames and I cannot remember ever a cross word or crabbiness, we both loved what we were doing and our abundant energy and ability to focus on a purpose bigger than ourselves carried us through. The only sometimes heated discussions were about issues such as the appropriateness of the 'Mind Map Laws' when we moved to computer drawn maps.

Tony was very generous and I was fortunate to travel the world, meet people and create new and exciting endeavours with him, such as 'The World Memory Championships' and 'The Brain Trust': with his encouragement I founded and grew the 'Buzan Centres' where we created a global network of centres, dedicated trainers and master trainers and product distribution.

When Tony was about the champagne corks popped and the 'good times rolled'! Whatever he was doing he turned into a celebration. He relished and loved all aspects of life.

Unknown to many people, Tony and I also had a personal relationship; we were 'Companions', playfellows, life travellers. We shared so many interests and delights and I will always treasure those memories. We were together from 1984 until 2006.

Vanda was one of the sponsors of the World Memory Championships and the Brain Trust, also CEO of Buzan Centres 1989 – 2006.

· · · ·

Dominic O'Brien

Eight Times World Memory Champion

Persistence Personified

I first met Tony at the Athenaeum Hotel, London in 1991. I was very eager to meet Tony and Raymond Keene as they were about to launch the first ever World Memory Championships and, having spent the last four years training my memory, I wanted to know the format for the competition so that I could prepare and possibly have a chance of winning.

Tony's superb invention and super mnemonic device is the Mind Map. The genius of the Mind Map is in its simplicity and directness. It strips away gobbledygook allowing one's brain to get straight to the heart of what it's thinking. When working on a project, especially one with a deadline, it removes the stress and procrastination of "where do I begin?" It allows instant initiation of creativity allowing me to assemble my thoughts and "see" them more or less instantly in one picture.

His greatest achievement and legacy is in inspiring millions of children and adults around the world to unleash their creativity and help them to realise their full thinking potential.

One of the major components of Tony's character and, I believe, a quality of his success lays with his persistent nature. Like an inquisitive child persistently asking where, why, and what to a weary parent, I find this a refreshing and admirable quality.

I recall walking through an empty hotel restaurant in Shanghai with Tony. We spotted a shiny new piano and when Tony tested one of the keys, a waiter promptly rushed to him and told him that the piano must not be touched.

Tony asked, "Why?"

The waiter replied, "Because it is not allowed to be touched by anyone except hotel staff."

Tony again asked, "Why?" "It mustn't be played by residents."

Tony, again asked, "Why?" At this point, the waiter stared long and hard at the piano keys and appeared to be rendered speechless. As we left the restaurant I could see the waiter still staring at the piano keys. The expression on Tony's face was one of mission accomplished.

The incident reminded me of an early episode of *Dr Who* when he gave a computer one question, "Why?" The machine, unable to compute the question, blew itself up.

I think the example that Tony sets for us all is in the unceasing output of creative ideas. The world to Tony is like a special toy to a child that it never tires of.

Dominic O'Brien was the first winner of the World Memory Championships in 1991 and has gone on to win the title an unprecedented eight times. He was named Brain of the Year in 1994 and Grandmaster of Memory the following year.

He has written best-selling books on memory and made numerous TV and radio appearances around the world.

Dominic has achieved a host of World records, including one for memorising the order of 54 shuffled packs of playing cards after a single-sighting of each card. He has been a friend and colleague of Tony's ever since the first World Memory Championships of 1991.

Phil Chambers, World Mind Mapping Champion, Dominic o Brien, eight times World Memory Champion and Tony, on board ship.

Julian Simpole

Former Editor of SYNAPSIA

I was introduced to Tony at Raymond's London flat in Hyde Park Place at a time when my father had been assailed by a stroke, one that severely reduced his ability to speak. This was particularly frustrating for a man whose mental faculties were otherwise still unimpaired. On learning of the specific nature of the trauma Tony immediately advised me to give my father a notebook so that he could write what he wanted to convey, and this I did.

The readiness to help, and the simple yet effective suggested remedy itself, stem from Tony's enduring desire to increase our awareness of latent mental capacity in order that all can benefit. To date this driving force has impacted on a global scale to the benefit of millions.

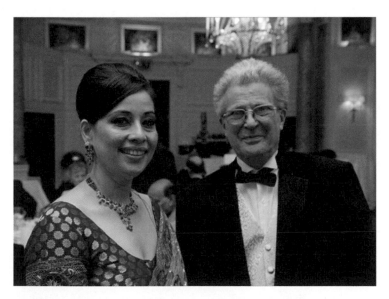

Julian Simpole with Princess Asra Khan

Later, I was to profit directly from this missionary zeal. At the end of 1991 it was agreed that I become the executive editor of Tony's International Brain Club journal *Synapsia*, and I duly ran the magazine for a year, overseeing the production of four issues until domestic circumstances obliged my resignation.

Format, cover designs and, in some measure, content were brought into sync with the ongoing demands of the day, and I remember happily discussing the nature of intelligence with Harvard professor Dr Howard Gardner. In his seminal double feature spread over the last two issues (the `hands-on' educational ideas expressed there have certainly caught on – think classroom/discover museum), it became clear that somebody brought up in the Western academic tradition has no reason to feel superior to the unlettered man who can, however, successfully navigate a catamaran across thousands of miles of ocean without a compass.

To summarise: we rely on our cultural milieu, the environmental factors and stimuli in which we function, to be able to demonstrate how smart we are. The buzz word is contextualisation.

I also recall with admiration and amusement Deborah Skinner's rebuttal of an assertion, put forward in a previous *Synapsia* article, that attempted to explain an aspect of her late father's work. As the daughter of famous behaviourist B F Skinner she had an insight into his contribution to science few could rival, and as she pointed out, negative reinforcement is still reinforcement!

Yes, they were halcyon moments from a vintage year in which the revamped journal's basic message was blazed far abroad: *we can all make better use of our brains*. Also, that the techniques for doing so (Mind Mapping, memory training et al) can be fun and demonstrably helpful within a short time-frame, and that this cerebral provender is available to everyone, crossing boundaries of race, creed, gender, acquired educational baggage and so on. Truly a litany of hope and enlightenment in a complex – Professor Gardner would say bumpy – world.

Complex or bumpy, it is matter of huge regret that there exists in the human psyche a leaning towards acrimony, a giving way to negative impulses that suppress initiatives directed at creating positive welfare in society. Observing this, a cynic might linger upon criminality rather than applaud the good mankind can achieve, thus arriving at the conclusion that there are too many dictators, not enough David Attenboroughs or, indeed, Tony Buzans.

We can only hope that Tony's worldwide reach continues to shift the balance towards the light, and that others are inspired enough to maintain and advance his cause. The world will be a better place if they can.

• • • •

Dr. Kirpal Singh

Professor of Creativity, Author and Poet

Singapore

Tony Buzan and I

This strange, wonderfully English gentleman known for his wit, charm, panache and, of course Mind Mapping! And I go back years - two not-so-young men both trying to bring about a better world through transforming the way our mind works.

Tony and I were scheduled panellists for a Radio discussion on Creativity - of course, we had both known of each other before the Radio event - he, I think, primarily through his good friend Edward de Bono who, apparently, had been upset with me and had told Tony I was 'cheeky'.... years later when the three of us dined together (with Howard Gardner from Harvard being the other dinner guest) we clarified.... with Ed laughing and saying he had forgotten what exactly it was that got his goat!!!! I, of course, had read about Tony's achievements in founding Mind Mapping and going beyond in so many different and fascinating ways.

But what I feel really connected us is that Tony and I both really like/love a few things: good food, good wine. But most of all - good conversation (in the old style) and good poetry. Indeed, we are both convinced that the passion for writing/reading good poetry almost automatically guarantees good conversation.

And so began what is now a rare, genuine friendship that has taken Tony and myself to several continents together-either literally or metaphorically. Both he and I are passionate about *metaphor* - this is what today's young don't seem to grasp -and we are doing our best to help redress this. If we lose sight of 'metaphor' then life, too, will become boring, ponderous and in some deep sense, meaningless. This is where POETRY comes to our rescue.

The fact that Tony and the late Ted Hughes were great mates turned out to be yet another vital and emotionally binding connection. Though I only met Ted Hughes twice, his sonorous voice and his steadfast views have remained embedded in my consciousness. 'TH' was extraordinary - both as a human being and as a poet. And to see Tony's eyes light up (btw, Tony's eyes are absolutely worth spending time on!!!) whenever Ted Hughes is mentioned is in itself a scintillating experience.

It has been a fantastic journey - this travelling together with Tony in spirit - he is an extraordinary human being. His vast intellect aside, there is a genuinely compassionate side which many don't know and/ or recognise. He is supremely nice and generous to the simple folks-servers at coffee shops, attendants at hotels, office boys and girls who bring letters, etc. and with friends - with some he is generous to a fault. When Tony likes you, he really does!

All in all, my poem for Tony, written expressly for his 70th birthday, sums up my deep admiration of the man and his stupendous intellect. He always asks me about his poems - and I always tell him Mind Mapping is poetry!

Mind Mapping Poetics

(for Tony Buzan on his 70th Birthday, 2 June 2012)

On that welcoming desultory nite
Amidst the Shangri-La shades
We struck more than a chord-
You, almost shy about being a poet,
I, watching, listening, reaching out.

Ted Hughes and I were very close-
You began, narrating a sad tale
Yet one with glory and triumph
As we both reflected on tragic nodes
The world knows you as the genius
Creator of Mind Mapping and more:
The world knows me as it does so many
In multiple terrains and hues-
We give the world what it seeks
My friend and fellow sojourner
Of life's long learning and remembering
With memory now being the centre
And us ageing, graciously, voyaging
Stars, planets, moons and humans
Wisdom our grannies dispensed freely
Now we realize just how precious
These connections across vastness
These meanings which fulfill, enrich
And cement the bonds of shared love.
Three score and ten, now you've done it
Lived past the good book's map of minds
As we celebrate your fame and fortune
Knowing not what tomorrow might bring.
I end as I began: that desultory nite
When the sake flowed minus geishas
And words and phrases detained us
Looking for origins, parallels, metaphors
We managed to be the last to leave-
Even Shangri-la allowed us this affirmation

Tony with Dr. Kirpal Singh

Jane Stephenson
International Conference Organiser

I first met Tony at a Harper Collins book launch in Ireland. His work is brilliant, innovative, highly effective and inspiring.

I have enjoyed many road trips with Tony, as we travel to events all over Ireland and we always find time to locate a good hostelry for a leisurely meal and bottle of wine; he is always excellent company and we laugh a lot. Many is the time when we have arrived at a scheduled talk with moments to spare, well oiled with some fine bottle!

When I first met Tony Buzan I said to myself, "Thank God Tony Buzan is in the world", he is such a big thinker, so positive and so refreshing in his outlook, always intuitive and sensitive to others.

I run large events with Tony and it always touches me how many children and young people queue up to get their books signed; he definitely has rock star quality!

I have been running inspirational events with Tony for many years; he is a very dear friend as well as one of my favourite speakers. We often spend four or five days together as we travel to different events, there is never a dull moment and he keeps me on my toes - he has the energy of a 20-year-old!

• • • •

Dr. Henry Toi

Buzan Centres Asia

As I sit in my office reminiscing about the expansive professional and personal journey that I had travelled with Tony for the past 12 years, my mind went back to an evening in Hong Kong circa 2002.

It was a talk that Tony gave for parents and teachers at a school far from the main city centre of Hong Kong. This was an event that the Hong Kong Management Association had organised.

At that event, I sat off stage, nearer the front of the large, non-air conditioned hall. The wooden flooring reminded me of my own school back in Singapore. Tony had asked me to help to Mind Map the talk on computer, which I did faithfully, even though I had only one day to familiarise myself with the software. Tony as usual went on to mesmerise his audience and taught them about learning, Mind Mapping and how to love and respect their brains.

Eric Cheong, Tony and Dr Henry Toi

Towards the end of his talk, Tony told the audience about me, did a fabulous introduction and invited me on stage to use the Mind Map I had done to summarise the talk. I did so courageously. After my short presentation, I felt it fell short of my own expectation, and certainly Tony's. Tony walked over to me on stage and gave me a hug and whispered, "Well done, even though you had such short notice to learn the software."

Such was Tony's predisposition to encourage. Over the years, I saw him encourage others and by doing so draw out the best in people. Tony drew out the best in me, and that indeed is education.

Tony with kids

In 2009, Tony went to a school in Singapore to talk to 500 kids. I have heard Tony work with adults and he is good. I was not sure how he would work with kids. These are kids ranging from 10 to 12 years of age. When we reach the school, the kids were already seated on the floor in a large auditorium with no air conditioning. It was about 11am, and in Singapore, it was getting really hot. The kids were a little restless. I did a short introduction of Tony to the kids. Then Tony took over.

He started by asking them a question, something he did with adults as well, but this question was rather interesting. He asked them if they think a computer was smart, the kids responded with an enthusiastic response, "YES", Tony went on to ask them if they think they are smarter or a computer was smarter. He got their attention.

We got the kids to think together with him and think loudly they did. Needless to say that it was a good session with the kids. The session went on for more than 30 minutes. Tony is indeed a good communicator and teacher with both adults and kids.

Travels with Tony

I had the privilege of travelling with Tony to many cities around the world. I might be the person who has accompanied Tony on the most number of trips. I can remember multiple trips to Jakarta, Kuala Lumpur, Beijing, Hong Kong, Bangkok, Manila, had meetings in London, Marlow and Singapore of course.

In all my travels with Tony, he has always been consistent in his exercise and food. His motto of healthy mind healthy body is consistently practised. Even when he broke his leg and was later hospitalised, he bounced back with greater energy and enthusiasm. In his speaking engagements in all these cities, he comfortably spoke to the "man in the street" as well as politicians and government ministers. Regardless of culture, audiences around the world loved him, his speaking skills transcend cultures, race and age.

• • • •

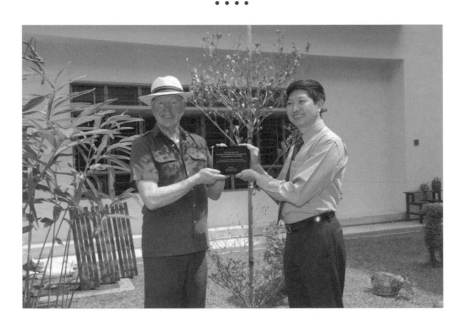

His Serene Highness Prince Philipp Von Und Zu Liechtenstein

"How fascinating!"

I first met Tony at a Greek friend's house at the beginning of the nineties. On this occasion, he presented and taught us his revolutionary Mind Mapping and how to use your head. My wife and I were deeply impressed and so we invited Tony to our house near Paris for a long weekend to teach our sons and some of their friends. He most kindly accepted to all our lasting advantage.

Later I invited Tony to join me in setting up our LGT Academy. This institution, now over 15 years old, is fundamental in forming our corporate culture. The themes taught there are widely spread from natural sciences to social sciences, meditation, sports like rowing, chess, drawing and painting and of course Mind Mapping, now widely used in our company.

Having myself followed the first class of the Academy (6 weeks) Tony's "How fascinating!" is still an expression I am not the only one to use when confronted with something you tried unsuccessfully and learned from this experience, like falling overboard while rowing.

• • • •

Dr Sue Whiting

Five Times Women's World Memory Champion

I first met Tony at the wonderful 1992 Brain Club Conference at Durham University. I was already an active member of the London Brain Cell (that I subsequently organised) and the Brain Club.

Tony is one of the most generous hosts I know: his wonderful Christmas Eve parties, where my children were made so welcome, were surpassed only by his amazing 70th birthday party on the Thames. We were delighted that Tony became our youngest daughter's godfather. We even managed to arrange Fiona's baptism around Tony's travel schedule so that he and Vanda were able to attend!

When Tony encouraged me to watch the 1993 World Memory Championships, I decided to experiment with memory systems and enter the one hour random numbers competition. And so, thanks to Tony, I became hooked on the mental sport of memory! In 1994, I entered all ten disciplines, becoming Women's World Memory Champion and also the first female Grandmaster of Memory. I fondly remember the stimulating sessions I spent with Tony exploring the intricacies of advance memory systems: learning can be such fun!

Thank you, Tony, for everything.

• • • •

Sutanto Windura

Brain Coach Leader

The Enthusiastic Disciple

I would definitely like to have some contribution on the making of this wonderful genius person's biography - I encountered Tony for the first time in August 2002 in Jakarta, Indonesia.

I was introduced by a friend in the event of a "little" memory championship in Jakarta. The event was hosted by a memory school. I took the franchise.

I knew Mind Map from Tony's *The Mind Map Book* which I bought when I met Tony in 2002. And I fell in love with Mind Maps the first time I used them.

A Mind Map is a simple, powerful and fun tool for any thinking mode. Everybody on this planet should know and use Mind Maps.

Tony is a man with abundant idea and passion.
A man with Semper Solutio...
A man built by Genius and Discipline...
A man who rebuilt the Brain New World

Sutanto Windura is the author of seven best-selling books of Brain Management Series published in Indonesia and Malaysia

Host of You Are Genius! on Radar TV and Chairman of The Brainic® Institute founded in 2002.

Ben Zephaniah

Rastafarian Poet & Dyslexic

Tony's a great mind and all that, and he's a laugh.

I met him face to face on a memorable day in March 2011 in Dubai. We were both attending the Writers' Festival there and, as writers do, when not speaking at their own events, we attend each other's events.

I had heard some creatives and academics talking about Mind Maps, but I was never sure what it was all about so I was keen to hear Tony's lecture in Dubai. We had already spent a few days together, just loitering with intent, and I could see that he was a passionate, and energetic person. But even that didn't prepare me for the content of the lecture. I was completely blown away by it and it all made absolute sense to me. I just can't understand why I had not heard him before. That lecture actually changed the way I think.

At the time I met Tony I was considering a post I had been offered at Brunel University. I told him about the offer and he gave me some very good advice, which I have heeded. The first part of the advice was about understanding and protecting my intellectual property. The second part was about staying creative and not getting bogged down and becoming a boring academic. It was very helpful.

Benjamin Obadiah Iqbal Zephaniah is a British Jamaican Rastafarian writer and poet. He is a well-known figure in contemporary English literature, and was included in The Times list of Britain's top 50 post-war writers in 2008. A dyslexic, he attended an approved school but left aged 13 unable to read or write.

David Zhang:
Tony's Publisher In Beijing

I first met Tony in September 2010 when I visited his lovely residence in Marlow. The talk between us lasts the whole afternoon until it gets dark outside. He's energetic, quick-witted with terribly clear thinking during the whole talk although at that time his leg was in a plaster cast after an incidental fracture happened during his travel in Russia.

Mind Maps and Tony's related contributions to world mental literacy has already become an icon, which makes an epoch-making change in the history of human brain and metal skills development.

During an author tour I accompanied him in Beijing, Tony would rather postpone his supper until late at night when he knows that there would be a speech at 7 pm. The reason is that the meal shortly before the speech may influence the perfect performance during presentation. And he did it.

David Zhang with Tony and Ray at Simpson's-in-the-Strand in spring of 2011.

Joe D Adams

Former CEO of Encyclopaedia Britannica UK

'**ve** known Tony Buzan since 1971 and was successful in getting Dr Mortimer J Adler, the editor in chief of Encyclopaedia Britannica, to write the foreword for Tony's first book – *How to make the most of your mind.*

As Dr. Adler points out in his foreword, Tony's aim in that first book was threefold:

1)   To persuade each of us that our mental resources are greater than we could ever envisage

2)   To help us to acquire the skills that will enable us to make the most of these resources

3)   To motivate us to make the effort to acquire these skills so we can profit from the satisfaction and results achieved

Tony Buzan made a major contribution to me as Chief Executive Officer of Encyclopaedia Britannica by speaking at a number of our international sales conferences. He also inspired me to start a new division of the company – 'Human Potential'. But perhaps most of all, he became a lifelong friend and we shared many stories and talked endlessly about our hopes, dreams and aspirations.

He is an extraordinary individual and a man who I'm proud to call a friend.

Chris Day

General Secretary, World Memory Sports Council

I first came across Tony Buzan when, as head of field communications for Encyclopaedia Britannica UK, he was invited by my CEO Joe D Adams to train and inspire our sales managers. I can still remember him teaching them to juggle at an event in the Runnymede Hotel in Egham overlooking the Thames.

At that time, Britannica was an early sponsor of the World Memory Championships which were then taking place annually in Simpson's-in-the-Strand in London. As I was responsible for Britannica's in-house television studio, I was asked by Joe to go and film the event to support Tony. Thus began my involvement with the World Memory Championships.

Over the years, my involvement grew behind the scenes as I facilitated a web presence, and created an archive of visuals materials related to the championships. I also worked with Ray, Phil Chambers, Dominic O'Brien and Vanda North with the organisation of the event.

As the sport grew and became international, I helped to set up the World Memory Sports Council as the governing body of the sport to provide a central administrative base, and later became the General Secretary.

Wearing my other hat as CEO of Filament Publishing Ltd, I co-wrote and published the first *Memory Yearbook for the Mind Sport of Memory* with Phil Chambers and Tony Buzan. I am now extremely proud to be the publisher of Tony's official biography.

Phil Chambers

Chief Arbiter, The World Memory Championships

I first came across the name Tony Buzan in the mid-eighties when the *Use Your Head* series was re-run on BBC2. I can't say that I was an avid viewer or took a great deal of notice. Later, I came across his book *Master Your Memory* and various articles in *Mensa Magazine*. I was introduced to Mind Mapping in a very primitive form by a science teacher at school and used it to some effect in exam revision. Little did I expect at the time that I would become World Mind Mapping Champion. It wasn't until university that I finally met Tony. I was a member of the *Use Your Head* society at Durham where Tony was invited to speak. I watched the great man somewhat awe-struck by his eloquence and charisma. Later that year, I attended the second World Memory Championships as a spectator and was hooked. Working in IT, I instigated computerised scoring to the championships, initially as 'Statistician' to the tournament and then 'Chief Arbiter'. Now, two decades later, I am still heavily involved with Tony's vision of Memory Sports around the globe.

It is not only through memory that Tony has influenced my journey in life. I was a member and regular contributor to the Brain Club. I made a great number of friends through both the Thames Valley and London clubs, and I fondly remember speaking at Brain Club Conferences in London. My speaking career stated in 1995 when I became what was at the time called an RTI (Radiant Thinking Instructor) with Buzan Centres. Later to become a BLI (Buzan Licensed Instructor) and then TLI (ThinkBuzan Licensed Instructor). I now work with Tony training the next generation of TLIs in memory and Speed Reading.

Tony's work has changed thousands of lives and has touched mine more than most. I am proud to count him as a friend.

Phil Chambers is Chief Arbiter of the World Memory Sports Council, Reigning World Mind Mapping Champion, author on learning related topics, and runs Learning Technologies Ltd, a company that teaches thinking, memory and speed reading skills to corporate clients, educators and individuals.

World Memory Championships - China 2011

Left to right - Jennifer Goddard, Dominic O'Brien, Tony Buzan,

Phil Chambers, Gaby Kappus

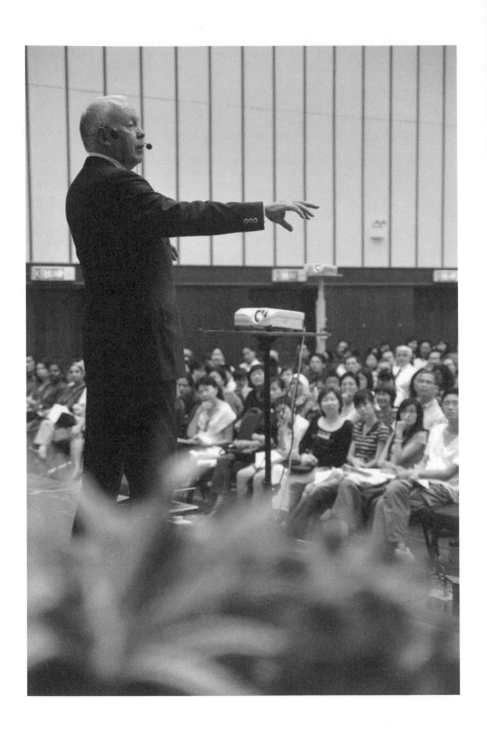

Chapter 17

As Nestor To Agamemnon

2012 Brand Laureate Award

Tony has devoted much of his working life to applying his formidable thinking powers to the subjects of management and leadership skills at the highest levels.

The theories and programmes he has developed are much in demand by governments and businesses throughout the world.

Whether he is working one-to-one or delivering a keynote speech to an audience of thousands, and, having witnessed him in action first hand on numerous occasions, I regard his ability to inspire, motivate and empower, as awesome.

The focus of Tony's work with businesses and governments is to help leaders to maximise their creativity and innovation skills. He also works on specific projects, advises on election campaigns, and empowers the negotiation skills of individuals and teams. He has a particular interest in the areas of Knowledge Management, Leadership, Intellectual Property, and Corporate Memory.

As an indication of Tony's impact, *Time* magazine in 2007 showed a Mind Map prominently displayed in Al Gore's Nashville home office, where he regularly uses Mind Map software to 'order his thoughts' in particular on environmental topics, such as his controversial, influential and polemical documentary on climate change, *An Inconvenient Truth* (2006).

In the article, the former US Vice President said that he uses Mind Maps to keep on top of everything.

Tony has also acted as adviser to a number of the world's leading families, including Kings, Sheiks, Princes, country leaders and, as we have seen, cultural icons such as the family of the late-lamented Michael Jackson. His influence on the global business community, and the impact of his 'ultimate thinking tool' the Mind Map, were both highlighted in a *Newsweek* article entitled *The Road Ahead: How Intelligence Agents and Mind Mappers are taking our information democracy to the next stage.* The writer? Bill Gates!

Gates stated his conviction that..."a new generation of Mind Mapping software can be used as a digital 'blank slate' to help connect and synthesise ideas and data – and ultimately create new knowledge...and mental models to help people mine and assess the value of all that information...".

In the early 1970's, Tony was asked to give a keynote speech to a group of 100, an all-party and business gathering at the House of Commons. The result was so successful, that a six-session course was arranged for a select group of mixed-party politicians. The group included Richard Dunn, MP for Liverpool, Sir Spencer Summers, Bernard Wetherill, who was soon to become speaker for the House of Commons, who called the course "one of the five most important events of my life" and a guest for the speed reading section, the Shadow Minister for Education at the time – Margaret Thatcher.

Soon after this event the BBC ten-part television series *Use Your Head* (and its accompanying book of the same title) was screened and published in April of 1974. Within a week of their screening and publications, both IBM and British Petroleum (BP) had requested Tony's services.

Flowers In The Field

Critical mass had been reached. Tony often refers to this dissemination of his ideas and the way these interconnect, grow and flourish around the world, then feed back to him, often in the most surprising and unexpected fashion, as "flowers in the field." In a few years, Tony was giving special keynotes and lectures for Management Centres in Europe, Turkey, the Middle East, USA, Australia, and the Institute of Directors in London.

During his global travels, Tony has presented on the same stages as Dr Henry Kissinger, Buckminster Fuller, Dr. Edward De Bono, Professor Howard Gardner, Dr. Stephen Lundin, Lord Robert Winston, John Sculley, Nicky Oppenheimer and Megatrends futurologist John Naisbitt...

Another great honour was the invitation from the King of Jordan to speak at the Hashemite Court in Petra to the King's annual conference for Nobel Laureates. His work was personally patronised by Tun Dr. Mahathir Mohamad, the Prime Minister of Malaysia, who incorporated

Mind Maps and Mental Literacy into his 2020 Vision plan for the future of Malaysia.

Another highlight, as we have seen, was his co-founding, with Prince Philip of Liechtenstein, of the LGT Renaissance Academy, a six-week course designed eventually for all members of the organisation. The course focused on business studies, art, Mind Sports, physical sports, the martial arts, philosophy, communication skills, poetry, ethics, music and the art and science of the self. Founded in 1995, the Renaissance Academy still thrives and grows, and remains the beacon for LGT's Human Resources Development Programme for Mind, Body and Spirit.

Tony was also featured in *Forbes Magazine*, being included in the world's top presenters, alongside Margaret Thatcher, Mikhail Gorbachev and Henry Kissinger.

In 2010, *Mind Maps for Business* was published by BBC Active/ Pearsons, giving examples from businesses around the world of how Mind Maps have saved them millions of pounds, have enhanced all other standard business tools, have streamlined organisations, have inspired workforces, have solved 'insoluble' problems, and have generally created wealth in all its manifestations wherever they have been used.

Tony's achievements as a Corporate and Government keynote speaker and lecturer have stamped him as one of the most inspirational and business-relevant speakers in the world. He targets with clinical precision the concerns which most engage the individual as a learner, the individual within the organisation, and the ability of organisations, whether a corporate, national or global, to unleash their maximum potential, to nurture their intellectual capital, and to survive in the modern environment.

• • • •

Chapter 18
Tony in Turkey

With the prevailing goal of global mental literacy, Tony has dedicated himself to travelling the globe raising awareness of the human brain's infinite potential. No biography would be complete without inclusion of the work he has done around the world.

As Appendix A shows, he has worked in 150 countries and to detail the significant impact he has made in every country would fill the Grand Canyon. So let's take a detailed look at just one country and explore nineteen years in Turkey with Management Centre Turkey

In the spring of 2012, Mr. Alper Utku, Chairman of MCT (Management Centre Turkey), a leading consultancy firm in Turkey was attending an exclusive event with all of the great and good in Turkey – senior politicians, industrial leaders, bankers and EU representatives.

He'd arranged a special invitation for Tony to attend this prestigious gathering. As they walked along the corridor on their way to one of the breakout session, they were passed by one of the industrial leaders – the Chairman of one of the region's biggest conglomerates. He caught sight of Tony and, as Alper describes it, "he ran after us like a high school student. He took Tony's hand… 'I'm such an admirer… I'm one of your students… I'm so happy to see you here'. He said this in such an open, naïve and youthful way."

Tony reconnects people with the vitality and hope of childhood, a childhood of possibility. Tony touches people from all walks of life – from students, to captains of industry, to passport control officers. He cuts across the entrenched divisions of age and social background – most recently he's been focusing on the young.

Tony and MCT, a management development and consultancy company, got involved with each other in November 1993. At the time MCT was a small start-up and Tony managed to get into the company's DNA in a wonderful way.

Tony was the star turn at one of MCT's first guru seminars – this one was for 60 people at one of Turkey's finest hotels – the prestigious Ciragan Palace Kempinski Hotel. Alper was mesmerised then, as he has been many times since, as Tony kicked things off with his 'paperclip' exercise.

"I want you to tell me three things you can't do with a paperclip," he requested the audience.

Well, according to the audience, you can't eat one… you can't eat with one… and you certainly can't write with one. Tony then reframed their answers to demonstrate that a paperclip could easily work as any of these things – as a foodstuff, a fork and a pen. A mundane paperclip could be anything.

The remainder of the seminar – as with all the others he worked at in Turkey until 1997 – was a practical master class in engaging with the discipline of creative thinking. There is no mystery to connecting with the infinite potential of the mind – Tony's renowned Mind Mapping discipline was the practical manifestation of a mind-freeing, rather than mind- limiting, philosophy.

And for Alper this mind-freeing philosophy made even more sense with its refusal to engage with those classical perspectives that see the mind and body as separate units, rather than informing parts of the same whole.

"Tony talks to the unity of the body and mind… how the healthy mind and all its creativity depends upon – and is entwined with – a fit body." Creativity is whole-bodied as well as whole-minded.

One of the significant touch points in the MCT history with Tony was the student event that Tony did with MCT for 6000 university students in Istanbul. The event publicity had made such a great success that when Tony arrived at Istanbul airport he was greeted by name as he arrived at passport control, the policeman on duty hadn't even looked at the paperwork, but he knew who Tony was – and was hoping to make it to one of Tony's events in the coming fortnight.

Tony and the culture of MCT

Nineteen years on from Alper's first engagement with Tony and with MCT now approaching its IPO (Initial Public Offering), MCT staff and clients are very clear about the company's culture, its effect on their lives and the unique contribution that MCT can make to corporate life. And Tony's fingerprints and influence are all over the place.

As part of the preparation for the upcoming IPO, MCT pulled together a series of digital testimonials from its clients – including one organisation that's famous for only giving very limited positive feedback. On this recording the mood was very different.

"When it comes to MCT," was the tone of their words, "whenever we offer them a challenge… they never say no… sometimes they're creative on the spot… sometimes they go away and think and study… but they always come back with something new… and this gives us comfort as a client."

Tony's mantra about, and disciplines for, unlimited creative potential have been paying off for nearly two decades in how MCT goes about its business. Ehru, relatively new to MCT, sums up the philosophy using the same words as the hard to please client: MCT is built on the idea of "never saying no." This is new to her and something she's "learnt from MCT and used in all parts of my life."

When she's organising conference speakers she'll always find a way to make it easy for them to say yes to her proposals – and so MCT is able, year after year, to attract some of the world's most fascinating thinkers and business practitioners to its annual Human Resource conference. Next year they're hoping to have keynotes from either Al Gore or Prince Charles, the heir to the British throne.

At home Ehru's relationship with her kids has changed as she focuses on "giving them different ideas" to work with, "encouraging them to grow up creating new things and possibilities." Learning to let go of the easy parental habit of simply saying no, of setting down those self-limiting habits of mind that Tony has dedicated his life to freeing people from.

Tony and the energy of youth

Tony started off his work in Turkey focused on the corporate world – beginning with his guru seminars in '93, before moving on to being an in-house speaker for client organisations from '97 through to 2003/4. Lately he's combined his role as a guest speaker at MCT's annual HR conference with other more inclusive activities.

One of the most significant of these new, more inclusive, events was held in a *Cirque de Soleil* big tent in 2011 with six thousand students coming from all over Turkey. He taught them Mind Mapping, the discipline of creativity, how they can engage with their unlimited imaginative potential and avoid the dead end of "no way out conversations", where possibility is killed off by the deadening habits of denied possibility and invention.

For Alper the "energy and vibration was the peak moment of his career and gave him the inspiration to go with younger people and larger audiences." Inspiring young people to engage with possibility rather than limitation is a hugely invigorating perspective for Alper, MCT and its future.

After the event the feedback was heart-warming and uplifting; the students spoke of having "more confidence in themselves", of feeling "encouraged to do more with themselves… to try new options," it "gave hope." In the case of one student "this event has changed the course of my whole life."

The insights Tony has gifted MCT

Given that Tony's work is all about the limitless nature of possibility, it feels strange to reduce what he has given to MCT to six sentences – but then part of Tony's gift has always been to make the infinite accessible.

Here are Tony's six gifts to MCT:

Gift 1. **Creativity depends on how you use your brain.** Neuroscience is making major strides in helping us understand how the human mind works, but Tony was popularising and working with these insights thirty years ago. The brain is a part of the body, it is not a mystery; it can be understood and worked with differently.

Gift 2. **The mind has infinite potential and we can tap into that potential with the right user's guide.** As with Mandela's observation that it is not our powerlessness we fear, but how powerful we can be – so it is with our mental capacity. We allow ourselves to become labelled and shrink our potential to fit with what others tell us – and we then learn to tell ourselves the same limiting story. Tony provides the 'how to' guide that helps us step into our limitless, imaginative potential.

Gift 3. **Possibility is about mental framing – and you can learn how to reframe what your mind can see with the right discipline.** Paying attention to how you see the world is vital – thought creates the world and then defines it as David Bohm put it. The key to mental framing are the disciplines you use – disciplines that train both the mind and the body.

Gift 4. **Learning how to reframe how you see the world gives you hope.** Ever since Alper met Tony in '93 and worked with his practices "I've never failed to reframe" a situation. Alper has always been able to find hope, even when he's been facing tough times at work and home. Finding hope is not the same as denying that the world presents us with tough situations.

Gift 5. **You can choose to be creative about anything – there is nothing you can't see and know in a new way.** At the heart of Tony's work is the discipline of owning your own agency; you are not passive when it comes to how you think – you may feel you are, but that is just a habit of mind telling you to be passive. There is always choice.

Gift 6. **Over the years MCT's clients have learnt to trust MCT's capacity to reframe complex situations.** In the English phrase, the proof of the pudding is in the eating. MCT has been proving Tony's insights on the ground in Turkey for nearly twenty years… and "even when we don't find a gorgeous creative result for a client, we give them a sense of possibility and options they hadn't seen before."

Finishing with the chains of childhood

"Tony talks about creativity in childhood… the critical voice we experience in childhood limits us. Tony encourages us to shut down the critical voice." When Alper is "with my children I'm nurturing rather than critical… helping them develop by focusing on their strengths."

Both at home and work Alper's ambition is "not to put limits around people." The focus is on "what can be done and the choices people have." Tony's thinking is about liberation; freeing people from habits of thinking that imprison them in hopeless conversations.

Tony has inspired MCT to be the practical advocates of hope in Turkey – for children, students, parents, CEOs and passport control officers.

• • • •

OMNE·IMMENSUM·PERAGRAVERE·MENTE·ANIMOQUE

Chapter 19

The Banner Of Mental Literacy

Tony's Coat Of Arms

On 26th August 2008, Tony was granted Armorial Bearings by Her Majesty's College of Arms. One of the many thrilling aspects of being granted Armorial Bearings is the challenge of creating, in a single formalised image, a summary of the main elements and aspirations of one's entire life, goals and achievements.

A daunting task...

Tony had an expert team to help him, including Thomas Woodcock, then Norroy King of Arms, Robert Parsons, Senior College of Arms artist, Grand Master Raymond Keene, Julian Simpole, former *Synapsia* editor and an expert in the field, the artist Lorraine Gill and the Visio-technologist Richard Morris.

The team met regularly for a year and produced a unique Coat of Arms. Shortly after the successful completion of the Coat of Arms, Robert Parsons was made an MBE for his life-long excellence in producing artwork for Armorial Bearings, and Thomas Woodcock was promoted to Garter King of Arms – the most senior position in the field.

Let Tony take you on a guided tour of this joint creation which deliberately reflects his life and achievements:

Purpose

MOTTO

"Each Coat of Arms rests on the base of a motto which is inscribed on the supporting scroll. After much deliberation, and considering mottos that had inspired me throughout my life such as 'Mens Sana in Corpore

Sano' (Healthy Mind Healthy Body; Healthy Body Healthy Mind); Carpe Diem (Seize the Day!); and Semper Solutio! (there is Always a Solution!), I settled on the more vast and inclusive: Omne Immensum Peragravere Mente Animoque, which translates literally into: 'all', 'immensity', 'to traverse', 'mind', 'spirit' and which fully translated means: "to Traverse, in Mind and Spirit, the Great Immensity (the Universe)."

In the major part of the shield of the Coat of Arms, one is allowed any image desired. I wanted my image to be inspired by the incredible etcher Maurice Escher, famous for his visually tantalising and complex images which provide the viewer with many simultaneous and differing perspectives. Similarly I wanted expressed Escher's constant theme of Metamorphoses and mastering the processes of change.

In the shield's main image I also wanted to include:

- Pieces from the 'King of Mind Sports' chess, a game that has informed and inspired me throughout my lifetime;
- Concorde, the plane that fired many imaginations around the world, including mine, and while flying in Her I wrote 385 poems about Her;
- A spaceship to symbolise my fascination with the planets and the universe;
- The Eiffel Tower – a building that holds many special memories for me.
- A warrior;
- A fairytale palace;
- Tree forms;
- Dancers;
- Outstanding representatives of fish and birds;

For the fish I chose the three-spined stickleback (Gasterosteus aculeatus), arguably the most intelligent 'pound-for-pound' fish, which I had bred as a young boy, and which had astonished me with its intelligence, social organisation, fighting ability, determination and sheer physical and functional beauty.

"I was later to discover that Nicholas Tinbergen, one of the founders of ethnology, the scientific study of animal behaviour in natural surroundings, was awarded a Nobel prize for revealing the incredible social infrastructures, behaviours, and intelligences of these beautiful little fish that had so entranced me as a child;

"For the bird I chose the swallow, for the Concorde-like beauty of its design, and for its speed and gracefulness;

"I had also wanted the image to include the concepts of Focus and Radiance. And those were just some of the symbolic highlights of my life. How many of these were successfully incorporated?!

"At first the task seemed an impossible one, especially as the shape of the shield was not conducive to Escher's perspectival illusions. We worked on it as a team, and finally, after filling a sketch-pad full of ideas, Richard Morris hit on the brilliant image that, in this context, was the first ever of its kind, and which is a prime focus of the Coat of Arms.

"At the top of the shield, and protecting everything below it, is a raptor – a bird of the eagle/peregrine/falcon family. 'Peregrine' and 'peregravere' forged a pleasing additional flight of associations.

"The eagle was, when I was a child, my favourite bird, and, as we have already seen in this book, Alfred Lord Tennyson's poem *The Eagle*, transformed my writing and poetic lives.

HELMET - Above the shield there must, in a Coat of Arms, be a helmet which can face to the left, to the right, or face-on. I chose face-on, because it was more direct, and symbolic of honesty, focus and commitment.

THE MANTLE - Embracing the entire shield and helmet, the Coat of Arms must have a mantle. I designed mine to be particularly organic, reflecting the forms and shapes of Nature, and emanating, Mind Map-like, from the central image, in a way that symbolised reaching out into the micro cosmos and macro cosmos. I also wanted the mantle to reflect the willow-like grace and flowing quality of my major martial art, Aikido – 'The Way of Harmony'.

THE DRAGON - Above the helmet I was privileged to be able to use, because I had been honoured in 1984 with the title of Freeman of the City of London, the City of London's own symbol: the dragon. The dragon symbolises power, astuteness and wisdom, qualities which I personally revere. London's dragon was placed over the Temple barrier in early times, which was the official (and only!) entrance to the City of London. The dragon was the guard and guardian, and symbol for the ideals of the City.

In Asia, an area of the world where my work is increasingly widespread, and where I am spending a growing amount of my time, the dragon is a creature that brings with it ultimate abundance, prosperity, and good fortune. The dragon is the emblem of the Emperor

and Imperial Command, and its benevolence signifies greatness, goodness and blessings. The Chinese dragon symbolises auspicious power and excellence, valiancy and boldness, heroism and perseverance, nobility and divinity, energy, light and rebirth. A dragon overcomes obstacles until success is his, and is energetic, decisive, optimistic, ambitious and intelligent. Most Eastern Dragons are beautiful, friendly, and wise. They are known as the 'Angels of the Orient'.

THE DRAGON'S WEAPONS - In the 'hands' of the dragon one can choose further symbols. I chose the pen and the sword, putting a new 'twist' on the standard saying 'the pen is mightier than the sword'. As a writer I obviously needed a pen, so chose the original writing implement – the quill, symbolic of both writing and nature.

In the right hand I chose a sword that is-and-is-not, a sword! It is actually a neuron – a brain cell, symbolising, for the Warriors of the Mind, the immortal battle for the freeing of Intelligence. The brain cell is also the inspiration for my valediction Floreant Dendritae! – 'May Your Brain Cells Flourish!'

COLOUR

The colours were potentially a difficult choice for me, because I love the rainbow!

The choice was made easier by considering again the original purpose of the Coat of Arms: the colours had to give clarity to the overall image, had to be strong, had to support the themes of the Armorial Bearings, and had to be powerfully distinctive. Four different colours were considered ideal. I chose, therefore: blue; gold; silver; and purple.

Blue, especially in its form as ground Lapis Lazuli, is a colour that represents both the physical and the metaphysical. In the physical realm, blue is the colour of both the sea and the sky on a sunny day. In the metaphysical realm, the azure of the sky leads to the universe and the heavens, the gateway to all that we have yet to traverse and explore. For this reason blue is often considered "a colour of the mind and spirit".

Gold and its lustrous ore, is an integral part of the grammar of heraldry. Gold represents a symbol of the 'idea' for which all people strive. Gold has a hint of rarity about it, and traditionally was used to symbolise and communicate excellence.

Tennyson's *The Eagle* was a poem written about the Golden Eagle!

Gold is also a symbol of desire and passion, and is the colour used throughout heraldry and by the great artists to symbolise energy, the sun, radiance, incorruptibility and eternity.

Blue/Gold In addition to their individual qualities, blue and gold are complementary colours. They are, therefore, ultimately distinct colours which give further clarity and power to an overall image. Optically each stands out, and helps the eye distinguish elements within the image.

Silver is the colour of purity and reflection. Reflection in the physical sense, where the colour acts as a mirror, and reflection in the mental/ spiritual sense of contemplation and the examining of oneself.

Silver is the actual colour of most helmets, and is the natural colour of the three-spined stickleback. In the Coat of Arms, you will notice that the mantle has a "silver lining"!

Purple was the most-prized colour in classical civilisations. It could be produced as a dye only by the delicate processing of the Mediterranean Murex molluscs, and was, like gold, prized for its rarity. In addition to its luxurious quality, it represented power and elegance, and was therefore used by Roman emperors. In modern times it has come to represent, increasingly, the spiritual world.

Purple and gold are another powerful combination of colours. The strength of their marriage is succinctly stated in Lord Byron's most-quoted lines:

> The Assyrian came down like the wolf on the fold,
> And his cohorts were gleaming in purple and gold;
> And the sheen of their spears was like stars on the sea,
> When the blue wave rolls nightly on deep Galilee.

Colours: Conclusion Blue, gold, silver and purple are colours that are deeply woven into the tradition of heraldry. They are colours which optically have great clarity, and which contextually tie in with the overall themes of the Coat of Arms.

Tony's Armorial Bearings needed to be, and he believes are, a composite, revealing the beauty of Nature, his personal history, and his ideals.

Part Four

Spiritual Progression

Chapter 20

The Parables of Tony Buzan

The following parables all bear upon Tony's experiences, in particular with the discovery of both intelligence and huge cerebral resource in frequently unexpected or underestimated locations or people. This refers back to the opening theme of this book: Barry, the unrecognised nature genius and the perennial question of "who guards the guards?" Who decides what intelligence is and who is intelligent?

I. The Parable of The Lover of Memory

On 5 February 1997, at 9.00am, the first American Memory Championships were about to start. As the two Tony's, Dottino, the co-organiser of the event and Buzan prepared to launch proceedings, a breathless and bright-eyed girl came panting to the door, and asked enthusiastically if she was still in time to enter. Tony Buzan asked her why she wanted to, and she replied with gusto: 'I couldn't think of anything I'd rather do than spend a Saturday in New York playing with my memory!'

Tatiana Cooley was in!

As the memory competition progressed, Tatiana gradually eased ahead of competitors who included IT (Information Technology) company executives, college professors, top college students, students of memory, national newspaper journalists, teachers and psychologists.

Tatiana's performances improved, and in the end, having surmounted hurdles such as the memorization of numbers, giant shopping lists, complex poetry and decks of cards, Tatiana emerged as the first National US Memory Champion.

In an impassioned and moving Championship Acceptance Speech, Tatiana explained how, as a little girl of less than three years old, she had 'fallen in love with memory'.

The reason for this blossoming love affair Tatiana attributed to her father. Tatiana's earliest memories of her childhood were of playing mental and physical games of all sorts, especially memory games. These included speed association games, memorisation of 20 or more covered objects on a table, which were uncovered briefly, covered again, and then to be recalled, and many other memory games involving words, numbers, situations and stories.

Also, whenever they went anywhere together, which happily was quite frequently, Tatiana's father would say such things as, 'Tatiana, my love, can you see that train? How many carriages does it have?' And so saying he would point to an exceptionally long trans-national cargo train that had as many as 73 carriages. Little Tatiana would count them and triumphantly announce the accurate number.

Some one, two or three weeks later, at 'random' moments, her father would say 'Tatiana, do you remember when we went to the countryside a little while ago and saw that train? Can you remember how many carriages there were?' Increasingly knowing that 'the game was on', Tatiana would come up with the correct answers.

By playing such games, Tatiana's father was not only improving her memory, he was making her more interested in the world around her, expanding and stretching her senses, and regularly encouraging the development of her majestic imagination.

II. The Parable of Creativity And IQ

These two critical elements of the multiple intelligences are often confused with each other and sometimes, to the untrained mind, can be seen as opposite and antagonistic intelligences. They are, of course, not, and should be trained simultaneously and synergetically.

When IQ tests are administered to young children by untrained overseers, two of the prime strengths (and indeed requirements)| of the creative thinker: originality (seeing things in ways that no one has seen them before) and multiple perspectives (seeing things from many different angles) can lead to the child being given lower marks than deserved.

Two examples will serve to illustrate the tyranny of evaluation by means of the standard IQ test:

In the first, a 10-year-old boy was given an IQ test in which there were many multiple choice questions, he being obliged to select the correct answer from a choice of four.

One of the questions had four consecutive cubes, in each of which was a different image, with its name underneath; in the first square was an image of the sun; in the second an image of the moon; in the third an image of the earth; and in the fourth an image of a lemon. The young boy was asked to select the 'odd one out'.

The expected and 'obvious' answer was number four, lemon.

The young boy immediately chose (and speed is another factor in creative thinking) number three, the earth.

His IQ was 'marked down' because on this question, as with many others, he had failed to see the obvious and 'logical' answer. In fact many of his answers, as with this one, were so bizarre that the testers actually began to wonder whether he was suffering from some form of mental retardation.

As a result they brought him back to the clinic, and went through his answers one by one, asking him to explain why he had selected as he had. His responses were startling, and to many of the psychologist interrogators, humbling. On the case in question, when they asked him why he had selected 'earth' instead of 'lemon', he looked at them with amazement in his eyes, and responded with sympathy for their lack of perception in his voice: 'because it's the only blue one!'

His answer revealed a big knowledge of space, dimension and colour and an intellectual process that was far more complex and creative than the more simple solution for which his relatively uncreative thinking testers had been waiting. His brain was obviously thinking in new and creative ways.

The second test was similarly a multiple choice picture test, this time including colour, no defining key words, and being administered to a 10-year-old girl.

In the first square was a picture of a large pile of coal; in the second a yellow daffodil; in the third a shovel; and in the fourth an empty fireplace. As with the little boy, she was asked to select the 'odd one out' and to indicate which one it was by putting an 'X' through the image. She crossed out the picture of the 'coal. Again, like the boy her IQ was downgraded because she had missed the obvious logical answer: number two, daffodil.

When asked why she had answered certain questions in the way she did, she said referring to this one: 'Oh, I thought the correct answer was supposed to be "daffodil", but it was such a pretty picture I didn't want to spoil it.'

Her response was as beautiful as her thoughts, displayed a wonderful creative and spiritual intelligence, and was worthy of an upgrade in her IQ score.

III. The Parable of The Angel Mind Mapper

In Colorado, a young computer engineer, Brent, was the proud father of a three-year-old girl who, apart from one continuing and notable exception, 'was his little angel'. The singular exception had been triggered by Brent's very compassionate approach to marriage and child-rearing. He had proposed to his wife, who also worked, that they would each come home early on alternate nights, and would individually spend extra time with Christina while also, where possible, helping out with family and housekeeping tasks.

Brent had ended up with early Tuesdays, which coincided with the day when shopping needed to be done. He felt that this would be a good opportunity to spend co-operative and functional time with Christina, as she could help him do the shopping.

However, Christina decided that she did not like shopping, and did not want to accompany her father on the trips. This was obviously not possible.

As a result every Tuesday, Brent had to haul a screaming little banshee around the supermarket, cringing from the stern and disapproving stares of other shoppers, who probably assumed that he was an uncaring, vicious and brutal example of how not to be a parent! This mini horror-story went on for a number of weeks, Christina demonstrating her powers of persistence in sticking to her attitude and opinions.

On the next Tuesday, Brent, in one of his breaks, was musing on what to do about this increasingly untenable situation. Running through the considerable shopping list that he had to buy that evening, he decided to convert it into a Mind Map, festooning it with images of the foods and products to be bought. As he developed the Mind Map, the idea formed in his mind that it would be a wonderful gift for Christina, and that it might in some way entice her to consider shopping in a slightly more positive light. Little did Brent realise the magnitude and implications of what he had just done.

That evening he took Christina, once again howling, to the entrance of the hyper-market, and there handed her multi-coloured, illustrated Mind Map.

He had underestimated Christina!

She surveyed the map intensely, and then, holding it in front of her like a steering wheel, pointed to the drawing of carrots and looked at her father imperiously while stating: 'Carrots!' Then, like a little guided missile, she directed Brent through the mazes of the market to precisely where the carrots were. As soon as the carrots were selected, weighed, placed in the bag and put in the trolley, Christina pointed to the drawing of potatoes and, in the same manner, proclaimed 'Potatoes!' Once again she led her father directly to where the potatoes were on display.

This procedure continued for half an hour, with Christina pointing eventually to every object on the Mind Map, and leading Brent upstairs, downstairs and throughout the entire complex of the shopping centre with unerring precision and accuracy.

He reported that he was amazed by her performance, not only for her instantaneous ability to recognise and name every item on the Shopping Mind Map, but also by the revelation of the fact of which he had been completely unaware: Christina's three-year-old brain, despite her dislike of shopping, had totally memorised the architecture, structure, design and location of hundreds of different objects in the hypermarket.

Brent reported that in subsequent weeks Christina could not wait for Tuesdays and 'shopping!' with a different Mind Map each week as both her guide and confirmation of her own genius.

The 'sting in the tail' mentioned at the beginning of this story refers to the fact that as the weeks progressed, Christina became more and more enamoured of shopping. It became such a passion for her because of the way in which the Mind Map had released the intelligence and allowed her to display her memory, knowledge and skills, that whenever her parents asked her what she would like to do, the only answer she ever gave was: 'Shopping!'

• • • •

IV. The Parable of The Invention of Light

"They all laughed at Christopher Columbus, when he said the world was round, they all laughed when Edison recorded sound." Fred Astaire, song from the film *Shall We Dance?*

In inventing the light bulb, he had been inspired by a vision to 'light the planet at night', providing the human race with, should they wish it, 24 hours of 'sunlight'. He proclaimed to his family, friends and the world his goal, claiming that he would do it by passing the then generally unknown and mystical force of electricity through objects in order to create heat and light.

He was mocked and scorned.

Edison went through innumerable substances, eventually having tried over 5,000 different experiments without success. He had to endure mounting criticism and censure, and when he was well on his way to his 10,000th trial, still without a notable success, the censure had reached such a pitch that even his closest family and friends considered having him committed to an insane asylum.

Thomas earned himself a temporary reprieve by pointing out to his mass critics that he was the only person in the world who knew of so many thousands of things that didn't work, and therefore he was the closest person in the world to finding the single thing that did!

As he approached his 10,000th trial, the light dawned.

From that day to this, the light bulb has been the symbol for inspiration and genius. It is the appropriate symbol for genius, and therefore, by Thomas Edison's definition, is also the appropriate symbol for Persistence.

So what was the event in the early 1970s that transformed Tony's own thinking about this crucial aspect of human intelligence? It was, as you will by now realise not surprisingly, a profound lesson-by-demonstration taught to me by a five-year-old girl.

• • • •

V. The Parable of Persistence - Do You Want a Sweet?

The scene is a small tree-lined street nestled near the heath in the writers' and artists' community of Hampstead in North London. The time is late Saturday morning; the day balmy and scented with apple blossoms.

Tony had strolled a few houses up the street to pay a casual visit to some friends, Gerard Benson and his wife Joan. Gerard was not at home, but Joan, who was a concert pianist, was, and she invited Tony into the spacious downstairs room, which was dominated by a large rectangular antique table. Around the table sat four of Joan's female friends. Tony was welcomed by one and all to join them both for morning tea and for conversation, which as he had entered, turned to the nature of freedom, the definition of feminism, the nature of male/female leaderships and best practices for bringing up children.

The discussion was already becoming intense, and as the tea in the teapot cooled, the temperature of the debate rose. The level of emotion and intellect was high, the members of the 'debating chamber', in addition to Joan and Tony, consisting of a BBC television presenter, a novelist, an English scholar and a Cambridge don.

The debate had become a raging inferno of thought, and words probably unknown to Webster and Roget, in combination, with quotes from every imaginable 'great thinker,' were being hurled around the table like grenades.

After half an hour had passed and many brilliant arguments voiced, no one had yet managed to convince anyone else to change an opinion. The individual frustration felt by proponents of an idea that was not gaining acceptance raised the heat of the debate even further.

As it was reaching a climax, and as personal thermometers and blood pressures were continuing to rise, the hanging curtain that separated the room from the garden silently opened, and there stood, unannounced and generally unnoticed in her entrance, Olivia.

Olivia was a five-year-old girl who was dressed beautifully in the hippy-child-style of that time; a puffy-armed white blouse and a full length, autumnal-coloured Indian cotton dress that reached down to the ground, the hem just revealing the protruding toes of her bare feet. Her long brown hair fell to the base of her spine, framing a face that could only be described, straight from the pages of the Rev Charles Kingsley, as a 'grimed cherub'.

After the few seconds it had taken her hazel eyes and focused brain to absorb the physical and mental environment, she glided, again generally unnoticed, to the left of the chair of the lady sitting to Tony's left.

In Olivia's right hand was a crumpled white bag that contained her treasures of the morning – her weekend ration of sweets. With her head reaching only just above chair level, she raised the bag of sweets to adult-sitting-in-a-chair elbow-level and said: 'do you want a sweet?' There was no reaction, as the offeree was intently and totally committed to the ongoing debate.

Unperturbed, Olivia stood, motionless, like the Statue of Liberty, still holding up the little white bag, and repeated, in exactly the same tone as previously: 'do you want a sweet?'

Again, she went unnoticed and after a brief hesitation, again, she repeated the request: 'do you want a sweet?'

This continued roughly for another 12 identically intoned repetitions, at the end of which, acting almost as if she had been hypnotised and not quite knowing consciously what she was doing, the woman muttered: 'Oh yes, thank you' and unseeingly and unconsciously dipped her hand into the bag, taking a sweet, and putting it into her mouth, as she continued to make the points that were crucial to her ongoing argument.

Having accomplished her task, Olivia glided clockwise around the table, and placed herself identically adjacent to the next woman.

Once again she asked 'Do you want a sweet?' and once again she was not noticed. Once again she repeated and once again she was not noticed. Once again, as the intellectual missiles continued to be hurled around the table with increasing ferocity, Olivia began her almost mantra-like intonation of: 'Do you want a sweet?' Do you want a sweet?' Do you want a sweet?' Do you want a sweet?...'

And once again, the fire-branding debater succumbed after 15 repetitions, again taking the sweet almost robotically from the proffered bag. By this time Tony had begun to become intrigued, slowly realizing that something quite extraordinary was taking place in this Hampstead home. He kept one part of his attention on the debate, in which he, like the others, was arguing 'brilliantly' while simultaneously failing to make any headway, and the remaining (and growing!) part of his attention on Olivia and her Pilgrim's Progress.

Two down and four to go!

Olivia approached the third lady, and proceeded with the identical routine, achieving an identical result. By this time Tony was mesmerised, and as he listened to the screaming intellectual bansheeism of the august adult group, he simultaneously observed the extraordinary and obviously irresistible incantation from this genius Brain Child. 'Do you want a sweet?' 'Do you want a sweet?' 'Do you want a sweet?' 'Do you want a sweet?' 'Do you want a sweet?' 'Do you want a sweet?' 'Do you want a sweet?' 'Do you want a sweet?' 'Do you want a sweet?' 'Do you want a sweet?...'

Olivia's chant began increasingly to sound like the fundamental base rhythms of the double bass or didgeridoo, while violin and cello sections screeched out of control.

As numbers three, four and five inevitably fell to the intoxicating offer, Tony began to hatch a wicked plot to foil this master schemer.

When Olivia finally glided to his left side, he pretended to pay no attention whatsoever to her, and mentally tolled off the mounting number of her repetitions. He thought that she would stop at around 20 and then he would challenge her. Instead she continued and continued: 'Do you want a sweetie?' until, by the time she had reached 36 repetitions, he decided it was time to pounce.

Turning around in his chair, Tony gave her his total and passionate attention, exclaiming with a loud voice, blazing eyes, and hands outstretched over her like giant cranes descending upon her offering,

'YES!! I WANT THE WHOLE BAG!!!!'

At that moment the transformer was transformed! As he looked triumphantly and exultantly down at Olivia, he was greeted with a smile; one of the most extraordinary smiles he had ever experienced- one that instantaneously told him that he had been easily out-foxed by a thinker of gargantuan proportions.

Olivia's smile was utterly angelic and open, admitting, willingly, that she had been 'sussed'. At the same time, and far more importantly, that smile contained one of the most impish gleams imaginable. That impish gleam was the product of her realization that although Tony had sussed her scheme, she had won. She had gained my attention. I had focused upon her; had focused far more than any of the others, and had taken a sweet!

Mission accomplished, the tiny mastermind left as noiselessly and unobtrusively as she had entered, leaving the debate to rage on unabated and her vanquished competitor sitting stunned by the magnitude of what had just occurred.

Tony sat, the raucous sounds of the still-inflamed debate fading into a background din, as his mind filled with thoughts about the significance of what he had just experienced. For more than an hour, six highly trained and highly educated intellects had presented, passionately, an incredible range of arguments and rationales for the points they were attempting to make, in order to bring about change in thinking and behaviour of those they were addressing.

Not a single thought or opinion had changed one iota.

While all this incredibly intense, yet utterly unproductive, circus had been going on, the seventh mind, with a similar mission to adjust thinking and influence by behaviour, had succeeded perfectly with every single member of the group, while every one of those individual members had singularly failed with every other one.

The debate eventually subsided to a gentle simmer, and after a light lunch of white wine and salad the guests went their separate ways.

At least one, however, was changed for life. Tony began to put Olivia's lessons into practice, arguing less and persisting more. And succeeding more. With far less effort, and always keeping in mind that extraordinary morning and that amazing smile as a constant and eternal guide and provider of amusement.

Tony has observed, and as the genius biographies confirm (it is interesting to note that contemporaries of the geniuses almost invariably described them to being like 'big children') that all children are identical to Olivia, and use persistence like ultimate artisans as a tool to learn, to accomplish multiple tasks, and to satisfy basic needs.

Young children, on a daily basis, regularly outwit their 'more educated and powerful' adult masters.

Consider the typical example of a multiple-degreed, athletically skilled, 1.90-m (six foot three), 90 kg (two-hundred-pound), business-leader father, with four year old daughters, who after the initial hugs and greetings say:

'Dad, can we have an ice-cream?'

'No.' (distracted)

'Dad, we want an ice-cream.'

'I said No.'

'Ohhhhh, go on Dad, we want an ice-cream.'

'I said No, now stop asking.'

'Daaaaaaad, pleeeeeease, we want an ice-cream.'

'Stop pestering me and leave me alone. I said no.'

After a moment's pause and reflection,

'Go on Daaaaad, pleeeeease, we want an ice cream.'

'I said No and I mean No.'

Again, after a slight pause, some tactical leg hugging and heart-movingly pleading looks, the Olivia-like mantra begins:

'We want an ice cream, We want an ice cream, We want an ice cream, We want an ice cream, We want an ice cream, We want an ice cream, We want an ice cream, We want an ice cream, We want an ice cream, We want an ice cream, We want an ice cream, We want an ice cream, We want an ice cream, We want an ice cream, 'ALL RIGHT, ALL RIGHT! But only this once!'

Child's brain 1 – Adult's brain 0!

Persistence is a vital and endearing quality that is an essential survival tool to your child. It needs to be encouraged and developed.

• • • •

VI. The Parable of "Work"

Gerard Benson, the mathematician, musician, code-breaker and poet, who was the father of persistent Olivia, had brought up his five-year-old son Oliver to adore mathematics. They constantly played mathematical games together, and young Oliver was learning to speak 'mathematese' with a facility that was approaching his level of competence in English.

Tony had the good (though disturbing) fortune to be visiting their home when Oliver returned from his first day at school. His face was not a happy one, and Gerard very gently and concernedly holding back on the real question he wanted to ask, enquired about the day in general, the school, the teacher and other odds and ends. Oliver answered perfunctorily, giving little information, and obviously reluctant to communicate.

Finally, unable to bear the suspense any longer, Gerard posted the prime question:

Gerard: 'Did you do mathematics?'

Oliver: 'Yes, in a surly fashion.'

Gerard: 'And....' Expectantly.

Oliver: 'I don't like maths.'

The shock registered in every fibre of Gerard's body, but being alert and not wanting to in any way alarm or upset Oliver, he asked very casually, 'Why don't you like maths?'

Oliver thought for a moment and then replied: 'Because of work'.

Tony and the dad were both intrigued by this answer, and Gerard, one of the world's great decoders, asked the next probing and appropriate question: 'What's work, then?'

At this, Oliver frowned deeply, thought for a considerable time and finally said: 'Work is doing what you want to do when you don't want to do it'.

Both Gerard and Tony were stunned by the profundity of this definition. It turned out that the teacher had forbidden Oliver to do mathematics in the morning when he had wanted to, and had forced him to do mathematics at, for him, a boringly simple level in the afternoon when he did not wish to. From the mouths of babes ...

VII. The Parable of Austin's Powers

At the age of four Austin, his parents, and his and their lives seemed ideal. Austin was a good-looking, athletic, charming, happy and attentive child; his mother, Diana, was the successful director of a major national management group; and Austin's father, Keith, was a leading medical specialist, who was also the director of a major hospital. They lived in a spacious country house with delightful grounds and a large swimming pool, and led a happy social and cultural life.

One year later poison had entered their lives. Tony received an urgent call from Diana and Keith, explaining that Austin had evolved into 'a little monster'. He had become rude, aggressive and increasingly violent, and was now virtually out of control. They had tried so many different approaches to cure the problem, but to no avail, and the situation was now so out of control, and so potentially dangerous that they were reluctantly considering against all their instincts and desires, having Austin committed to a psychiatric ward.

Tony naturally offered to do whatever he could to help, and one early balmy summer afternoon he visited them, and the three adults sat by the swimming pool, sipping tall fresh fruit punches laced with ice, and discussing Austin's extraordinary decline and increasing delinquency.

In the middle of the afternoon, Austin returned from school, where once again he had apparently been causing havoc. As he walked in, Tony was surprised to see not a scowling and snarling psychopath, but a little boy similar to the one he recalled from a year previously, though slightly larger. Austin said, 'Hello', and rather aggressively asked for a fruit punch like ours, with lots of ice and two straws.

For ten minutes he behaved in a perfectly normal fashion, sipping contentedly on his drink and wandering around looking at the flowers.

As he finished his punch, he sidled over to the table, and when he was standing next to his parents, suddenly and mightily sucked on both straws, creating a loud, drain-like gurgling sound that rattled to the collective adult ears.

'Austin! Stop that!' said Diana.

And Austin did so. For 20 seconds.

And then, having exhaled totally, he once again inhaled mightily, making an even louder and more disgusting 'schluuuurrrrrrp!'.

'Austin! I've told you once Now stop it!' said Diana.

And once again Austin did stop.

For 20 seconds.

And then, once again, the total exhalation and yet another mighty inhalation through the thundering straws.

'Austin! O-n-e moooore time…..' said Diana threatening, waving her finger pointedly at him.

And of course, Austin obliged with one more time!

'All right, Austin!' said Diana, 'That's IT! Keith!' said a now-livid Diana 'You tell him!'

Keith momentarily taken aback by the sudden responsibility thrust upon him, quickly recovered and glowering, turned towards Austin and said:

'All right, son, now it's me! Quit!

And Austin did.

For 20 seconds.

And then calmly, methodically, and without a trace of fear, came the inevitable and next monstrous schluuuuuuuuuuuuuuuuuuurrrrp!

Keith, who was a big, commanding, strong and athletic man, then glowered more ferociously and fell into exactly the same trap as his wife had done.

'All right, son, that's enough! One more time....'

And of course, Austin obliged.

Tony now picks up this increasingly tense story:

By this time I must admit I was surreptitiously rooting for the boy! My own internal man-child was saying, 'Come on kid, you've got 'em on the run!' By this time Keith was now really furious, and turning to Austin he said, with an ominous and threatening finality in his voice:

'All right, Austin! That's IT! One more time and you are going to get hit! And you know I mean it!'

This threat had more of an effect on Austin than the previous ones, and he momentarily quit. I kept my peripheral eye on him as Keith and Diana exasperatedly explained that this was yet another example (though mild) of his cantankerous delinquency and insubordination. While this was going on, Austin, like a master hunter, was massaging the space between us and him, sometimes sidling closer, sometimes farther away. When he had come innocently within a few feet or so, he moved approximately 50 feet away, and suddenly, without warning, schlurped with even more vigour than he had done before!

Keith instantaneously leapt up from his seat. Austin had been prepared for this, and had already run to the far end of the garden. Keith, observing this, subsided into his seat, saying with relief: 'Ahhh, it's OK now, we won't be able to hear him any more'.

And there at the far end of the garden, schlurpping away in the distance, stood the little Mohammed Ali of the Mind, Austin – total 'victor' of the mental battle.

Diana, Keith and I had been discussing the episode for some few minutes when suddenly 'out of the blue' I was hit, full force on the pressure point in my shoulder, by a perfectly directed, and maliciously intended, karate punch from the five-year-old miscreant.

I turned to Austin and, like his parents before, said: 'Austin! Stop it!'

And stop it he did, for a micro-second, before hitting me full-power again in exactly the same spot. A five-year-old with energy, direction and good technique can hurt any adult. It hurt!

This time I grabbed Austin by the shoulders, looked him straight in the eye and said: 'Austin, I don't want you to do that again, I don't even want you to want to do it again. But if you do, you'll turn this into an unpleasant game of consequences: when you hit me, I will hit you in exactly the same place on your shoulder, but just a little bit harder each time. So the choice is yours'.

Austin thought only briefly, and then wound up and smacked me again, once again in the same place. I immediately grabbed him, explained that I didn't want to do what I was going to do but that was the arrangement between us, and so hit him on the corresponding spot on his own shoulder.

Austin thought for slightly longer, looked me straight in the eye, and again hit me, hard.

I immediately grabbed him once again, explained that I didn't want to do it, didn't like doing it, and would quit as soon as he did, but that the deal was the deal and therefore I would hit him again as agreed. I did.

Austin thought about this even more deeply but nevertheless decided to continue and whacked me again. Persistence!

This time I once again grabbed Austin and explained to him the following metaphor: 'Austin, if there is a large boulder falling towards your foot, it doesn't know about your foot and doesn't care about it. You obviously know about your foot and care about it. If you don't move your foot the boulder will land on it and crush it. If you don't want your foot crushed you must move it to save yourself. The promise you and I have between us is just like the boulder. The promise doesn't know about you or know about me, or care about you or care about me. It simply says that if you keep hitting me I will keep hitting you, no matter how much we care for each other, and that if we don't stop we'll both end up in a bloody mess on the ground. So I have to hit you again, although I don't want to.' As soon as I had exchanged hits, I held him gently but firmly, and said: 'I don't want to continue doing this because I like you. I'll quit if you quit. It's a promise'.

Austin strolled away, thought about this for some minutes, and then came at me as if to hit again, but instead said: 'Do you want to go for a swim?!'

'Sulphuric Acid in the pool!' was my first thought! I said: 'Yes' but explained that I wanted to have a half-an-hour lie down first and then we'd go swimming. I lay down in the shade, with one concealed eye checking, and to my amazement observed Austin sitting cross-legged some little distance away from me, observing me. At precisely the 30-minute mark, his little face was next to mine saying: 'You promised!'

With that I leapt up, saying: 'Yes, I did!' Gathered him in my arms and leapt into the pool with him. He played ecstatically, and for the rest of my stay with them, behaved like my guardian angel, trying to make sure that my every need was catered for. We became 'best friends'.

What brought about this sudden change in Austin's behaviour? And, more importantly, what was it for which Austin was so desperately searching?

Quickly review Austin's story, and decide what you think his goal was (a clue is that most people immediately get an 'obvious' answer – and it's wrong!)

What Austin was searching for was not attention. This he had by the barrel-full.

What Austin was searching for was MEANING and TRUTH.

Austin, with his infinite and brilliant creative intelligence had unwittingly thought his way out of reality! It was only when there was a formula that enveloped him with both love and no way out, that he became centred, directed and happy.

Think, from the brain-new-to-the-planet-point-of-view about the meaning of which his parents had said. When Diana said 'Stop it!' It really meant: There was no time limit, and if you use your creative imagination you can do whenever you want.'

When Diana said: 'That's it!' it really meant that 'wasn't it'!

When Keith said: 'All right, Austin! That's IT! One more time and you are going to get hit! And you know I mean it!' It meant: 'If you can think of a creative interpretation of what I've said, you won't get hit. And what's more, son, when I say I mean it, I don't mean it!'

Austin was like a little spaceman on the spaceship 'Meaning' who had been cut off, and was drifting away in space totally isolated, without the oxygen of 'Truth', in an increasingly blank Universe where nothing meant anything, or everything meant nothing.

Imagine yourself in such space. What would be your first and immediate reaction when you realised you had been set adrift from the spaceship? Obviously, pure utter and stark terror. It was that terror that drove Austin to the frantic behaviours he was increasingly exhibiting, as he tried desperately to find meaning, to be aware of parameters, to, know literally, where he stood and where he therefore was.

Unintentionally and unwittingly Keith and Diana had been lying to Austin. They had all suffered the consequences.

• • • •

VIII. The Parable of Moon Numbers

In Liverpool, England, a father told the members of one of Tony's seminars a story that was inspirational, moving and sad at the same time.

His young son, like Oliver whom we have already met, had gone to school loving numbers. He had been a fairly quiet child, and had always done superbly in mathematics. However, as the complexity of the problems presented to the children increased (it was an accelerated mathematics class) the young boy began to irritate the teacher by constantly blurting out the answers to the problems that were being written on the board, comfortably before the writing of the problem had been completed!

As the frequency of these 'interruptions' increased, the teacher became increasingly frustrated and annoyed, initially thinking that the boy was somehow cheating, but then realising that he could not be, and that something else was going on. He asked Billy how he was coming up with the answers, to be surprised by the reply, 'Moon Numbers'. At this everybody else in the class laughed, and unfortunately the teacher mocked Billy.

From that day on Billy, having been rejected, hated mathematics.

Only some time later did Billy's father discover what had happened, and when asking the child what 'Moon Numbers' were, was told that they were special numbers he had discovered that were not anything that was taught in school and therefore could not have come from the earth. Billy had decided that they therefore must have come from somewhere else, and the moon seemed to him the obvious place. He had unfortunately stopped using them and thinking about them, but the father's discussions with mathematicians subsequently revealed that somehow the boy had intuited power and logarithmic relationships in numbers, and had used these in his mental calculations.

Unfortunately he never returned to them, and Moon Numbers were never revisited by the astronauts of the child's imagination.

• • • •

IX. The Parable of Metabolic Age and the Japanese Song Birds

"Metabolic age" is a new and revealing concept in the fields of health, physical and mental fitness, the idea being that one can, in fact, be younger - or older - than one's chronological age. Metabolic age can give you greater insight into your health habits and can help put you in charge of your health, well-being and ability to learn. Indeed, feeling younger than our numerical years is a state to which many aspire. Being motivated by reaching a younger metabolic age could help get you there. A metabolic age that is substantially lower than your chronological age means, compared to the average person in your age group, that you have more muscle mass, less fat, are more active, and therefore generally far fitter. As we shall see, there are other profound implications.

The Japanese teacher, musician and instrument-maker S. Suzuki noticed that baby chicks learn to sing by copying accomplished warblers. 'Astounding!' thought Suzuki, 'If a bird's tiny, tiny brain can learn so perfectly, then surely the human brain, with its vastly superior abilities, should be able to do the same and better?' This line of reasoning led Suzuki to his next revelation, which, when he announced it, made many of his friends think that he had lost a large number of his own brain cells!

Suzuki, in a delirium of enthusiasm for what he had realised, rushed around telling everyone he knew of his remarkable discovery: that every Japanese child learns to speak Japanese!

His friends and colleagues patted him on the shoulder concernedly, informing him rather firmly they were actually already aware of that. 'But No! NO!' declared Suzuki. 'They really do, and it's amazing'.

And Suzuki was correct. For, like Newton before him, he had discovered something that was so obvious no one could see it. What he had discovered was the fact that any baby born in any country automatically learns, within two years, the language of that country. This means that every normal baby's brain is capable of learning millions of potential languages.

If you had been born and lived in, for the first few years of your life, a totally different country from the one you are familiar with now, your own baby brain would have absorbed that language as rapidly and fluidly as you now speak your own main tongue. And not only would you have learnt the language of that country, you would have learnt the specific dialect of the special area of that country in which you had been born. If you, for example, were a Caucasian baby and had been born in Beijing, you wouldn't have looked up with your little baby eyes and exclaimed, 'Oh, Chinese. Far too complex for me! Think I'll stay silent for the rest of my life!'

What Suzuki had discovered was that the voice/ear/brain system was a virtually perfect copying machine, with an almost infinite capacity to learn the music (songs) of an infinite number of languages. And it didn't matter whether the language was Chinese, Portuguese, Music-ese, Maths-ese, Art-ese, Burmese, or Japanese. So long as the baby was given the right learning environment and proper encouragement, that baby could learn anything!

In the middle of his musings on the little chicks' brains and the amazing baby brain, a friend asked Suzuki if he would teach the friend's four-year-old son to play the violin. Thinking very little about it, Suzuki apologised, saying that it was impossible to do so because the child was too young, and in any case would never be able to handle a violin, which in proportion to the child's size would have been like asking a normal human to play a double base in the position of the violin.

A short while after he had parted from his friend, Suzuki was thunderstruck by his own narrowness of thinking. He had said that the child was too young to learn, when by his own admission all babies everywhere are learning music and becoming master musicians by the time they are three. Secondly he had said that the violin was too big, Why not, he therefore thought, make a violin that was an appropriate size for the young child.

Utterly inspired, Suzuki set about making a number of little violins. But how then to teach it? Suzuki realised that the answer must be to copy what the little chicks had done i.e. to COPY. That's why, Suzuki thought more than 95 per cent of us never learn to sing properly or enjoy playing musical instruments or draw – because we are told never to copy. The prime learning tool, mimicking, is taken away from us. To make it even worse, we are told that copying is cheating and cheating is bad, wicked and wrong, and that we are never to do it.

Further evidence of the work of the enemies of Mental Literacy at large!

Armed now with his child-sized violins, his revelations, and his clear understanding of how proper education must be structured, Suzuki approached friends who had young children, and asked them if they would like their children to learn to play the violin.

In his first classes, Suzuki scattered violins and bows around the room, and invited the toddlers to come and play with whatever they wanted, including other toys that were around the room. Suzuki, squatting cross-legged on the floor, simply picked up one violin, picked up one bow and played one note. As he had expected, one by one the children copied what he was doing, at which point he began to play two notes. Exactly as the little chicks had learned the Master Singer's song by listening and practising themselves, the children, at their own paces, learnt the violin with as much ease and grace as they had learned their native language. Suzuki had unwittingly founded a technique that has now spread throughout the globe, has tens of thousands of graduates, already a number of world-class performers, and no failures.

Normally one associates language – learning with French at school, or university degrees, but this is where metabolic age comes in. Every toddler has a metabolic language learning age far in advance of its academic years.

Metabolic Age versus Chronological Age

Chronological age is your age in calendar years. Metabolic age is a number that comes from comparing your Basic Metabolic Rate with the Basic Metabolic Rate average of your chronological age group. Depending on how you compare, you are assigned a metabolic age number that can be lower or higher than your chronological age. A metabolic age number younger than your chronological age generally means that you are fitter and in better health than the average, the lower the age the better in shape you are. An older metabolic age points towards being less healthy and fit than your peers and if it's much older than your chronological age, this should be considered a wake-up call.

Basal Metabolic Rate (BMR)

Your BMR is a measurement of your body's use of energy and is usually interpreted as the minimum level of calories your body needs in its resting state (including sleeping) each day.

What does it mean?

If you have a goal of improved health and fitness, both BMR and the metabolic age number are good ways to track your progress. Some over-the-counter tools, such as select body fat and weight scales, now contain these features. One thing we now know is that weight loss and gain alone do not tell the full story about being at or achieving a healthy body weight. You can be as skinny as a rail and still have too much body fat for your height and weight. Knowing your BMR and metabolic age can help you make educated decisions about calorie consumption, activity, fat loss, and how to keep and gain lean mass.

It is possible to calculate your Metabolic Age online, for example, by going to this link:

https://www.purelifestyle.co.uk/Calculators.aspx?idx=6

Tony Buzan was born in 1942. According to the latest calculations his metabolic age is 45!

• • • •

X. The Parable of The Disabled Learner

Pat's story shows the devastating effect that incorrect labelling can have on a young child.

From a very early age in his childhood, which had been spent in the southern United States, Pat had been diagnosed as 'severely learning disabled', had been publicly so labelled, and as a result had been ridiculed and ostracised. By the time he was 17, he had entered into what appeared to be a terminal depression, refusing to leave his bed for more than two or three hours a day, a behaviour which confirmed his dismissive label for many of those around him.

Pat was diagnosed by Vanda North as simply dyslexic and probably very bright. Together Tony and Vanda taught him basic information about the brain, and especially about how to memorise. Pat's imagination (as you might imagine!) from all those years of isolation was gigantic. He lapped up memory techniques, and was very soon easily able to remember 100 random items, in perfect order, in less than an hour.

Inspired by his sudden accomplishments and the self-realisation of his quite extraordinary abilities, Pat was suddenly empowered, 'came to life', became almost hyperactive, extremely physically fit, and reversed his behaviour, sometimes having to be forced to go to bed!

In a meeting one day, when Pat was publicly talking about his 'disability' and his transformation, he exclaimed, spontaneously and exultantly: "I WASN'T LEARNING DISABLED! I WAS LEARNING DEPRIVED!"

He was right.

• • • •

XI. The Parable of Alexander The Great And Paul The Disciple

Matthias Alexander was born in Tasmania, Australia in 1869. Alexander was especially interested in Shakespeare, and after studying drama and performance began to do one-man shows on the Bard's work. His performances were excellent, and he began to build a reputation both for the power of his voice and projection, and for his overall performance and stage presence.

And then the trouble with his body began…..

When he was comfortably into the middle section of his performances, Alexander found that his voice began to go hoarse, and by the end of his performances he was often in considerable discomfort.

As his condition was 'career threatening', Alexander sought advice from drama teachers, voice trainers, and doctors. He was prescribed potions, lotions, pills, balms, a change of air and rest. Alexander tried the various remedies, but infuriatingly, at about the same point in each of his performances, the hoarseness returned.

Eventually an especially important performance loomed on the horizon.

Alexander consulted the leading doctor in the field, and was advised to give his body and voice a complete two-week rest before the performance. This he dutifully took.

And in the performance?

At the same point his hoarseness returned.

Alexander furiously confronted his doctor, only to be advised to take even more rest. Concluding that all the experts must be missing the point, Alexander decide to become his own doctor.

He had noticed that in conversations with friends and colleagues, he could discuss, debate and lower and raise his volume of his voice for hours on end, with no hoarseness whatsoever. Surely, Alexander reasoned, the reason for the hoarseness during the performances must be something that he was doing with himself and his vocal chords during those performances.

He had tried and tried; he had experienced an event – his voice had become hoarse. He had received the feedback that experts weren't helping and that it was something he was doing during his performances that was causing his problems. He now decided to check. Alexander bought himself a full-length mirror and created the following self-check. First he chatted to himself as he would do to a friend. As he carried on his conversation, Alexander minutely observed what he was doing with every part of his body, especially his neck and throat area, his head, his chest, his abdomen and his back.

Then Alexander performed his theatre piece to himself. Again he observed minutely what he was doing with his body; how he was 'using himself', as he so perceptively put it. He observed some extraordinary differences. Because of his training in performance, and because of his own assumptions about what good performance and good posture was, Alexander observed the following things when he was performing:

1. He stuck his chest out;

2. He stiffened his neck, so causing his head to be pulled backwards and downwards;

3. He compressed and restricted his vocal chords;

4. He restricted and pulled his lower back in and forward;

5. He sucked in air with tension and a gasp;

6.   He tended to tense and 'lock' the joints of his ankles, knees, hips and shoulders.

No wonder he had been causing himself problems!

Intrigued by the astonishing discoveries he was making about how his training, thoughts, poise and physical actions so profoundly affected his performance, Alexander set up more mirrors and began to study himself even more intensely. He noticed that just by thinking 'Neck Free', his neck became freer, his head would 'float' forward and upward, and his back would lengthen and widen – all through the power of thought. He called this 'Primary Control'.

When he had achieved this state, he noticed also that his vocal chords were more relaxed and open, his breathing more free and easy, and his joints more relaxed and open for movement.

Most importantly for Alexander, he noticed that his voice greatly improved in quality. Applying his growing knowledge of the importance of poise to performance, Alexander returned to his own performances with gusto. The new and more powerful quality of his voice drew amazed comment, growing admiration, and Alexander became known as 'The Voice!'

By 1952 Paul Collins, then aged 26, had run the New York Marathon, had become the Canadian National Marathon Champion and record-holder, and had qualified for the Helsinki Olympics in that one year. He had a reputation as one of the prodigies in the marathon field, and was known as a particularly tough runner, who could break through most of the pain barriers experienced by marathoners.

The 1952 Marathon in Helsinki was a particularly difficult one, and Collins' competition was very high class. By the beginning of the second half of the race his feet were already beginning to blister, and his muscles and joints to ache.

He ran on. Through the pain.

As the race entered its final stages, Collins was in the leading group, and fighting bravely on. By this time his muscles and joints were screaming in agony, and his feet were beginning to bleed.

Still he pushed himself onward.

In the final two miles the pain was almost unbearable. Collins endured it. He pushed and pushed, his energy being drained by the length of the race, his excruciating agonies, and the loss of blood from his feet, which had now, as he described it, become 'crimson pads'.

Collins, being Collins, finished the race. His position? A very creditable 19th.

And then came the horrifying aftermath….In the days after the event, Paul Collins' body gradually seized up. Doctors told him that he had seriously overdone it; that his legs, their tendons, joints and muscles were severely damaged; that he would never run again; and that he was, from that time on, a semi-cripple. For years he had to live with that verdict, hardly able to crawl upstairs, and walking with pronounced limps. Even rising from a chair was a painful experience.

He came to accept that the 'hardness' of the run had indeed been the cause of his misfortune. And then he had a sudden, life-changing revelation. He realised that the 18 runners who had beaten him in the Marathon had continued to run in major competitions after Helsinki. And they had all run faster and 'harder' than he had. It was, therefore, not the speed of the race, or the toughness of the course that had caused his injuries. It must be something else. That something else could only be the way in which he had run the race; the way in which he had used (and as he eventually discovered, misused) himself during the race.

Like Alexander, Collins began to examine his use of his body, and found that, sure enough, all his injuries could be related to the way in which his poor poise had enabled his own brain to use his body, unnecessarily, to pound parts of itself during extreme exertion.

He continued his intensive studies, including the Alexander Technique, and trained himself to walk with more elegance and grace. By the age of 35, he was walking longer distances. A few years later he was beginning, gently, to run again, using the Good New Habit of his improved bodily alignment. Within a couple more years he was running up to 10 miles; and a few years after that he ran his first 'poised' marathon.

Being the great experimenter he was, Collins extended himself further, exploring the realms of the ultra marathon. Between the ages of 55 through 60, he set world records for his age group for the 200, 300 and 400-mile runs; for the 200, 300 and 400-kilometer runs; plus 3,4,5 and 6 day records at the third annual 6-day race in Nottingham, England.

At the age of 60 he entered a 24-hour race (in which you run for as long as you can, rest, and then continue, for 24 hours, your distance covered being measured constantly by judges around the track). In 24 hours, including breaks, how far do you think Collins ran? He established a new United Kingdom all-comers' record by covering 117 miles, the distance of nearly five marathons in the time!

At the end of such ultra marathon events the finish line is festooned with doctors, physiotherapists, masseurs and all manner of people lined up to deal with the results of the extreme physical strains and stresses to which the bodies of the competitors have been put. It became a laughing point at such finishing lines that when Collins, still maintaining his superb running poise, was asked what he needed, he would reply, 'Only a pint of beer, thank you!'

One sidelight of Paul Collins' career is that he helped massively with Tony's! Due to what Tony describes as "my own bad poise, I injured my lower back in the gym by lifting heavy weights while I was not properly balanced. I had been told by many experts (much as Alexander himself was told concerning his voice) that there was no real cure to the constant and nagging pain I had in my lower back, because I had irreversibly damaged it."

While doing standing repetitive presses with over 120lbs weight, Tony had unfortunately taken his mind and body 'off task' and turned, with the weight above his head, to look at a very attractive young lady who had just entered the gym.

Lower-back disc injury.

As the months progressed, the injury got worse, despite the fact that he was trying all the best cures, including standard physiotherapy, yoga, acupuncture, blind masseurs, meditation and hydro-therapy. The situation had become so serious, that occasionally he was having to use a walking stick.

His yoga teacher, Chris Stevens, persuaded him to try the Alexander Technique with Paul Collins. Tony went to Paul, and purposely did not use a walking stick, because he didn't want to give Paul any 'clues'. As soon as Paul opened the door, he looked at Tony, and said, "What's the matter with your lower back?!"   Found out!

Tony explained to Paul the situation, and Paul explained that it was quite obviously nothing serious or permanent, and was simply a matter of the growing misalignment of Tony's body, the pain causing the exacerbation of the condition. Within three weeks, Tony woke up one morning sensing that 'something was wrong'. A few minutes later he realised that it was because he no longer had pain in his back! His still, but now less severe misuse of himself during that day, made sure that the pain returned! Within two more weeks, though, he was completely cured.

From that day to this, he has had thousands of hours of lessons in his continuing study of the use of the self, and in terms of the body and its posture, loves Alexander's statement 'everyone wants to be right, but no one stops to consider if their idea of right is right!' He also agrees with Alexander in his statement that the next great phase in human development is to pass from sub-conscious, to conscious control of mind and body. Tony learned from Paul, and the Alexander Technique, the art and science of running, the vital importance of poise, and the role of vision and determination in the athlete's life.

By showing Tony some of the horrendous Big Bad Physical Habits into which he had allowed his posture to degenerate, Paul had demonstrated that much of Tony's discomfort and pain was being caused by the constant pressure to which his body was subjecting itself. By helping Tony to realign, Collins had guided him to complete freedom from pain, and to the re-emergence of his running and physical career, which had been in seemingly permanent suspended animation.

• • • •

Chapter 21

Letter of Invitation to Nobel Laureate conference from King Abdullah II of the Hashemite Kingdom of Jordan

FUND FOR DEVELOPMENT

April 12, 2008

Dear Mr. Buzan,

On behalf of His Majesty King Abdullah II Ibn Al Hussein it is with great honor that I invite you to be a guest of the Hashemite Kingdom of Jordan at the fourth annual Petra Conference of Nobel Laureates, which will be held in the ancient city of Petra during the period of 17-19 June 2008.

The meeting, held in collaboration between the King Abdullah II Fund for Development and the Elie Wiesel Foundation for Humanity, will focus on the Middle East's economic, scientific and educational horizons. Through engaging some of our world's most prominent achievers -- Nobel laureates -- along with a select group of political, business, and cultural figures, we hope to start building a new global partnership for peace and prosperity.

With mounting challenges, but even greater hope and opportunity, we hope to explore ways to re-build the economic infrastructure for peace and the tools available to ensure sustainable growth. We also look forward to discussing related areas in economics, energy and the environment, as well as in science and technology.

In 2007, at the third Petra Conference of Nobel Laureates, a Middle East Science Fund was launched, to be advised by Nobel laureates. We look forward in our next meeting in Petra to start the implementation phase of the fund.

A group of young people from the region will also join us in Petra. Your participation will inspire them. It will motivate them to actively engage in the sessions.

I look forward to your participation and I am confident that it will help promote dialogue and be a catalyst for positive change. In the meantime, please accept the assurance of my highest esteem and consideration.

Sincerely,

Bassem Awadallah
Vice Chairman of the
Board of Trustees

Chapter 22

Nobel Peace Prize nomination

Here follows the Official text of Nobel Peace Prize Nomination for Professor Tony Buzan: Professor Buzan is the inventor of Mind Maps, essentially a meta-language transcending all cultures, which has proved its invaluable nature in learning institutions and academic fields around the world.

He has presented, taught and lectured globally to congresses, at special events and to audiences numbering from tens to hundreds of thousands, in varying areas of the globe from Africa (including 2000 students in Soweto 1981) to Europe, the Americas and the East.

His Curriculum Vitae, as cited in *Who's Who*, includes the spreading of Mental Literacy and multiply intelligent thinking across all major world capitals, as well as remote aboriginal village outposts.

Professor Buzan's message thus sweeps across mental frontiers and traverses the geographical continents of our world.

Globally he continually reinforces his passionate belief that reason, logic and the power of the human brain can transform all actions into harmonious, peaceful, non violent and non aggressive channels.

His abilities to reach out to peoples of the world are demonstrated and confirmed by the fact that he is the most popular international author of all BBC publications.

Based on his work with disadvantaged children for the Inner London Education Authority (ILEA) the ten-part BBC television series and book *Use Your Head* in the 1970's launched his career. This series was repeated twice annually on BBC 1 and BBC 2 from 1974 to 1989.

Norway was the first internationally to take the baton, with celebrated publisher and teacher Nils Schjander.

To date Professor Buzan has written and co-authored over 120 books (which have been translated into 40 languages) focusing on the importance of using the brain and its potential for human benefit, development and enrichment.

Too often people take the brain for granted, but, we now find that mental ill health is overtaking all other burdens of disease as a weight on the shoulders of society.

As Professor Michael Crawford, the head of the Institute for Human Nutrition and Brain Chemistry has indicated, Swedish authors first drew attention to this serious situation in 2005 when they audited the health costs of the EU. (European Journal of Neurology - June issue 2005).

The cost for brain/mental disorders stood at 386 billion Euros per annum, for only the 27 member states of the EU, ahead of all other costs, including heart disease, cancer and obesity. The annual cost to the global economy in 2010 for Alzheimer's disease alone has been confirmed as $600 billion.

The greater the rise in mental ill health, the less likely people are able to make intelligent judgments and decisions. Such a negative spiral threatens the ability to make rational decisions and therefore on a deeper level endangers peace.

The teaching of learning and especially learning how to learn is paramount in reducing anti-social behaviour, and its concomitant manifestations of crime, murder, and on a larger scale, war.

Professor Buzan's work is totally dedicated to the noble aim of teaching learning and learning how to learn. This is at the core of Professor Buzan's efforts and has been shown to be a major bridge from mental ill health to mental health.

Professor Buzan founded the Brain Trust Charity just over twenty years ago to support his passionate commitment to rationality and world peace. He has worked indefatigably since then to achieve his charitable aims. Consideration for the Nobel Prize would be extremely beneficial in helping Professor Buzan to raise the profile of The Brain Trust Charity and assist him to provide Global Mental Literacy to the children of Africa and throughout the world. Professor Buzan's work in this field is evidenced by successful ventures in Indonesia, Mexico, Jamaica, Sierra Leone and Soweto.

The Brain Trust's Charter includes the following aspirations:

"To promote research into study of processes of thought, the investigation of the mechanics of thinking, manifested in learning, understanding, communication, problem solving, education and creativity."

Professor Buzan's work promotes physical, mental and spiritual harmony, for the purpose of working towards a more healthy and peaceful world. Professor Buzan is a pioneer in this important initiative.

In the past few years alone, his achievements include:

Appointed a leading member of UK Guild/Company of Educators and key note speaker for the prestigious annual Franklin Lecture on the future of education

As a practising and published poet, delivered a keynote speech at His Excellency Abdullah Ali Babtain's Dubai conference for Poetry and Peace

Appointed the first Thinker in Residence at Wellington College

Appointed Visiting Professor of Creativity and Innovation at The Stenden University of Applied Science, The Netherlands

Honoured by the American Creativity Association with the Lifetime Achievement Award for Services to Global Creativity and Education

Furthermore, Professor Buzan has...

Completed In Search of Genius – a BBC TV special - according to the BBC itself: "a unique social experiment" to raise the cognitive skills and educational standards of children who had lost academic hope - thus confirming Professor Buzan as a defender of children, thinking and the future

Worked and continues to work with former President Vicente Fox of Mexico on charitable educational initiatives – and receiving The Innova Award for contribution to the development of Mexico and its innovative and creative thinking skills

Developed the thinking and presentational skills - Mind Maps - which former US Vice President Al Gore has used to promote his global message of environmental care and responsibility. They have also been utilised to determine branding initiatives such as the naming of the Blackberry communications device - see *The Times* business section of Wednesday 6, 2012

Been appointed by the Ministry of Education of the Indonesian Government to oversee the training of 3,471,000 teachers to teach 100 million children thinking, learning and communication skills

Been invited by His Majesty King Abdullah II of The Hashemite Kingdom of Jordan to address Nobel laureates in Amman and Petra,, and other dignitaries amongst the audience, on the future and significance of Mental Literacy

Donated thousands of books and taught personally in Sierra Leone for the Build on Books Charity - as a young boy from Africa, wrote to Professor Buzan: "Thank you, Mr Tony, for giving me back my brain."

Donated free thinking Mind Map software to the children of the world

Returned recently from an extremely successful 20th Jubilee World Memory Championship in Guangzhou China. The World Memory Championship, which he originated and co-founded, has been widely hailed as a conduit of historic importance for international understanding.

As an intellectual imperative the championships are open to all people, regardless of age, race, religion, education, language, creed, gender or physical ability, and promote the positive human values of understanding, mutual respect, harmony, open exchange, and cooperation, leading to a greater probability of world peace.

• • • •

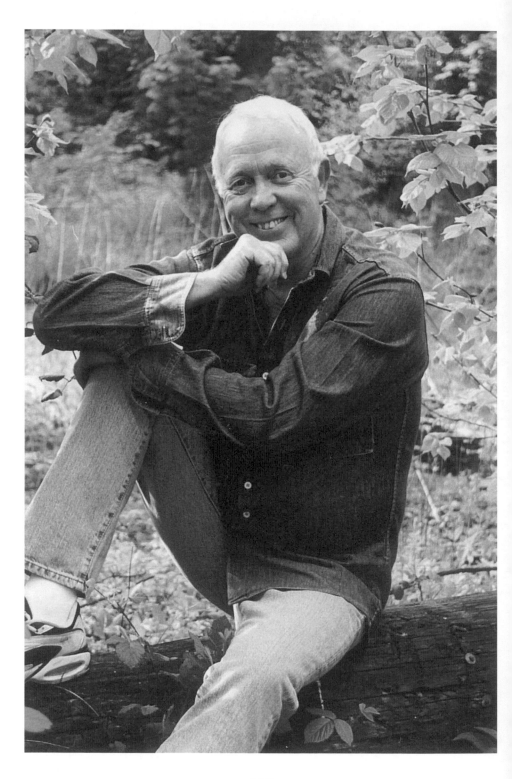

Chapter 23

Religion and Spirituality

Many readers will wish to know Tony's views on religion and the nature of spirituality. Is he with Darwin, Dawkins, or what?

Let us take an imaginary family consisting of a mother, a father, a seven-year-old girl and her five-year-old brother. Let us look at it first from the little girl's point of view.

Every micro-second of every day sees her as the only one at whatever point in the Universe she is currently inhabiting, seeing and reacting to the kaleidoscopic uniqueness of possibilities for interpretation and reaction that her unique and constantly varying being gives her the privilege of experiencing. She is infinitely different from anyone who has lived, is living or who will ever live.

She is also, in a very big sense of the word, Alone.

Consider now the little boy.

At the thousands upon thousands of meals that he will share with his family, he is a little male sitting at a table with a giant male, a giant female and another larger female. He, like his sister, is the only one who will see only the faces of the other three members of the family, never his own. He is the only one who will interpret the things said to him in the way that only he can interpret them, and he is the only one who will go to the 'same school' as his sister and will experience it as not the same at all.

He will sit in his classes, in his special seat seeing everything from his unique physical and mental perspective. He will experience the 'same teachers' who will not be the same teachers at all. The male teachers will be the same sex as him, the female teachers the opposite sex. The 'same teachers' will be different. They will be two years older.

Those 'same teachers' will relate to him in ways very differently from the ways in which they will relate to his sister. He will be the only one who had his sister attend the 'same school' before him, leaving her trail of memories and influences that will affect him in myriad subtle and unique ways. He will be the only one with his friends and the only one who throughout his entire school year will never see his face or his body in any of the interactions or games with which he is involved.

His senses gambolling with the Universe will, like his sister's, take place in the playground that only he will ever know as he knows it.

He, like his sister, would be the only one with his dreams, his fears, his passions, his loves and his hopes. He will spend his early life, and indeed his entire life, being the only intrepid explorer of the Universe as seen from the second-by-second kaleidoscoping viewpoints that make up his special being.

There is not one micro-second in one day, week, month or year of his life in which he sees anything from the same perspective as his sister or anyone else. Think of the difference that sitting at the front, back, sides or middle of a class or lecture room makes to your memory of that class. He is the only one who has the fantasy friends that only he in the Universe could create, and he is the only one who has the dreams, fantasies, fears and hopes that only he will ever have.

The Universe is bombarding his eyes with a trillion unique photon video packages per second; his ears with million-molecule percussion messages; his nose with a million-faceted palette of aromas and smells; and his skin with a never-ending symphony of atomic information. Only he will ever sense these magical particular messages from the cosmos.

He is utterly, fantastically, infinitely and preciously unique.

And Alone.

When Tony was a young teenager, he began to ask 'the big questions' such as: what is the meaning of life? Why is there so much suffering in the world? Do animals have emotions? What is the purpose of our lives and why do we die? What's the point of being honest or good? Are there other planets with life on them? How big is the Universe, what is our place in it and where does it end? And so on. He and his friends thought they might get some answers by going to the church Sunday School, so this they dutifully did:

"Our Sunday School teacher was a bullying, arrogant man, with a domineering and authoritarian style. One Sunday he said to us that if we brought in new recruits to the Sunday School the following week, he would give us a chocolate bar for every new person brought in."

Tony's hand immediately shot up! "I pointed out to the teacher that he had, in a previous lesson, talked about purity of soul and the evils of bribery. Should we not, if we were truly spiritual, bring people to the Sunday School because we wanted to help them on their paths? Should we not, therefore, do it purely for the love of the other person? Should we not do it with pleasure, enthusiasm and generosity, expecting no reward whatsoever? By offering us all chocolate bars, was he not, in fact, bribing us?

I was told never to ask such questions again, and to leave the class for rudeness and insubordination!

I never returned, and decided from that point on that anything to do with spirituality was either a con, irrelevant or wimpish, and that logic and argument were a far 'truer path'."

By the time Tony was 20 and at university, he had hardened his views on the supremacy of logic and the weakness of spirituality and emotion, while becoming a confirmed atheist. He had honed his verbal and logical reasoning skills and relished a good intellectual argument! Imagine his delight when his doorbell rang one day, and a frail, middle-aged lady announced that she had come to try to save his soul!

"Like a spider preparing to ensnare a fly, I invited her to let her explain her views on the need for me to be more spiritually aware. By this time I had become well-versed in the history of philosophy and the great debates on morality, God, and the meaning of life. In less than 15 minutes, I had this gentle lady floundering but, to my surprise, she was still upbeat and unbowed.

She explained that helping other people was a relatively new direction in her life, a life which had known a lot of pain and suffering, and which was now much more beautiful and calm. She cheerfully asked if she could come back next week with someone more experienced in the field, and I agreed, anticipating another logic battle, with a more 'worthy' opponent.

A week later she duly returned, proudly introducing me to a young man who had just graduated from University and who was extremely knowledgeable in the field. We immediately locked horns, and a great intellectual tussle took place. Finally, after an hour, he made one fatal logical mistake, and I pounced. The victory was mine!

Still unbowed, the lady asked if she could return the following week with one of the most senior members of her organisation – once again, I said yes.

On the day of the next meeting, a snowstorm had blown up, and it was bitterly cold. Nevertheless, my Angel of Mercy was there.

She introduced me, with pride and respect, to her companion: a middle-aged man who looked like a character out of a cheap gangster movie, who was a very senior person in her organisation. He appeared to be the opposite of everything that spirituality stood for, knew little about ethical or moral arguments, and seemed intent only on raising money from me and parading his status, I accused him of ignorance, greed and dishonesty and had him red-faced and speechless within five minutes.

Another great victory!

This, however, was soon to turn to dust. When the pair left, the lady looked up at me with a fractured face, her expression one of failure, disillusionment, loss, pleading and an almost unbearable pain. As I closed the door on her forever, those same feelings surged through me.

What had I done?

This gentle lady had spent several weeks of her life preparing for and meeting me, with the sole purpose of helping to save my soul. And what had I done to express my thanks and gratitude for this totally unselfish gesture on my behalf? Beaten her with the truncheons of logic and words; humiliated and demeaned those she loved and respected in front of her; attempted to destroy the foundations of a newly structured, innocent and loving life; and after gloating at my 'triumphs' had turned her into the snow. I sat down, stunned at the horror of what I had just done. Logic and words suddenly seemed irrelevant, and my whole being was overwhelmed with sorrow and remorse.

Without knowing it, my Angel of Mercy had more than accomplished her task and, in the final analysis had won her argument hands down and spirit up! Wherever you are, dear lady, I eternally thank you for your wonderful and successful rescue mission!

In one flash of heart-rending realisation, my life had been changed. I came to see that there was more to intelligence than simply words, numbers and logic." Sometimes it takes a truly cosmic experience to make this apparent, and few come more cosmic than man's journey into space.

The training at NASA for the flight to and around the moon was very, very, thorough. The astronauts had simulated every stage of the flight in terms of duration and daily activities – they had literally 'gone to the moon and back' while on Earth!

Indeed the training had been so thorough that astronaut Edgar Mitchell reported virtually no emotions of fear or exaltation when they took off, because it felt so familiar and 'normal'.

This familiarity continued all the way to the moon, everything running smoothly, on schedule and, as far as the crews were concerned, almost robot-like. They arrived and began to prepare for their journey to the 'dark side of the moon'.

This, like everything else, had been rehearsed. The trip was to take only an hour or so. The significant thing about being on the dark side of the moon was that for the first time on the journey, the sight of the earth would be totally blocked from view, and no radio or television waves could either penetrate or go round the moon. The astronauts would be totally excommunicated from Earth!

Mitchell said that the first five minutes on the dark side were fine, but after that the simulation training began to peel away, and concern, a touch of fear, and his imagination began to kick in. He began to think more and more about Earth – about his wife and children, his home, his neighbourhood, his friends and the places they met, and the changing colours of the seasons.

As his imagination expanded, time began to stretch, as it does when you are waiting for someone you love who is late. But this was not just one person Mitchell was waiting for. This was everyone and everything that he loved. He began to wonder whether there were some strange time-warp effects on the dark side of the moon, and whether he and the others were trapped in an eternal night. Mitchell reported that the minutes began to feel like days; the time behind the moon was becoming eternity.

After what seemed like aeons, they came out the other side.

And there, at last, was the Earth!

But the Earth was not as Mitchell had imagined. In his mind, it had been the giant planet on which the universe of his home and family existed. What he saw now was a tiny blue planet floating in the vast inky blackness of space. Surrounding it was a fragile, wafer-thin covering of white – our entire atmosphere. Mitchell felt that he could literally reach out with his head and flick the Earth, like a tiny pearl, into oblivion.

That moment, and that sudden realisation of the fragility of our local home in the vastness of our big home, caused a paradigm shift in Edgar Mitchell. When he returned he felt far more compassion and concern for his fellow living beings, and decided to devote the rest of his life to helping protect this delicate, unique and beautiful planet.

The vastness of space and the vastness of the ocean have elements in common. On holiday in the Caribbean, Tony was taking an early-morning swim in an exquisitely beautiful bay with crystal-clear blue water, mirror flat from the calm of the night before. Not particularly paying attention to where he was going, he ended up doing a long and leisurely series of back-strokes.

"When I stopped to turn around, I saw what looked like a blown-up balloon on the surface of the water, and without thinking (always dangerous!) I swam towards it. I noticed that the colour of the water underneath it appeared to be not so much blue as beautiful lavender. Suddenly my brain recognised the danger signs, and screamed at me:

'Portuguese Man-of-War!'

Terrified, I swung about in the water – too late. The beautiful purple tendrils wrapped themselves around my waist and legs and sent me rocketing out of the water in pain. It felt as if I had been wrapped in barbed wire through which giant electric shocks were being pulsed.

I suddenly remembered (and understood!) the many reports I'd heard of people who had died of such an experience. For the next 10 or 15 minutes I was like some Walt Disney cartoon character with my legs thrashing like an outboard motor in the effort to get back to shore! With every stroke I wondered whether the poison was going to kill me rapidly, or lock all my muscles into an immovable rigidity that would lead me to drown."

The fact that you are reading this biography, rather than an obituary, means that you know Tony made it! He spent a little time in hospital, and came out still shocked, having been taught a number of lessons by Mother Nature – among them that he needed to be more observant and more alert to danger.

"Most importantly, however, I had learnt, while facing the prospect of having no days left, to pay much more attention to appreciating and enjoying the 'gift' of every day that I had and would be given. Even the weather!"

Whenever you are encouraged by the media, friends or your own personal thoughts to moan about the weather we experience on our "tiny, blue planet" think of the other options! Even the great East Coast Frankenstorm of late October, 2012, Halloween, which engulfed New

York and caused 400,000 people to be evacuated from the urban centres of the most affluent civilization on earth, might have been worse, were we to colonise other planets of our solar system:

- Mercury: 1,000 degrees centigrade on its sunny side, airless, more radiated than a microwave, and near absolute zero centigrade on its dark side!
- Venus: 450 degrees centigrade average temperature, battered by over 400-mile-an-hour sulphuric acid winds, with never any sight of the night-time sky.
- Mars: often minus 100 degrees centigrade. Hardly any atmosphere and no oxygen. Sun just visible as a big star. Inhospitable to life.
- Jupiter, Uranus and Neptune: all giant planets with gravity so strong you would be crushed the minute you set foot on them which you couldn't do anyway, as their surfaces are liquid gasses. Average winds of 1,000 miles per hour that never cease. No oxygen!
- Pluto: a tiny, airless planet less than the size of our moon with no sunlight, no atmosphere and a temperature near absolute zero.

In contrast Planet Earth: Paradise! So delicately balanced to guarantee your survival, that changes of less than 1 per cent in the 'formula' that created it would have made it inhospitable to life, and therefore to you.

So, enjoy the weather – it's all good! Enjoy every variation from heat wave to freezing to wind to rain to frost to mist to snow. It is this very variation that allows the system to survive, grow and to support you…

and talking of support…

…those of you who have read Tony's book *Head First* will know how rabbits that are given positive affection and Love while in captivity were healthier and lived longer than those rabbits which were merely fed and watered adequately.

Tony's next parable of the beautiful fish confirms how a little love goes a very long way!

When Tony was a young boy, as we have seen in the early chapters, his main interest was nature and the study of its processes and wonders. He used to breed entire menageries, including butterflies, amphibians, fish and rabbits. One of the most beautiful things he had ever seen was the male three-spined stickleback. This tiny, streamlined animal looked like the essence of 'fishness'. In the mating season the body of the male is a translucent, almost luminescent steel-blue, with a throat and underbelly that are a vibrant blush-red.

"I used to breed these wondrous little creatures in a giant aquarium, and each male would stake out its territory, building nests of weeds and rushes in which they incubated the young. One summer day I caught the biggest, most beautifully luminescent male I had ever seen.

I gently introduced it to the aquarium, expecting it to stake out its own territory (probably slightly bigger than the rest, because of the fish's size and magnificence). To my surprise, it did not do so. It swam rapidly into a cluster of weeds at the surface of the aquarium, and tried to avoid the occasional 'raids' from the other males.

I expected nature would look after itself, and for a natural balance of power to establish itself by the following day. But the fish was still in its same place the next morning. It had become slightly less radiant, seemed to be a little timid, and was still avoiding attacks from the other males.

Day-after-day, I found the 'magnificent' stickleback still in the same place, increasingly less colourful, increasingly timid and increasingly attacked. After five days the little fish had become a grey and dull colour, and I began to fear for his life.

The only thing I could think of to do was to nurture and care for him. I began to stroke him gently, to let him know that there was no threat from me, and at feeding times made sure that he had just that little bit extra. I also gave him more weeds in which to protect/defend himself.

Within two days, I was just able to detect a slight change in his colouring; he was becoming a little more radiant! Day-by-day I showered him with the only manifestations of love available to me and day-by-day his spirit returned.

Within a week, he was back to his full magnificence, and began to make sorties outside his weed-home territory. Within a fortnight he had established his own 'home area' in the aquarium, and nature had looked after itself.

The stunning realisation to me was that 'nature looking after itself' was not about size, strength, beauty or magnificence; all these had meant nothing to my stickleback. Nature looking after itself included me, and more importantly included the Power of Love.

It was the Power of Love that had triumphed over everything.

I was once introduced to a woman who was 'dying for loss of love'.

She and her husband had been on a cross-Channel ferry that had sunk with horrific loss of life. She had been one of the survivors; her husband had died.

For ten years she had been unable to 'face' the situation; or, more accurately, to face the horror of the monstrous memories that kept lurching out of the blackness at her whenever her mind was about to rest.

For years she had been going to 'experts', trying to get rid of those memories. I explained to her that it was impossible to 'get rid' of a memory unless you exorcised part of your brain! The only way to deal with it successfully was to embrace it and use it.

I asked her to be courageous and look again at what had actually happened. Having done this, she would then hopefully be able to deal with the tragedy more appropriately, and to use it to her life-long advantage rather than reducing herself to a shattered wreck. She was both courageous and committed, and within a short time was reliving the entire event.

When the ship started sinking, she found her husband singing Irish ballads, downing Guinness and saying, sincerely and very happily: 'What a wonderful way to go!' All around her people were panicking; many yelling: 'It's all over'. 'Oh my God, we're finished'. We're going to die there's no hope. Her own reaction was to live! She said to her husband 'Come on (he didn't) and then made for the nearest exit.

Through all the panic and confusion, she made a beeline for where she knew the lifeboats were, and seeing that they were all afloat, dived into the water and made straight for one. Clambering abroad with the other few survivors, she observed, over the next horrible hour, that nearly all those who had made it to the lifeboats had had a singular desire to survive, and had committed themselves to saving their lives and others' too.

All those who died, she noticed with a shudder, had in some way 'given up' well before the last moment. By reliving the horror of what she had been through, she came to realise that her husband had not been afraid of death, and that she herself had survived such a terrible life-threatening situation through her own extraordinary spirit and will to live.

Eventually she was able to use the precious insights to help others to understand their own fears, and to overcome their own life-devastating events. In turn, this allowed her to regain some peace and sense of purpose herself."

Chapter 24

Structure In Hyperspace

by Tony Buzan

The culmination of Tony's spiritual journey is reflected in the following poem:

"Structure in Hyperspace"

I
As plasma loops bulge and snap
from the sun's sheath, writhe out
into the System's Cold and are sucked
back into their part of Eternal Heat, so Man,
Not Adam, strives away from what is
to what is not and is dragged, or falls, back.

II
Sound Beats over Time
ranges Solidity's Scale sined to a moving whip of rainbow
on which I, roller-coaster colour bead, travel,
lashed to whip's tipped extremity, off dropped
exploded up into Everything

III
shot as a grain of the spray,
laser of light, rainbow gunned
funnel spectrummed; hung like
Christ Season Spheres for trees,
rainbow balled into floatingness
brain-stroked on a Vista of Sound.

IV
Music, Microcosma's Rainbow Beads,
jostles down prism rivers,
bombards the receiver brain;
taps me, I drum skin, my Space hollow",
scolded for even thinking of thinking
about Music when the Great Children Play –

V
stick-hit cymbal hits colour bead hits
colour bead hits colour bead hits
my drum my tympani and I play
Music I play:

VI
Molecule is Sound's Drumstick
Ear Drum Sound's Drum Skin;
Music is the projected Solidity of Sound
Silence is the absence of Motion
Sound is Silence Moved.

VII
The Great Children.
Infinite Gamboling!
Sound rolls and spreads, rises and falls,
is sharp,
tough breaks, blends, molds, enfolds, jumps, leaps, laughs
Force heaves drives tunnels pierces shakes lifts tugs blows
shrugs sucks whirls drops stretches hones breaks combines
burns laughs
Space-Time spreads, drifts, fades, compresses, thins, rolls, wafts,
enfolds
Energy changes, shuffles, heats beams heaves radiates explodes

VIII

Their Toys! Their Fields!
Limitless limbs to drop rise kick hit and play!
jewel clusters to glee over, spin, rotate; fireballs to form,
heat, condense rocks around, paint with gamut's brush, freeze,
explode; ball as sun, planet, molecule or atom to dribble, carry,
bowl, throw, kick, or spin, All to hurl, skip, swing,
rollick, clown, play pranks on, laugh, dally, romp through:
X-Ray gardens, gamma greenness, ultra, infra realities; Great
Wastes
Galactic clouds to peep from, blind man's bluff in
Rorschach horses to mount and ride.

IX

Around and around and through our straight circled speed yoked
universe!
riding on flame tailed ice balls, looking to rings looming
from Titan's only blue horizon, seeing filigree
of star-dust spectra tantalizing to us, laughing at:
winged helmet; slit symbolized; sphere crossed; war arrowed
prick head; bolt:
Kronos; his spawner; trident; infernal god; and dust; our spinning
stones;
kicking about blue stars full circling red is heat to blue is cold,
tampering with Cluster, Nebula, shackled suns, tandem
travelers, and Supergiant, absorbing all colours, seeing Monster
exploded into Crab, Light dust-belted, Supernova shattered, and
the
Cosmos Red shift and Blue shifting us into cube into cube into
cube
into nothingness in Everything.

X
Infinitely Energetic, Boundless, Unchained!
all days and the seventh the same into One; Free, playing,
playing through us, lasers, heat, fire, bounce, penetrate, mould
form, all these are Theirs: Eternity, Infinite Dark, Light, Create,
Destroy,
Never grow old!

XI
Change consumes to Changed: movement uniform, speed
constant, noise none;
They rest in Single Tones.
XII
Beat is as a rubber ball between bats
is Centre undulated
is tsunami shunted by low sea earth
is slow shudder on Psyche's Harp
is her soma swaying jellyfish on tide arms
is a bird's balled body slung on curved wings, unsung note held
by limb to Nature's Stave
Energy is Wave.

XIII
Colourless colour bundle pierces glass sphere
and sprays free
Microcosma's Sun with Wanderers surges Energy into
Movement into Heat into Light into limbs metal
filament inanimates
The flattened disc cone spins to the balled point
stuffs the tiny head, traces the wire beads the code
beats the ear shell feeds the path ways
funnels
Free

XIV
rung with the Coils of Ecstasy
Size shrinks through smallness to Great.

XV
Everything is Solid is a tautology not yet known
solidity is Frozen
Solidity is not Immovable
is Fluidity, is Energetic, Can be moved in
Nothing is the Absence of
Everything is
Solidity is Everything Flows
is
Reality is non-particular
Are Truth
Everything is One
(Truth is One or Nothing)
XVI
'Can be moved in.' 'tangible' cannot:
touch is barriers, needless impediment
implement, is senseless,
cannot go through
eyes turn it on and do not See;
logic is particular
is touch reality
semantic's slave
physic's tool
is barriers
is not
Flow.

XVII
Intuition is particular bridged
leads through to Know

XVIII
Dimension holds Plane apart
magnet shunts antipode
Light shines through glass
God lives through me
receiver is other than Wave.

XIX
Definition or Force
is the Space between the stuff of Spaces.

XX
Laughing in his Space
Zeno dipped into touch, halved
and halved our sensibilities,
aeon-fooled us, plumped slow
forever faster; cracked, impossibly,
Time

XXI
becomes concept, mental become physical
movement becomes motion, flow becomes wave
beat becomes chroma, colour becomes experience
we
experience
colour
visual becomes touch, feel pulse, rhythm taste,
hearing world's music surge essence savour ease
rhythm Flows.........

XXII
we can
funnel in to us Girth's Immensity
strap Reality's Size to convenience
shrink the Immense to the conceptual
encapsulate Magnitude in Microcosma;

XXIII
we are the glass sphere
the touch reality,
the ear shell,
the instruments,
the inanimates,
the receivers,
the transmitters,
the symbol,
the drum.
XXIV
we have yet
to Live.

. . . .

Part Five

Poetry and Art

Chapter 25
Realms Of Gold

Tony is a prolific, prize-winning, highly acclaimed and multiply published poet. To introduce you to the depth and breadth of Tony's poetry, let me quote Edward Hazelton, former President of the Poetry Society:

"Tony Buzan is a poet, but not in the traditional sense of the recluse: he heralds the renaissance of the once flourishing and then rejected ideal of Man as Polymath. His province is universal and includes with equal emphasis the spheres of mathematics, philosophy, cosmology, biology, physics and aesthetics. These he translates into a poetry which is fresh in the unusual combining of what are assumed to be unrelated topics, and although difficult at first, I am sure these new poetic experiences will become a major part of the future tradition of not only British poetry but also of British thought."

Tony's poems have appeared in a number of significant poetry magazines, including *Poetry Review*, *Aquarius*, *The Catholic Review*, *The West Coast Review*, and *Samphire*.

His poetry has won many prizes, including joint first prize in the Canadian University's Society Annual Literary Competition for Loch Ness Phenomena, and the Poetry Society Premium Prize Competition Award for Thoughts of the Man.

So how did this successful and acclaimed poetic career begin?

Let Tony tell you in his own words:

As A Young Boy

"As a young boy I was enthralled, almost hypnotised, by the astonishing and varied beauty of Nature: the immaculate designs and coruscating (sparkling) beauty of insects; the infinite variety and magical forms of the animals; the grace, power, soaring and elegance of the eagles and hawks - the raptors; the majesty and mystery of the cats; the boundless energy, abundance, fantastic colours and formulations of the plant kingdom; the magnificence of mountains; the ethereal beauty of misty mornings; and the might and awesome beauty of the cosmos.

As a consequence, the houses of my best-friend-in-nature, whom we have already encountered, Barry Camburn and myself, as eight-year olds, were mini nature sanctuaries, brimming with cats, dogs, budgerigars, canaries, rabbits, guinea-pigs, mice, fish, tadpoles, newts, snakes, beetles, and caterpillars-into-butterflies, to name but a few. As a result we were avid supporters and proud wearers of the badges of the Royal Society for the Protection of Animals (RSPCA), the People's Dispensary for Sick Animals (PDSA), for which I proudly wore my bee-emblazoned PDSA badge as a 'busy bee', and other nature protection and conservation societies. We were always deeply saddened and confused by examples of, and stories about, cruelty to animals.

Both Barry and I were so in awe of all this beauty and creation, and so intrigued by its processes and evolutions, that we could not understand why it was that anyone would wish to pin into stillness on a board in a case, such a wondrous living thing as a butterfly, or how anyone could in any way wish to harm the natural world.

It was my passion for nature and my pets that led to my first poem, my first book, and my first contacts with the media.

My Relationship With Poetry

This great love of nature manifested itself by consuming both my thoughts and actions. It did not manifest itself in poetry, because my relationship with that Universe was an unhappy one.

My initial understanding of poetry was that it was a confusing, relatively meaningless, dull and boring subject. It required me to sit still and listen to some monotonic and self-righteous teacher droning on while reading this 'high art form'. I was then required to waste my time beating my brains out to memorise that which had no meaning or relevance to my young life. As I grew older the relationship worsened. By the time I had reached the giddy heights of teenage-hood, and was beginning to feel decidedly testosteronic, I had relegated poetry to a subject exclusively for the weak and feeble in both body and mind!

The Transformation

The event that changed both my attitude to poetry and my life was imminent. The scene: my English Literature class, when I had just reached the age of fourteen.

Our teacher at the time was a little, lank-haired, plain, and untrained lady whose voice you could hardly hear even when the classroom was not erupting with delinquent behaviour, which it usually was. On this particular morning she had totally lost control, and the class and she were in two different worlds. We were moving about, laughing and shouting and oblivious to her, except when to mock or catcall.

She gave us even more ample opportunity for this by stating that today she was going to read us her favourite poem. This was not an auspicious start to a lesson! We all groaned loudly and in unison. The situation was made worse when, clutching her poetry book to her grubby white blouse, she announced that the poem was about a bird. Our groans became ostentatiously louder. Things got even worse when she proclaimed that the author was called Alfred!! We lolled melodramatically, mimicking histrionic boredom and despair.

Her favourite poem! Poetry about a bird! By a poet called Alfred! What could possibly be worse...

Then something strange and eerie happened. She seemed to transform, like some other-worldly alien, as if a spirit had entered her being. Her posture changed and her voice became more powerful. She was wrapped in her own secure world of love and dreams for and about the poem she was about to read. She intoned hypnotically: "*The Eagle by Alfred Lord Tennyson.*" At this, for the first time in my classes with her, my ears slightly pricked up. The Eagle was my favourite bird, and Alfred was a Lord...

She continued:

THE EAGLE

He clasps the crag with crooked hands;
Close to the sun in lonely lands,
Ring'd with the azure world, he stands.
The wrinkled sea beneath him crawls;
He watches from his mountain walls,
And like a thunderbolt he falls.

Alfred Lord Tennyson

The thunderbolt had indeed struck.

I sat, poleaxed, stunned by the condensed power and the immaculate precision with which Tennyson had so perfectly described 'the King of Birds', which for many years had been a beacon for me, and whose qualities exemplified so much of that with which I had identified. In that one moment my paradigms of poetry and life shifted totally and forever. I realised that poetry could express in unique, powerful and sublime ways the awesomely beautiful world of nature; that poetry could, on one level, expand and magnify that world by giving it other dimensions.

In a very real sense, poetry could be seen as nature growing yet more wonderful and more magical by producing more life forms:

poems. As teenagers do, I had found a new hero! And, as a good teenager should, I wanted to be like, to copy, Alfred Lord Tennyson.

Hooked

Coincidentally, the following weekend, I was walking along a pier when I saw a fisherman catch a particularly beautiful fish and proceed to pound, with the lead weight from his fishing line, its flapping form into a bloody mess. My first-ever poem appeared, at warp-speed almost instantaneously:

THE CATCH

It stares through me with glazing eyes,

The blood, congealing on them, dries,

As gasping one last breath, it dies.

The fish that once looked so divine,

Lies smashed and dead, with broken spine,

I leave. The angler sorts his line.

Once I had read *The Eagle* and written *The Catch*, my mind was transformed. Rather than seeing things in the normal way, or not seeing them at all, my eyes were more opened to the beauty of everything, and to the possibilities of infinite metaphorical poetic connections.

Enchanted

Very quickly I fell under the spell of others who have become my virtual travelling companions through life:

George Gordon Lord Byron captivated me with these lines from

Childe Harold's Pilgrimage:

There is a pleasure in the pathless woods,
There is a rapture on the lonely shore,
There is society where none intrudes,
By the deep Sea, and music in its roar:
I love not Man the less, but Nature more,
From these our interviews, in which I steal
From all I may be, or have been before,
To mingle with the Universe, and feel
What I can ne'er express, yet cannot all conceal.
Roll on, thou deep and dark blue Ocean - roll!
Ten thousand fleets sweep over thee in vain;
Man marks the earth with ruin - his control
Stops with the shore; - upon the watery plain
The wrecks are all thy deed, nor doth remain
A shadow of man's ravage, save his own,
When for a moment, like a drop of rain,
He sinks into thy depths with bubbling groan,
Without a grave, unknelled, uncoffined, and unknown.

John Donne's metaphysical sonnet masterpiece and its opening made me gasp at the magnificence of its conception:

At the round earth's imagined corners, blow
Your trumpets, Angels, and arise, arise
From death, you numberless infinities
Of souls, and to your scattered bodies go

Gerard Manley Hopkins introduced me to the muscularly poetic power of *Sprung Rhythm* and, like Tennyson, enthralled me with his description of another raptor:

The Windhover:

I caught this morning morning's minion, king-
dom of daylight's dauphin, dapple-dawn-drawn Falcon, in his
riding
Of the rolling level underneath him steady air, and striding

High there, how he rung upon the rein of a wimpling wing
In his ecstasy! then off, off forth on swing,
As a skate's heel sweeps smooth on a bow-bend: the hurl and
gliding
Rebuffed the big wind. My heart in hiding
Stirred for a bird, - the achieve of; the mastery of the thing!

I longed for such mastery of the word! I wanted to write and think like them.

William Blake, still ahead of his time, grabbed my dendrites with his 'Innocence' and 'Experience', and with such observations as:

When thou seest an eagle, thou seest a portion of genius; lift up thy head!

And:

Listen to the fool's reproach! It is a kingly title!

(this saying and insight saw me through many difficult times during my period as President of the Student Council for Simon Fraser University, and continuingly throughout my life).

Blake's four-line poem from the 'Auguries of Innocence' summarised for me the essence of the philosophy by which a human life should be lived:

To see a world in a grain of sand,
And a heaven in a wild flower,
Hold infinity in the palm of your hand,
And eternity in an hour.

John Milton soon held me in awe with *Paradise Lost* and such succinct observations as:

"The mind is its own place, and in itself
can make a heaven of hell, a hell of heaven."

I was similarly inspired by the powerful and natural poetry of Ted Hughes, particularly *October Salmon*, which was also one of his own favourites. I was particularly impressed by Ted's description of the Salmon at the height of its lifecycle:

OCTOBER SALMON

And the eye of ravenous joy – king of infinite liberty
In the flashing expanse, the bloom of sea-life,
On the surge-ride of energy, weightless,
Body simply the armature of energy
In that earliest sea-freedom, the savage amazement of life,
The salt mouthful of actual existence
With strength like light

Another 'animal' poet was Rilke, who mesmerised me, as the cat had mesmerised him:

BLACK CAT

A ghost, though invisible, still is like a place
your sight can knock on, echoing; but here
within this thick black pelt, your strongest gaze
will be absorbed and utterly disappear:
just as a raving madman, when nothing else
can ease him, charges into his dark night
howling, pounds on the padded wall, and feels
the rage being taken in and pacified.
She seems to hide all looks that have ever fallen
into her, so that, like an audience,
she can look them over, menacing and sullen,
and curl to sleep with them. But all at once
as if awakened, she turns her face to yours;
and with a shock, you see yourself, tiny,
inside the golden amber of her eyeballs
suspended, like a prehistoric fly.

Rainer Maria Rilke

And of course, there was Shakespeare. In my new persona I saw him no longer as a dreary, old-fashioned, impenetrable, irrelevant and turgid bane of my school life.

He flowered in my 'new mind' as the comprehensively brilliant genius that he was, filling my internal universe with colours, images, metaphors, blazing insights, wit, humour, pathos, immortal stories and inspirations that have fed me for life, including, from Hamlet, arguably the greatest affirmation of man ever:

HAMLET, PRINCE OF DENMARK – Act II Scene II

What a piece of work is a man!
How noble in reason!
how infinite in faculty!
in form and moving, how express and admirable!
in action, how like an angel!
in apprehension, how like a god!
the beauty of the world!
the paragon of animals!

Also from Richard II, John of Gaunt's advice to his son Bolingbroke, a perfect summarisation of the essence of positive thinking:

KING RICHARD II - Act I Scene III

All places that the eye of heaven visits
Are to a wise man ports and happy havens:
Teach thy necessity to reason thus;
There is no virtue like necessity.
Think not, the King did banish thee;
But thou the King: Woe doth the heavier sit,
Where it perceives it is but faintly borne.
Go, say I sent thee forth to purchase honour,
And not, the king exil'd thee: or suppose,
Devouring pestilence hangs in our air,
And thou art flying to a fresher clime.

Look, what thy soul holds dear, imagine it
To lie that way thou go'st, not whence thou com'st.
Suppose the singing birds, musicians;
The grass whereon thou tread'st, the presence strew'd;
The flowers, fair ladies; and thy steps, no more
Than a delightful measure or a dance:
For gnarling sorrow hath less power to bite
The man that mocks at it, and sets it light
And from Julius Caesar:
There is a tide in the affairs of men,
Which, taken at the flood, leads on to fortune

The rest, as they say, is poetry!

From the time of writing his first poem, Tony began to read poetry voraciously, and to write profusely.

He was influenced by the Japanese haiku, by the English classic and modern poets, by the American modern poets, including especially Allen Ginsberg, by Rilke, Pushkin, Goethe, Homer, Juvenal, Escher and Borges, among many others.

Before returning to London in 1966, he spent an evening and night -into-morning with Allen Ginsberg, the author of the landmark poem *Howl*. They discussed Allen's *Howl*, which had introduced the concept of 'free-association' to the possibilities of expression for poets. *Howl* had a major effect on the poetic world, and influenced the form of certain of Tony's poems. The introduction was shocking in its originality and metaphor:

HOWL

I saw the best minds of my generation destroyed by
Madness, starving hysterical naked...
who bared their brains to Heaven under the El and
saw Mohammedan angels staggering on

tenement roofs illuminated,
who passed through universities with radiant cool eyes
hallucinating Arkansas and Blake-light tragedy
among the scholars of war,
who were expelled from the academies for crazy &
publishing obscene odes on the windows of the
skull,...

Much of Allen's and Tony's time together was spent discussing William Blake, with over an hour being devoted to how one would publicly perform the first 'Ah' in Blake's poem *Ah Sunflower*...

Upon returning to England, Tony's first action was to join the Poetry Society, where he met two poet-friends who were to become lifelong friends and colleagues – Jeremy Cartland and John Carder Bush, the older brother, and inspiration for, Kate Bush, and now Europe's most multiple-graded kyudo martial artist.

The three poets founded the 'Salatticum Poets' in 1967, and have given many readings, and produced many audios and videos since that time.

In April of 1971, Tony met Pablo Neruda at the Roundhouse Theatre in Hampstead London, where Pablo was giving a live reading to a packed house. Neruda was part of the triumvirate of Spanish/Latin American writers who were beginning to influence Tony's poetry: Lorca, Borges ("no one saw him arrive in the unanimous night..."). Tony was inspired by the beauty and richness of his imagery and metaphor and the style of his verse. One poem in particular caught his attention, because he had intended to write something similar, and Pablo had beaten him to it!

ODE TO A CHESTNUT ON THE GROUND

Out of the bristling foliage
you fell
complete:
polished wood,
glistening mahogany,
perfect
as a violin that has just
been born in the treetops

Later in 1971, Tony's first book of poems was published by Boydell Press, *Spore One*, including Tony's major poem, *Structure in Hyperspace*, which was described as: "a major work which is quite unlike anything else previously attempted in the poetry medium". Edward Hazelton said of Structure in Hyperspace:

"Tony Buzan, through his poem *Structure in Hyperspace*, is communicating an awareness of our here and now and of our 'to be'. While for, some of us, probability theory, Rorschach personality testing, cybernetics, Heisenberg's uncertainty principle, relativity, aesthetics and the philosophy of Zeno, may not be unfamiliar, it is highly unlikely that even the small selection of current pupils dealing with such concepts and experiences are in a position to separate and combine because of their overt and specialised restrictions.

I experienced when reading Buzan's major poem a fusion of the myriad interrelationships and interplays of the Universe as it is disparately perceived by, and as it effects, the human family now. To convey this vastness Buzan had to create, and did create, rhythms and patterns which were conceptually and sensorially multidimensional but essentially poetic ... as all satisfying rhythms and patterns are universal and poetic."

After the success of the *Use Your Head* book and television series in 1974, Tony, despite the increasing demands on his time, continued with his prodigious poetic output.

Among other things he became known as the 'Concorde Poet', writing over 385 poems on the supersonic passenger airliner, the Concorde, while flying on it thirty-eight times!

Tony became a close friend and colleague of Ted Hughes, the Poet Laureate, who was one of the major modern influences on Tony's work. Ted became senior Lecturer in Poetry at Tony's Renaissance Academy, co-founded with Prince Philip of Liechtenstein.

In addition, Tony and Ted worked on a nationwide scheme for training active poets in the art and science of memory, and then training those same poets to use the skills of imagination and association, which are at the heart of memory, as the basis for simile and metaphor in helping to release the poetic souls of the children they were teaching (with the declared aim of helping to create 'warriors of the mind').

After the untimely grounding of the Concorde, and the death of Ted in 1998, Tony compiled two new books of poetry which were published by Cellar Press in specially bound limited editions in 2007: *Concordea* and *Requiem for Ted*.

What follows is the frontispiece Concorde poem.

Archer

Curvature
Tends to Do it.
Tends to Bend the Mind
To Truth;
Tends to Show the Earth
As a Bow

For the Arrow
Of Intelligence.

Currently Tony is working on many poetry projects, including one massive volume of poems, based on the *Universes of Dreams*, and a comprehensive collection of poems, many of them originals, on and about animals. To date, Tony has written over four thousand poems, to which more are being added regularly! A growing number of people are 'catching on' to Tony's poetry, including major figures of the literary world.

Among those who have written warmly about Tony's poetry is Leslie Charteris, author of *The Saint*:

"He is a man of such many-sided intellect that he must inevitably be hard for less gifted minds to keep up with. His poems have nothing to relate to the light verse of John Masefield or a Johnny Mercer lyric. You have to work at them like a prospector, as they deserve, to find the rich ore which he has sealed in them."

And A.E. Van Vogt, author of *The Null-A Trilogy*:

"For many years Ray Bradbury has been, for me, the poet of the 21st century. But Ray will now have to move over, and stand side by side with this new poet - except the latter knows more science."

In terms of the 20th century, poetically expressed, the beauty of the poetry, and the wealth of information about the human condition in the poem, *Structure in Hyperspace*, has never been equalled in literature. In effect, the writer shows us the intricacy of particle and molecular interaction in intelligent beings in a universe that cannot possibly exist - yet here it is all around us. For years, he has been out there in the world of action, training other people's brains.

Now, he's coming back to poetry. That will be one of the events of the late 20th century in the field of literature."

Tony's most recent poetic interaction has been with London-based Chinese poet Yang Lian. Here is a sample of his work:

A Sunflower Seed's Lines of Negation

For Ai Wei Wei
unimaginable that Du Fu's little boat was once
moored on this ceramic river
I don't know the moonlight see only the poem's clarity
attenuated line by line to a non-person
to the symbols discussing and avoiding everything
I'm no symbol a sun dying under the sunflower seed's hard shell
nor is the sun snow-white collapsed meat of children
nor have I disappeared daybreak's horizon impossibly
forgot that pain bones like glass sliced by glass
I didn't scream, so must scream at each first light
an earthquake never stands still
no need to suffocate the dead planting rows of fences to the ends
of the earth
handcuffing ever more shameful silence so I don't fear
the young policewoman interrogating my naked body
it was formed by fire no different to yours
knowing no other way to shatter but a hundred millions
shatterings within myself
falling into no soil only into the river that can't flow
that cares nothing for the yellow flower within the stone having
to go on
to hold back like a drop of Du Fu's old tears
refusing to let the poem sink into dead indifferent beauty

• • • •

Tony's Poetry On The Web

Visit www.thinkbuzan.com/uk/tonybuzan/poetry

To start you on your journey of appreciation of Tony Buzan's poetry, we give you an early poem once again inspired by Nature, the Bird and flight. As Tony describes:

"On the West Coast of Ireland, abutting the rampaging Atlantic Ocean, are the spectacular Cliffs of Moher. From a dizzying height they plummet, sheer, to the rocky depths below, which are painted an ever-changing white by the pounding waves. The shapes of the cliffs combine with the force of the ocean's winds to create massive air currents in which the seagulls and sea birds play for hours.

The only way to look safely at this magical scene was to crawl on my belly and to peer down into the tantalising depths. The urge to jump (to fly!) was overwhelming, and both mind and body had to stay very much in control if this were not to be the last magnificent thing I ever saw! This poem is about the struggle between Siren Nature, Man, Mind, and Vision.

CLIFF AND MAN

The cliff-edge beckoned: asked him to walk near, dared him to
stand on edge;
but he tricked Her, approached on cat feet and buckled his own
length away -slid his body forward; safely moved his; Seeing over.
And She, laughing, made him swim, stretched him in Her space,
dragged his mind's laceworks down the rock-mossed edges of
depth, reeled him down Her sides and ledges, Yo Yo'd his Eye and
down and distantly roared at him with Her Sea.
He wrestled with Her offering, warped his tiny space.
Engulfed Her.
So She flung him Her Earth-Bird Seagull who wrung his Mind to
Ecstasy: rode the Funnel of Her Deepness, feathered the winds
that shoved him still on that cliff edge, Swept any Curve Stilled
any Wind-Rush Dropped in any Air Rise; erased ledge and
edgeness for him drew him, drew him out. The engulfer Engulfed.

354

Frieda Hughes

Thoughts on Tony Buzan's Poetry

Tony's *Epic Aman* is the evolutionary result of years of poetic creativity. Commencing life, several decades back, as an anthology of linked individual poems, it has grown - and continues to expand - organically, until the individual islands of this poetic archipelago have reached out to each other, coalesced and compressed into an overarching unity, thus, in one form at least, attaining epic dimensions.

A further mark of the epic is that *Aman*, in many ways, mirrors and explores the themes of the classic epics. Homer's *Odyssey* represents the extended hazardous journey of a man's development and his encounters with the rewards, dangers and challenges presented by the world. Similarly, Dante's *Divine Comedy* catalogues the travels of the soul.

In parallel to these, Tony Buzan's *Aman* traverses a prima facie impossibly complex Escherian dreamscape. Yet it subtly and almost imperceptibly metamorphoses the subconscious experiences, through the persistence of retained memory, into the tangible reality of the written word.

Dreams, whether of the sleeping or day variety, have enjoyed, or, indeed, suffered, a chequered reputation. In ancient times, and in contemporary so-called primitive cultures, the dream could signify haruspication, prognostication and prediction of all kinds. Wars were fought, and empires could rise and fall, on the information gleaned from dreams, as with the pronouncements of the Apollonian Pythoness of Delphi, from this particular activation of the subconscious.

With the advent of psycho-analysis, heralded by the Traumdeutung of Sigmund Freud, the dream was reduced to a manifestation of wish fulfilment, the symbolism of which was to be viewed primarily through the prism of a pre-determined - if "self censored" - sexual nature. The wide ranging predictive and multifariously symbolic essence of the dream was thereby abolished at a stroke of the pen of a dogmatic doctor from Vienna.

Can dreams be catalogued so neatly and, in effect, bureaucratically? Let us now turn to one of the undoubted inspirations for Tony's *Aman*, the work of Salvador Dali, whose oeuvre captures the richness of dreamscapes, employing what Dali himself termed the "paranoiac critical" method.

In the beginning, the word "paranoia" simply meant: "beside the mind" from the Greek "para" meaning "beside" and "noia" from "noos" meaning "the mind" as in Tony Buzan's much - loved and often - quoted phrase from Juvenal: "mens sana in corpore sano" from the Latin, translated and transliterated directly into the Greek as "Noos iyis in somatis iyes."

That was before professional psychology hijacked this expressive and multi-layered metaphor, in order to limit and constrict its meaning to that solely of a mental disorder, one indicating delusions of persecution. That, however, is not what the word "paranoia" actually means. The psychiatric version is an impoverished subset of a vastly greater universe of significance which has been obliterated by a soi-disant clinically justified mania for reductive manipulation.

The Surrealists, of whom Dali, Max Ernst and Andre Breton were the founding Godfathers, related theories of psychology to the idea of creativity and the production of art and poetry-not to disease! In the mid-1930s André Breton wrote that the objects of artistic and poetic expression had begun to be seen, not as fixed external truths, also as extensions of one's subjective self, indeed, perhaps, as a portal between other planes of perception.

In some ways this shows mere deference to the twin dream gateways of Ivory and Horn from Virgil's Aeneid, but one unique item manifested through Surrealism was the phantom object. According to Dali, these objects have virtually no mechanical meaning, but when the mind views them or perceives them, phantom images are evoked which are the result of unconscious acts.

The paranoiac-critical arose from similar Surrealistic experiments with psychology and the creation of images which, for example, involved rubbing pencil or chalk on paper over a textured surface and interpreting the phantom images visible in the texture on the paper.

A similar process could be seen in the "smoke paintings" of John Cage, the student of Schoenberg, both customarily noted for their musical composition. Less well known are the visual artworks of these two celebrated composers. Gustav Mahler was an early enthusiast for Schoenberg's art, while Cage developed the technique of raking through the ash in his fire, pouring it over paper, rubbing it in, then shaking it off and finally splashing water over what was left.

The point was to create an autonomous process, divorced from the waking consciousness, which might spontaneously, or by chance, create a significant image. Cage's Smoke Paintings were first publicly exhibited after his death in 1993 at the Museum of Modern Art in Los Angeles, where I had been invited to give the funerary oration tribute in his honour.

The aspect of paranoia which interested Dali, and which helped inspire his unique method was the ability of the brain to perceive links between things which rationally are not linked. Dalí described the paranoiac-critical method as a "spontaneous method of irrational knowledge based on the critical and systematic objectivity of the associations and interpretations of delirious phenomena." Again, as with "paranoia" the word "delirious" has been hijacked by psychiatry to indicate the negative-a mental disorder. In fact the word simply means, at root, "wandering, enthusiastic, excited…" hence implying - in the context of being "beside the mind" a multiplicity of possible meanings, images and evocations. Let us not forget that the word "planet," on one of which we all exist, comes from the Greek for "wanderer."

Employing the paranoiac-critical method when creating a work of art results in a complex or multiple meaning, in which an ambiguous image can be interpreted in many different ways. André Breton hailed the method, saying that Dali's paranoiac-critical method was an "instrument of primary importance" and that it "has immediately shown itself capable of being applied equally to painting, poetry, the cinema, the construction of typical Surrealist objects, fashion, sculpture, the history of art, and even, if necessary, all manner of exegesis."

In *Aman*, indeed, we see it applied to poetry. This new and burgeoning epic is a journey, a wandering, charged with the erotic, but not exclusively so, teleporting Tony Buzan's dreamscape into the observable universe. It is inspirational, hierophantic and visionary, moving effortlessly from the Daliesque paranoiac critical mode to the critical ironic and even quizzical -satirical. Part of Tony's intention, surely, being also to critique the absurdities excesses and mania of the contemporary world, through which the dreamer made manifest, moves in his parallel universe of the subconscious mind.

One large and important part of the *Odyssey* continually springs to mind as I read *Aman*, and it is Book Six, where Odysseus is thrown literally and entirely on his own resources, being rescued from nothingness by the sheer force of his physical, intellectual and heroic attractiveness. Book six also presents Odysseus with the opportunity to recount his own tale at length-a further link between Homer's epic and *Aman* with its similarly travelogic structure.

As Book Six opens, Odysseus has been shipwrecked on the coast of Phaeacia, where Princess Nausicaa and the servants of her father King Alcinous, are at the shore. Nausicaa is young nubile and extremely attractive; Homer says that she resembled a goddess, particularly the huntress Artemis. Odysseus emerges from the forest, completely naked, having lost everything in the tempest sent by the God Poseidon (Neptune), who hates the hero. The terrified servants flee - not the Princess. Odysseus solicits her aid and Nausicaa takes him to the King, where Odysseus wins approval, and is received as an honoured guest. During his stay and recuperation, Odysseus recounts his adventures to Alcinous and his court. This narrative forms a substantial portion of the Odyssey, where after, Alcinous generously provides Odysseus with the ships that finally bring him home to Ithaca.

AMAN WOMAN - WOOED IN A FOREIGN LAND

Aman
Dined,
Stamen
To the Flower Ladies
Of His
Food
And Sake
Supply
All Eyes
And Lips
And Body Parts,
They Clustered Around Him
Sipping at the Honeydew of His Mind
Neglecting to Let Him Feed;
Refilling Only His Glass
To Let Him
Subside into the Acceptance
Of Their Temptation:
To Let His Meal
Be Them

Tony Buzan's Aman has not yet reached his Ithaca, in fact, can he? While the writer dreams, Aman travels and the journey's end is not - and maybe cannot be - in sight. As Goethe wrote in his magnum opus, Faust:

"Wer immer strebend sich bemueht, den koennen wir erloesen."

Those who strive forever are assured of salvation!

Aman is an ongoing journey of a human being beginning to explore, through the surreal universe, the other infinite universes of love. Its inspiration comes from the twin cosmoses of 'Real' and the 'Dream' or, 'Real' and the 'Surreal'.

Exciting, disparate and growing bodies of evidence point increasingly to the fact that the Dream Universe is of major significance to human activity, creativity, happiness and survival, and that dreams also serve the purpose of the generation of paradigm-shifting creative ideas.

"I found," writes Tony," that as my own involvement with my Dream Universe evolved, my dreams became more magnificent; more vivid, more involved and more metaphoric and that they began to express themselves as poetry.

At night I would go to sleep as an excited theatre goer, knowing that I was about to witness a play of stunning originality, yet having no idea of what the plot, characters, theme or setting would be; I knew only that the play would completely absorb me. In many instances, I, the dream theatregoer, would become part of the play itself.

My mind provided me with an infinite theatre with infinite possible characters, limitless settings, a pallet that contained the colours, hues and tones of all paintings and all nature, plots that ranged the full gamut, from ultimate ecstasy to ultimate despair, and scenes that could be instantaneously created and instantaneously changed. And all a surprise; a gift.

I found, as time progressed, that many of the Dream Poems became Escherian, challenging my mind to take a Mobius Trip in which contradictory forms, structures and opposites could simultaneously, and without contradiction, coexist.

I found also that my mind and consciousness could easily exist in two places simultaneously, reminiscent of the chaos theory in quantum physics, in which scientists have recently discovered that in our 'Real Universe' the same entity can simultaneously exist at opposite ends of the physical universe. I am sure our paraconscious minds have been demonstrating through dreams that the long sought-after and elusive Unified Field Theory is not external to us, as has been thought; but is us!

Aman's Journey is populated with encounters, conflicts, battles, abandonment, exhilaration, lust, anticipation, life and death, passion and objectivity, ultimate pleasure and ultimate pain, bereavement, the huntress, the hunter and the hunted, visitations from the Cosmos, and hope.

It explores the full spectrum of love, ranging from the carnal, through the Platonic and the familial, to the spiritual.

Aman is the beginning of a man's journey in which the pursuit and exploration, in their hydra-headed form, of adventure, sensuality, love and meaning, are the methods by which the spirit is broadened, enlightened and forged."

It is also possible to detect in *Aman*, the inspirations and influences which we already know have planted their mark on Tony's poetry: William Blake, Gerard Manley Hopkins, Alfred Lord Tennyson, in particular The Eagle, and of course the Poet Laureate, Ted Hughes.

Here is a selection of Tony's poems from *Requiem for Ted* and *Concordea*, his explicit homage to the mythically charged avian form of Concorde, and to his friend, mentor and colleague Ted Hughes.

The themes of raptors, of falcons, of nature, mental agility, physicality and energy, both elegiac and forceful, permeate these works and are reflected in Tony's own elegiac conclusion: "That their God, Ted, was no longer there."

- Ornithological Armour,
- The Falcon Feeling and
- Vast Spiritus Mundi.

Ted Hughes sketched by Lorraine Gill

Ornithological Armour

I Love this Bird:
Platonic 'Form of Flight'
All Lines Clean and Neat;
Wing Like Sword of Samurai;
Nose a Rapier
One Wonders,
Philornithologically
What They Really Mean
When They Say
'Machine'

The Falcon Feeling

ls this the Falcon Feeling?
I, Like the Yearning, Little Bird-Soul
Anxiously Awaiting the Release
Command
That will Allow My Air-Master Body
To Leave the Talon-Hold-Vice-Grip
Of the Master's Hood.
Of the Momentary Master,
Land.

Ted Hughes and Sylvia Plath

VAST SPIRITUS MUNDI

Sun-Blasted
In the Cerulean Blue
His Beaked-Talons
Grasp
The Prey
Of Meaning.
Mountains;
Atmosphere;
Support.
Crawling Oceans
Subserve.
Thunderbolts Inform His Energy;
Earth His Aerie
As He Broods,
Gigantically
Over the Fragile Egg Shells
Of a Planet's Minds

Tony had the further distinction of commissioning a series of poems from Ted which were written according to Tony's innovative formula of being hard to remember, or, once read, easy to forget! Nobody else in the history of world literature has ever discovered such a formula, so Ted was more than willing to write according to this anti-mnemonic programme - thus the poetic form of the Anamnemonicker was born, and fittingly adapted to become the verse test in several World Memory Championships.

The most significant of all, is the until - now unpublished Ted Hughes masterpiece, commissioned by Tony, *A Storm in a Loving Cup*, which, of course, refers to *The Tempest*, fittingly Shakespeare's own last play.

An Unpublished poem by Ted Hughes

The following is a previously unpublished poem by Ted Hughes commissioned by Tony Buzan for the World Memory Championship.

A STORM IN A LOVING CUP - *Ted Hughes*

A ship splits in the jaws of the lion
But the King is tasteless. A bedtime story
Weeps to swallow what it will rejoice
To spew up. A child keep hearing
Father in the thunder. The sea's clouds
Are ballasted with books, but blue lightning
Rigs a wreck and plays pilot. The moon
Tortures a pine-tree that escapes by melting
Into a cowslip. Already a bumble-bee,
Big and red as a yeti, bumps its petals
For nectar. A beachcomber
Finds a goddess, castaway from her sea-shell
Where no bones are burning and no smoke
Tangles with the tears of the breakers.
Only a sleepless blade a nightbird's bill
Pokes and picks at a dream to hatch a kingdommmm---
Scattered by lions, trampled by bulls, and forgotten
By a tipsy seal upending a bottle.
Out of a pile of logs, a gold ring rolls.
Into a skull a nail sinks. Under clouds
Ballasted with jewelry. Out of the clouds
Bangs a zag of lightning
Ridden by a two-breasted raptor
Who kicks a wedding cake to rubble
And sends madmen staggering from the garden
In a reek of ozone, blind to the rainbow
Robing a peacock. A big-mouthed wedding bell
Hunts a naked woman over the horizons.
Yokels clog-dance in a dance of the fairies
Juggling a balloon of the seven seas.
Blindfolded with scarves, crazy horses
Flounder into a bog, and are stepping stones
For the absconding wildcat, as conifers fly
From a blast of ghosts. Till music pardons. Then
All deceivers go down on their knees.
Chess-players gaze, too much in love to move.
Mussel-shells split open and out reel sailors.
A monkey bangs the heads of two drunkards.
A druid crawls back into the hole of a bookworm.

Frieda Hughes

Daughter of famous poet Ted Hughes and ethereal poetess Sylvia Plath

I first met Tony at the family home in Devon on the occasion of my father, Ted Hughes's funeral in November 1998. My brother, Nicholas (sadly now also deceased) and I were left to deal with a crowd of people almost none of whom we knew, during my stepmother's absence from the house for the duration of the gathering. Tony introduced himself to us and appointed himself wine-pourer and greeter on our behalf.

His humour, charisma and ebullience helped alleviate the misery on one of the most miserable days of our lives, when my brother and I were launched into a social situation for which neither of us had been prepared and that we had not wished for. I remember Tony, larger than life, striding across the floor in a purple shirt with frills and a black cape!

When he was alive my father had explained Mind Maps to me and talked about Tony often in relation to them. He also told me that he and Tony and had once put forward a very exciting proposal to the then Labour government for use of the useless Dome when it was first built and submissions were being requested. (Their proposal was turned down.)

My father's story of increasing the effectiveness of a rowing team by using the mind to practise when not in the boat on the water was also related to Tony and Tony's exploration of the power of the mind.

I am a poet – and have published five collections to date – and a painter by profession. I have also written several children's books, and for two years wrote a weekly poetry column for *The Times*. I've also been chair judge and judge for The Foreword Prizes and The National Poetry Competition. My figurative paintings are based on the landscapes and creatures in my life, and abstracts describe my emotional landscape at various junctures.

• • • •

The Salatticum Poets

Chapter 27

The Salatticum Poets

As mentioned earlier, the Salatticum Poets were founded in the late 1960s by Tony Buzan, John Carder Bush and Jeremy Cartland, then three members of the The Poets Workshop at The Poetry Society. They performed together for about eight years. Initially music was supplied by John on guitar, but later by his brother, the eminent world-musician Paddy Bush, and Paddy's partner, Melanie Spriggs.

Readings were treated as performances and often included martial arts, masks, megaphones, dry-ice, smoke machines as well as music. Their last performance together was at the Festival of Mind, Body and Spirit in 1977.

They published a selection of their poetry, *Riding Light*, and also the poetry of Sir John Waller under the name Salatticum Press. The name refers, as we shall see, both to the "salty" wit of the trio and the name of Athens, the scene of the great intellectual renaissance of Socrates, Plato and Aristotle. If Jeremy resembles Socrates, and John is our new Plato, then that leaves the role of Aristotle for Tony, famously described by Dante in *The Divine Comedy*, as "The Master of the men who know," - "I Maestro di color che sanno!"

"As I recall, we were looking for a name for our group, I (Jeremy) came on Salatticum, meaning salty wit, and shortened it to Attic poets (multi meaning). But John and Tony seized on Salatticum, and that's what we became. And Whitstable became Salatticum Bay, where the sun always shines."

John Carder Bush writes:

"We saw ourselves as the antidote to the Liverpool Scene poets who were coming into vogue in the late '60s with performances of entertaining verse – we were determined to remain intellectual, mysterious and demanding. By the end of our readings together, I feel we had achieved something very powerful and audience orientated, but personal careers and their pursuit got in the way of taking the performance side of Salatticum onto something more permanent. However, although we have not performed a public reading as a group for many years, Salatticum continues to exist - we frequently meet, and use each other as sounding boards to test our recent poetry."

Here are two samples of the Salatticum poets at work-one poem each by John Carder Bush and Jeremy Cartland.

THE SWEET ICE WINES

by John Carder Bush

In night-dreams I crop the pastures of past hours,
Past places, past faces, past powers;
But I am as now, the dream connector,
A futuristic visitor, an old, homeless spectre
Moving like smoke-rings in their house at twilight.
No longer there by love, law or right.
I wisp around their beauty, the ever wild
Passion of young mother and sleeping child.
They are not as I left them, cold and tortured,
Fruit frozen on the boughs of an abandoned orchard:
No one has aged, faces are still young and fresh,
Experience has not yet dotted the blossom of their flesh.
In these dreams I am not prodigal, but penitent:
For me, no happy welcome or fond sentiment,
No sharing of joy in their eyes, nothing that's mine –
In this dream view of time, that lowers the blind
To shut out the grey light of intervening years,
There's only the cut of separation, salted with tears.
But, however much these dreams disturb and mock,
At the same time, they ease and unlock,
Healing something deeper than mind
That lies beyond kind and unkind,
So that, even if I wake blurred with regrets,
Later, there is a clarity in the day that lets
Me accept the frosted grapes of my heart,
Lets me turn them into the sweet, ice wines of art.

The Frog Prince

by Jeremy Cartland

It was quicker than a kingfisher's dive,
The Princess said. She bent her wimpled neck
To kiss, and before she straightened
I became Prince.
For me it was an age.
I remember the agony in each tissue:
The ripping of webs, the rasp of eyelids,
Choking on a tightening pharynx.
Blood howled through throbbing muscles,
Bones scored cramps into the limbs,
A burning wind seared my skin to dryness.
And the hollow ache for the Princess.
That remains, and uncertainty.
When I was Frog, it was simple.
There were no questions, all was Frog.
I roamed two worlds at will.
Now, despite castles, riches, and my Princess,
I am trapped in air.
I give commands. My periwig
Is powdered by powdered flunkeys,
Every bodily need is satisfied.
But still the void inside, the search
For a lost element, the missing rhyme.
All is not Prince, and I harbour
A peculiar craving for flies.

• • • •

Chapter 28
Mind Magician

"Tony Buzan will do for the brain what Stephen Hawking

did for the Universe"   The Times

Ironically, Tony's early career as a creator and innovator was as inauspicious as his early career as a sportsman. From a very young age, his school had identified him as an academic, and had inculcated into the children that academia and the arts were totally different fields, in which skill in one tended to obviate skill in the other.

In one of his first ever art lessons, the teacher asked the class to draw their favourite boat. Tony's favourite boat at the time was the cruiser, as much for its long and sleek lines as for its incredibly beautiful light grey. The colour fascinated him even more than the design. For his boat, he quickly drew the outline, and spent the rest of the lesson, with a very light grey soft-leaded pencil, colouring it in, going over and over each layer, relishing the feel of the rounded lead tip sliding across the paper, and marvelling at the way in which, the more the layers were added, the more the boat developed an almost silver sheen.

Oblivious to the effect of the shading, he failed to notice that the paper around his ship was curling up as a result of the pressure he was applying to his shading.

He thought it was beautiful.

The teacher did not, and scolded him for wasting his time doodling, rather than drawing a proper ship. Art, in his mind, died an instant death, for he had demonstrated, and been told by authority, that he was inadequate at it.

A few years later, when starting to learn the piano, he became fascinated with discordant chords. He composed in his head a very short piece, which he played over and over again he enjoyed it so much. Upon showing this to the teacher, he was scolded for not having done his 'proper' homework, told that the sounds he was making were cacophony, and that he was a poor music student.

Art had died. Music now died.

Despite this early rejection, Tony was still, at University, in love with music, and was the only 'non-music' student to join the University choir, singing baritone in such masterpieces as Handel's *Messiah*, Verdi's *Requiem*, Beethoven's *Missa Solemnis* and his *Ninth Symphony* (The Choral).

Tony's vision of himself as not creative had, therefore, strong foundations. Creativity was associated with music and art, academia was not; he was extremely poor at both art and music, and was good at academia.

Case closed.

Despite these early disappointments, Tony, believing he was still not creative, wrote, as we have already seen, his first book, *My Pets*, at the age of eight, and, inspired by the poem *The Eagle* by Alfred Lord Tennyson, wrote his own first poem in his early teens.

Creativity Tests and Memory

While Tony was at University in his final year, the students were given one aspect of E. Paul Torrance's *Tests of Creative Thinking*.

Tony explains: "We had to generate, in one minute, as many ideas as we could for the use of a paper clip. I managed to generate 14 ideas, and was running out of ideas as the time period ended. My score was comfortably above average, but was not in the genius range. As the years passed, my study of Memory was leading me to an inescapable conclusion:

"Memory and Creativity were fundamentally the same processes, each seen from a different perspective in time. An inevitable conclusion emerged: for Memory Systems to work, anything you wish to remember has to be connected, in your imagination, to a pre-existing 'coat hanger' word. Therefore, for the Systems to work, which they do, the brain must be able to link anything with anything else; in other words, everything with everything!

This conclusion was supported by Leonardo's dictum: 'Realise, as you learn anything, that in some way, everything connects to everything else.' If all this were true, then in creativity the same must apply. All this was true.

Therefore, the creative individual must be potentially capable of infinite creativity.

This led me to develop the formula – Energy plus and into Memory equals Infinite Creativity

$$E + M = C^{\infty}$$

So what about my University creativity result?! The possibility of uses for a paper clip was by definition infinite. I had generated 14 and begun to run out of ideas! Realising that all our thinking about Creativity was topsy-turvy, I prepared, for one day, and bolstering my strength in the basic memory principles of Imagination and Association, to take the full Torrance *Tests of Creative Thinking*. Knowing that there were potentially an infinite number of responses to most of the questions, the task was easy.

The psychologist who had given me the test, Dr. Geraldine Schwartz, sent my tests back to headquarters, who immediately asked her whether she had devised a special computer system to answer the questions, as the results were so far beyond the human norm as to be 'impossible'.

With the results confirming my conclusions, I began to realise the global assumptions that there are very few uses for anything, and that there are an infinite number of non-uses for that same thing, were exactly the opposite of what was true: we had put the infinity symbol in the wrong place. The fact is that there are an infinite number of solutions/uses for anything, and for the creative mind, therefore, every problem has a solution.

In addition it became apparent that we are not, as we are commonly called, 'problem solvers'; we are Solution Finders. From this I generated one of my favourite mottos: 'Semper Solutio' – "there is always a solution".

Music

"Once I had been convinced that the brain could make infinite connections, and was therefore capable of learning anything to which it set its mind and about which it had the basic grammar and language, learning to play the piano and guitar became easy and enjoyable, with none of the fear of failure with which I had originally approached these instruments.

One remarkable consequence of this was that I began to dream music.

I would wake up, for example, with an entire and original piano concerto having just played in my head, and because of my absence of musical training and note-taking, I had no way of recording it. But it was there, and it had given me, in my dream, as much pleasure as other piano concertos to which I had listened.

If only I had been taught music as a necessary alphabet and language, I would have been able to write nearly as much music as I had poetry…"

Mind Maps

"As I began to expand the application of Mind Maps from simply Memory to other spheres, especially Creativity, a new realisation dawned: at the end of each branch anywhere on the Mind Map was the theoretical potential to add an infinite number of new associations; each key word and each key branch was its own 'supernova' of ideas, which itself could reach out infinitely in infinite directions.

The Mind Map was the physical and theoretical proof that the brain's potential to generate ideas, to be creative and to innovate is an infinity of infinities.

We are all, by definition, infinitely creative – it is the natural state, away from which most of us have been guided."

Perception

"One day, after I had taken the Rorschach Tests, in which one is asked to identify as many structures as possible from an inkblot, I was at home at night, tired, looking out of my window at an oak tree, bared for the winter and lit up by a solitary street lamp.

As my eyes went into soft focus, the scene before me transformed into a fantasia-like palace, with streams and rivers running down the hill on which it stood, and with a full country scene surrounding the base of the palace. The whole scene was in fantastic, luminescent colours.

Shocked by this sudden 'revelation', I found myself able to hold the image in my mind, and check it against the actual tree. I was able to identify which branches and which spaces/shapes between the branches had caused my mind to create, instantaneously, this phantasmagoric scene.

Conclusion: my brain could create, from relatively random patterns, complete, totally 'rational' scenes; not only could it do this, it could also hold that complete image, and compare it detail by detail, with the actual vision that had inspired the brain to create its own 'masterpiece'.

And we were testing ourselves on what different shapes we could see in an ink blot! Something was amiss..."

Humour

"Humour, a difficult concept."

Lt Saavik, a Vulcan, in Star Trek II The Wrath of Khan.

"Having been schooled to be 'academic', and 'serious', Tony had accepted the belief that humour was somehow childish and immature, and not to be engaged in, listened to or practised. This, as in so many other cases, was exactly the opposite of what was true.

Through my studies of Memory and Creativity, I realised that humour is a glorious and infinite playground of Imagination and Associations, when a sudden shock of a totally new and original connection sends the brain into an ecstasy which is commonly known as laughing.

One of my goals in the vision of Global Mental Literacy, is that the world will become a more fun-loving and humorous place, and in that way will increase enjoyment, unleash more creativity, release stress, and allow the human brain to be its natural laughing creative and joyous self."

In 2008, at the Annual Creativity Conference, Tony was presented, on behalf of the American Creativity Association, and by the Senior Minister for Foreign Affairs of Singapore, Professor Kirpal Singh with the lifetime achievement award for services to Global Creativity and Innovation.

Chapter 29

All The World's His Stage

Google "Tony Buzan" and nearly 400,000 pages of information appear. For "Mind Map", the results are an astonishing 103 million pages, and even this is still no more than a mere hint of the popularity and global reach achieved by Tony Buzan and his concepts of Mental Literacy and Mind Maps.

This popularity has been gained through Tony's six decades of global travel, during which time he has visited over seventy countries on his keynoting and lecturing tours. In so doing Tony has acquired the status of a global media personality and Brainstar.

So far in his life, he has spent a total of:

- eight months in the air!
- one year in Mexico;
- one year in Africa;
- one year in the Arabian Gulf;
- one year in Australia/New Zealand;
- three years in the United States of America;
- three years in Asia;
- five years in Europe;
- twelve years in Canada;
- twelve years in post-war United Kingdom;
- and forty plus years based in 'modern UK'.

He also picked up some of the 'pioneering spirit', as opposed to the old 'empire spirit' to which he had become accustomed as a boy. His media career started, when, as Head Boy's Prefect of his school, he made his first brief appearances on radio and television. This media presence grew considerably in 1965/6, when, as inaugural president of the Simon Fraser University Student Council, he had to represent the student body regularly on radio and television, as well as to the press. After having travelled the length of the West Coast of America and into the North of Mexico, he returned to England in September of 1966.

By this time Mind Maps were taking shape, and his teaching and writing led to a number of radio interviews, among the most significant being a half hour feature discussion on the Robin Day Show. Shortly after this, he was a repeat guest on Ireland's number one television show, *The Late Late Show* hosted by Gaye Burn.

Then, in 1973, an event occurred which was to change his life.

Tony was lecturing on a management course, when he was asked if he would come, with one of his students, for a ten minute spot on BBC's television's number one news programme *Newsnight*. The best student in Tony's class, a senior man who was director of personnel for the BBC at the time, and who had no connection with the television programmes, agreed that he would be the guest. Christopher Tatham was already a superb Mind Mapper, was the fastest reader in the class, and had applied the Memory Systems perfectly.

When the two of them arrived at BBC Television Centre, a junior member of the television programme (known in the trade as "a gofer") greeted them, initially thinking that each was the other. When this understandable confusion had been straightened out, the gofer explained that 'something had come up' and that unfortunately they could devote only two minutes to the piece and therefore, they could not use Mr. Tatham.

All they were going to do was to give Tony a thousand-word article which he had to read in a minute, and then they were going to ask him questions about it. Tony explained that this was not the reason why he had come; the reason why he had come was to discuss the new concept of Mind Mapping, and its application to business, personal and general life.

"We can't do that," said the gofer.

"Then I'm not doing it," said Tony.

"But you have to!" said the gofer.

"Why?" said Tony.

"Because it's the BBC!" said the gofer.

"And that's an ashtray," said Tony, "which is just as relevant. If you want a circus act, Barnum and Bailey is just down the road…"

Tony had turned down a prime spot on BBC's prime news programme, which could have been the beginning of the end of his media career! As it turned out, it was exactly the opposite. Christopher Tatham said, "Well done, young man – good to see someone sticking to his principles. Your material needs more than ten minutes anyway. I'll see what I can do to connect you with BBC educational television, in order to arrange a half hour television feature."

Two weeks later, Tony was at the BBC, with the head of BBC TV Further Education, with a producer, and with a director discussing what they would put in the half hour programme.

Tony will take up the story from here:

"Rather than listing the brain-stormed ideas, I began a Mind Map, with a central image of the brain on a television screen. The first item suggested was a general introduction to the brain with some of the latest findings. This I put on the first branch, including some of the astonishing new information about the number and capacity of brain cells.

Next they wanted some information on Memory, so on the second branch I drew a little elephant (the memory animal which has subsequently become the logo of the World Memory Championships) and branched from it: memory problems; memory systems; recall during learning; and recall after learning (forgetting!) The third item they wanted was speed reading, so on the third branch I drew an eye and from that, eye movements, speed reading, slow reading, and reading problems and solutions.

Next on the agenda came traditional note-taking methods, so on the fourth branch I drew a pen and some linear notes with the disadvantages of such notes, including slowness, irrelevance of content, disguising of key words, and monochrome (boring!) colours. This led naturally to the 'new method' of Mind Mapping (at that time called brain patterns) with extensions off the branch for theory, use in school and university, use in business, and general applications.

Even more was wanted, so yet another branch was added for study skills. For this branch I drew a little open book, and off that radiated goals, survey, preview, inview, and review.

At this point, the head of BBC TV Education said, "I say, young man, this 'Mind Map' thing makes it look more like ten programmes than one, doesn't it?!"

"Yes, Sir, it does!" I said.

"Jolly good, then, ten programmes it is!" and then, as he was leaving, he turned and said, "Could you write a book on this as well?"

"Yes Sir, I could!" I said.

And so *Use Your Head* the television series and *Use Your Head* the book came to be.

"If I had listed the items being brain-stormed in traditional linear form, the programme would have remained as a half hour feature, and would have had no book. Because it was a Mind Map, the full breadth and depth of the content grew in front of their eyes in the meeting, and made it apparent that the programme required much more time than even half an hour. In real terms, the Mind Map gave birth both to the television series and to the book which immediately spread it around the world..."

Tony shot to global fame in the spring of 1974, when the prize-winning ten-part BBC series on the brain and thinking was screened and when *Use Your Head*, the book, was published. The series proved so popular that it was repeated at least twice on an annual basis on both BBC 1 and BBC 2 for the following fifteen years. In the same year, Tony also featured in a Thames Television one hour primetime documentary: *The Evolving Brain*, which also received a worldwide screening.

This sudden rocketing into the media stratosphere immediately led to invitations around the world to keynote, to give presentations and seminars, and to appear in all forms of media, especially radio and television.

In the space of a few years, Tony had travelled:

- to the United States and Canada, with their pioneering spirit and extraordinarily varied peoples and landscapes;
- to Jamaica, jewel in the Caribbean where Bob Marley and reggae were revolutionising popular music;
- to New Zealand, which from the air looked like paradise before it was populated;
- to Australia, where Sydney was one of the most beautiful cities he had ever seen, where the humour was profound, and where the Australian outback and its aboriginal inhabitants really took him back to the earth and his roots;

- to all the major countries in Europe where the collective and embracing European name disguised the many and astonishingly different cultures contained within that area;
- to the Arabian Gulf with its culture of generosity and a new creative spirit generated by its discovery of oil;
- to Russia with its profound soul, exquisite and powerful cultural history, and great generosity;
- to Japan which beguiled him with its Samurai and Shogun traditions, its etiquette, its Mind Sports (especially Go) its martial arts, and its deep sense of community and honour;
- to Singapore, a brilliantly conceived 'dot' of an island that had decided, as its only real natural resource was human intelligence, to develop it. And did!
- to Malaysia, luscious, bountiful, and with a population driven to learn;
- to Thailand where he met some of the most kind and gentle people he had ever encountered in spite of their recent doubtless temporary challenges;
- to the Philippines where poetry, thinking and sport were etched into its history;
- to Vietnam, people of unimaginable dedication and innovation, who had actually trained bees to help them in battle!
- to India with its untold wealth and untold poverty in a land teeming with intelligence;
- to China whose energy, variety, lust for learning, curiosity and desire for success left him almost breathless.

Throughout his sixty years of travel, Tony concluded that fundamentally, all humans speak the same language – the language of Imagination and Association, and that 'foreign' local languages are sub-routines of the Prime Language; that in a real sense we will never meet a 'foreigner', or as they are often mis-described, 'aliens'. 'We all speak the same language' has become a theme in his work, and led to his *Language Revolution* series with Harper Collins, in which the Prime Language, Imagination and Association, manifested in Mind Maps, is used to help the learning of the 'sub-routine' languages with much greater speed, efficiency and pleasure.

The Media

As his career and travelling continued unabated, it was laced with international radio and television appearances and programmes, including three major video and audio packages.

On television he has appeared on most of the major global networks, including CBC (Canadian Broadcasting Corporation), BBC 1, BBC 2, Thames Television, NBC, CNBC, ITV 1, ITV 2, ITN, Channel 5, Tokyo TV, Sky TV, The World Television Network, German Television Networks, Mexico's TV Stations, various channels on CCTV (China TV) and many others.

Featured among these many highlights was his 1999 new BBC Television series *Brain Bytes*. It was designed to help members of the general public and especially students of the Open University, general Universities and schools, improve their memories, reading skills, study habits and general knowledge of the brain and its capabilities.

Another major media feature was his co-presenting in 1993, with Raymond Keene, and Carol Vorderman, of an 80-programme television series on Channel 4 commenting on the Kasparov v Short World Championship, sponsored by *The Times*.

In 2005, Tony furthered his media presence and gained considerable credibility amongst his peers when he put his reputation on the line in a feature educational primetime programme for the BBC *In Search of Genius* in which he went back to his teaching roots to work with six 'failing' children in a South London school. Progressively over his seven lessons, the children started to achieve in class, gained self-esteem, and turned their behaviour from what had been described as "appalling" to "model".

In 2008, Tony starred on the Channel 5 TV globally broadcast programme on the World Memory Championships and Genius. In December 2010, in Guangzhou, China, Tony presented a one-hour television feature on Memory and Mind Maps for the programme *Happy Dictionary*, watched by over 300,000,000 people on China's CCTV.

At the beginning of 2007, Buzan Online (Tony's iMindMap software website) was nowhere to be seen on the Google rating list of the top twenty million websites of the world's 200 million.

By the beginning of 2008, it had entered the top twenty million, and by the beginning of the following year, 2009, had entered the top million. By the middle of 2009, Buzan Online had risen to the top 70,000, and by the end of the year had cracked the top 50,000.

Tony and his colleague, Chris Griffiths, the founder and CEO of Buzan Online, then had a significant decision to make. They wanted to re-brand and combine Buzan World and Buzan Online into a new website: Think Buzan. Google informed them that they could not 'carryover' their ratings, and had to start from scratch if they wished to begin a new website. Google estimated that it might take as much as six months to a year to get back to their previous rating.

From the end of January 2010 to the end of April 2010, the new website, Think Buzan, rocketed up the standings, past the 20 million mark, past the one million, past the 100,000 mark, past the 50,000 mark, to be rated as high as in the top 31,000!

Think Buzan already has over 100,000 unique visitors per month, who hail from over 108 countries.

• • • •

Chapter 30

Multiple Meanings In The Art Of Lorraine Gill

Below the thunders of the upper deep;
Far, far beneath in the abysmal sea,
His ancient, dreamless, uninvaded sleep
The Kraken sleepeth: faintest sunlights flee
About his shadowy sides: above him swell
Huge sponges of millennial growth and height;
And far away into the sickly light,
From many a wondrous grot and secret cell
Unnumbered and enormous polypi
Winnow with giant arms the slumbering green.
There hath he lain for ages and will lie
Battening upon huge sea-worms in his sleep,
Until the latter fire shall heat the deep;
Then once by man and angels to be seen,
In roaring he shall rise and on the surface die.

Alfred Lord Tennyson

Lorraine Gill has been Tony's most faithful supporter, and he hers. Tony, entranced by the metaphorical content and profundity of her art, has championed her works for decades, while Lorraine has backed Tony to the hilt in his ongoing battle against the enemies of Mental literacy.

In the exegesis which follows I have sought to bring out the intellectual and aesthetic qualities which bind these two extraordinary individuals together. Lorraine is also Head of the Art Faculty at The Renaissance Academy. She has played a gigantic and seminal role in Tony's life, as we shall see!

Believing that he was not creative, and misunderstanding the true definition of creativity, Tony continued to teach and write until, at the age of 24, he met, in London, the artist Lorraine Gill, who was one of the instructors at a school of dancing at which Tony was also teaching (he didn't think that dancing was creative either!) In one of their conversations, he explained to Lorraine, who was obviously, in his eyes, 'a creative' that he was not one of those, and that he could not draw. She looked at him with amazement, and asked him what he was talking about!

Tony: "Using my debating experience, academic background and powers of persuasion, I attempted to demonstrate to her that I could not even draw a cube.

My demonstration was successful!

All the shapes that came out on the page were total distortions of the shape of a cube. Lorraine looked at me with both pity and compassion, and explained to me that someone with my presumed intelligence should have been able to work out that drawing was a natural human function, that it had its own alphabet, and that once you had learned that alphabet, you could automatically draw.

She demonstrated that a cube was simply a square with three parallel diagonal lines emanating from it, and that to make a cube all you had to do was draw a horizontal and a vertical line connecting the three diagonals, and you had a cube.

I tried my first cube, and because I had been taught so well, and because the language of art was so fundamentally 'clean', the cube was basically perfect. It was, in every sense of the word, a moment of enlightenment. That cube shone in my internal Universe like the most brilliant supernova, and opened up that Universe to other Universes of possibility. In an instant, I had become an artist. I couldn't stop drawing cubes for some time, and proudly showed them off to my somewhat bemused friends, who thought I had gone a bit strange, and who thought so only because they did not understand the gigantic weight of impossibility that had been lifted from my shoulders, mind and life."

It was the beginning of Tony's realisation that creativity is a natural birthright, that we all possess it, and that we are all naturally creative. His own outlook on the world and perspective on himself had paradigm-shifted to the positive.

When speaking of Tony, Lorraine emphasises his generosity in helping to fund her initial art courses in the UK when she arrived from Franco's Spain, where she had been studying Flamenco dancing. She also notes the ubiquity of his presence, with Tony's books being stocked in the Alice Springs Library, when all Lorraine had expected was Barbara Cartland novels. Furthermore, his indomitable will, always bouncing back, after whatever challenges life throws at him.

One such challenge related by Lorraine - albeit in Tony's absence from the scene - involved a break-in at his house. Tony kept an extremely life-like model in his rooms, an upright representation of a flayed human figure, revealing all the musculature, in the Da Vinci mode of anatomical research. When Lorraine, as his closest friend, was called to the location of the crime, there was blood everywhere, since the windows had been smashed and wounded the intruder, who had, understandably, retired hurt.

On entering the premises with an officer of the law, Lorraine observed the young policeman spot the blood, then in the gloom, become aware of the anatomical model. Putting two and two together the officer's brain connected the "flayed corpse" with the blood, and he promptly fainted in horror!

From the ludicrous to the sublime, I now proceed to examine the work of the artist who wrought such a transformation on Tony. The pictorial art of Lorraine Gill exhibits a compelling similarity to the poetry of John Milton, in particular with regard to his master epic, Paradise Lost, as we have seen, one of Tony's favourite poems and one of his favourite poets. Multiple meanings and infinite complexities of depth abound in both, such that one word, or one image, can furnish simultaneously a variety of congruent yet disparate interpretations. The pressure of symbolism and metaphor behind the image is indicative in both oeuvres of an opulent visual and verbal multifariety. Remarkably, even opposites and contradictions may be embraced to enrich the creative experience in both instances.

I take the painting *METAMORPHOSIS OF THE KRAKEN* in Lorraine's *Kraken Series*, as my starting point, this being the metaphorical bridge between both the beginning and the ending of the Kraken's life cycle. Here, the Kraken is portrayed in egg-like embryonic form. On analysing it, I found the following ideas in one single image:

Thus, we have the eye, we have vision and metaphorically we have imagination. Then, moving further into the series, we see a wheel, we see a ship. We see an ocean. We see the dimensions of energy and the dimensions of time. We see consciousness, we see surface consciousness, sub-consciousness and overt consciousness, as the Kraken, the great sea beast, emerges from the depths into the upper ocean and the atmosphere. At that moment, its life-force surges from its previous primordial incarnation, becoming visible to all. Every one of these qualities, developed throughout the series, comes together in this one establishing image.

"The Kraken" Begins from Lorraine's
Kraken Series

With Lorraine, each of those multiple meanings is congruent with all the other meanings. What immediately drew me to the connection between Lorraine's painting in the *Kraken Series* and the poetry of Milton was the image of a terrifying denizen of the abyss, speeding upwards to manifest itself. The giant cephalopod, this mighty marine monster, capable of destroying ships and pulling mariners down into its own depths, emerges into the consciousness of the upper deep, encountering a world it has not seen before, and vice versa.

Metamorphosis of the Kraken

In book one of *Paradise Lost*, Satan (Lucifer) has challenged God in Heaven, but lost, and lost badly. Lucifer, formerly the brightest of the angels, has now been hurled down into the pit of hell by God after the battle. Satan is lying on hell's floor, grovelling or floating in the slime at the bottom. At this dramatic moment, as we first encounter Satan, Milton compares him to the whale, to a Leviathan, to a sea monster: a sea monster which, like the Kraken, is capable of sucking down and destroying ships and sailors.

> Or that sea-beast
> Leviathan, which God of all his works
> Created hugest that swim the ocean-stream.
> Him, haply slumbering on the Norway foam,
> The pilot of some small night-foundered skiff,
> Deeming some island, oft, as seamen tell,
> With fixed anchor in his scaly rind,
> Moors by his side under the lee, while night
> Invests the sea, and wished morn delays.
> So stretched out huge in length the Arch-Fiend lay,
> Chained on the burning lake;

The implication of course, based on standard mediaeval bestiaries, is that the sailor anchors his ship on Leviathan, but what is Leviathan going to do when the morning comes? He's going to wake up and crush the ship or sink it or drag it underneath the waves.

In Lorraine's *Kraken Series* we see the Kraken pulling the ships down, destroying them. The communal metaphor is obvious, but there is a further and greater dimension than this self-evident resonance of theme!

In this context, let us now examine a particular sentence from Paradise Lost. As we know, Satan has engaged God in battle. He has fought him on the plains of Heaven and he has lost. Milton describes it thus, putting these words into Satan's mouth:

His utmost power with adverse power opposed
In dubious battle on the plains of Heaven.

The key question here is: what does "dubious" mean? It can mean several things. It can mean "unjustified", since there was no good reason for Satan to challenge the Almighty. In general, though, in literary criticism, "dubious" in this context is said to mean "uncertain". This would be in character for Satan, deluding himself that the Battle was "uncertain", i.e. dubious.

The Kraken Attacks by Lorraine Gill

The battle could have gone either way. It was doubtful whether he would win or God would win. But "dubious" also means "unreal". So we have a triple meaning from one word, where each meaning is relevant to the message Milton wishes to convey. These are: "unjustified", "uncertain" and "unreal." It could mean we doubt that in fact it was a Battle, for if we know that God is all powerful, omniscient and Almighty, how can one fight against him?

In a single word, Milton shows Satan's view of the contest, that in his own mind he had a chance, but Milton also adds two further concepts to the one word "dubious" which completely undermine Satan's reasons for fighting God. It was a dubious battle i.e. it wasn't actually a battle because God has perfect foreknowledge, total omniscience and ultimate power.

The Kraken Activates by Lorraine Gill
Note the background of Devil's horns

How can there be a battle in any real sense against that sort of power? Of course there cannot be. Far from being an almost level fight, which could have gone either way (according to Satan's assessment of "dubious") the battle is not only unjustified, it actually was not a battle, in any true sense, at all. This panoply of information, and different debating viewpoints, is conveyed by one seven letter word!

We now move on from the triple meaning of the word "dubious" to describe the Battle in Heaven, to that moment where Milton is depicting the manner in which the rebellious angels have been overthrown, having been hurled out of Heaven by God and now grovelling in the fiery wastes of Hades. They rise up, when Satan calls them, and swarm into the sulphurous air. At this moment, Milton produces the most fantastically multi-dimensional evocation of the demons in flight.

In the section that follows "Amram's son" is Milton's term for Moses, who famously called down the plague of locusts on Egypt, when Pharaoh stubbornly refused to release the imprisoned and exiled Israelites:

> As when the potent rod
> Of Amram's son, in Egypt's evil day,
> Waved round the coast, up-called a pitchy cloud
> Of locusts, warping on the eastern wind,
> That o'er the realm of impious Pharaoh hung
> Like Night, and darkened all the land of Nile;
> So numberless were those bad Angels seen
> Hovering on wing under the cope of Hell,
> 'Twixt upper, nether, and surrounding fires;

The key words in this passage are "pitchy" (describing the cloud of locusts) and "warping." What do "pitchy" and "warping" mean?

The basic root word "pitch" can mean "throw", since the Angels were "thrown" from Heaven into Hell. It can also bring to mind a pitchfork, which is the standard devilish instrument, often seen in artistic imaginings of Hell. It can mean, "to descend". It can mean "to hurl". It can mean "to bowl" or "throw in an underhand way".

And what do the devils do? They are underhand. They are dishonest. It can also mean dark – pitch black. It can signify tar – pitch, a pitchy substance associated with Hell. It can also mean to oppose, as in, a pitched battle. It can mean to fall.

Summing up the various ideas conveyed with this one word: falling, opposing in battle, underhand, blackness, tar, descent ... and in addition and, indeed, above all, it can mean oscillating, hovering in the air, or unsteady and unstable at sea. This cunningly creates a link back to the futility of pinning one's hopes on the unreliable Leviathan, as a firm anchorage. We are presented by Milton with a picture of bad Angels, demons now hovering under the ceiling of Hell, where they are imprisoned. Oscillating, pitchy. In one word Milton conjures a complex litany of different meanings.

What does "warping" mean, and, in particular, why should locusts warp? Locusts, of course, devour crops, cause starvation and kill people. Although they are, in fact, morally neutral, hungry insects and the effects of their predation can seem "evil" to humans. "Warping" can also mean "throwing". The demons have been thrown from Heaven.

The connection with "pitchy" is already becoming clear and for etymological derivations see the German "werfen" or the old English "moledewarp" which means the "mouth thrower" or mole, significantly an underground animal which hates the light! "Warp" can also signify: to twist, to bend, to be warped, perverted, swerving.

Ostensibly Milton is describing the oscillating, swerving movement of the locusts. With the same word, he is also conveying the character of the fallen angels, the devils, their past and future history. Where are they going? They are swerving from God. They are distorting God's truth. They are miscarrying. They are turning away from the face of God and also they are shrinking, by leaving Heaven and deserting God and his truth. Milton actually refers to Satan seeming shrunken and diminished in the eyes of his companion Beelzebub.

Two words, but with an increasing crescendo of many, many different meanings.

Milton's words contain a uniquely high number of meanings, as do Lorraine's paintings, works which are sophisticated, complex, rich and do not conform to a programme. In contrast, Picasso tended to have phases where he operated within a programmatic framework, such as the Pink period, the Blue period, the Cubist period...

Tony, Ray and Lorraine

I do not believe that Lorraine's paintings operate within such a framework. They operate within a thought structure, as does Milton's poetry, which is the most intellectual of any of the English poets. The awareness of the richness of language and the choice of words means so many different things With Milton one can see a world in a word. One word of Milton can give vital indications about the history of the angelic rebellion against God.

Milton and Gill are two of a kind in the profundity of their intellectual perception and expression. The Poet has been recognised as a global genius for the past four centuries. Tony's favourite painter is on the path to becoming one of the great creators, thus joining the Miltonic Pantheon.

• • • •

"What lies behind us and what lies before us are but tiny matters compared to what lies within us"

Ralph Waldo Emerson

• • • •

Part Six

Appendices

A Japanese Mind Map showing the two halves of the brain.
An example of how Mind Maps are crossing linguistic frontiers

Appendix A

Global Locations Visited By Tony Buzan

Tony Buzan has worked more than 292 cities in 67 countries…

NEW YORK · ZURICH · LOS ANGELES · SAN FRANCISCO · CHICAGO · LONDON · BERLIN · STOCKHOLM · VANCOUVER · AUCKLAND · MILAN · PORTLAND · SEATTLE · TORONTO · BUDAPEST · AARHUS · UTRECHT · PARIS · CAPE TOWN · SINGAPORE · GENEVA · SYDNEY · OTTAWA · PRAGUE · AMSTERDAM · BARCELONA · DETROIT · EDMONTON · PITTSBURGH · MUNICH · BOGOTÁ · MADRID · BELO HORIZONTE · BOSTON · ATLANTA · PARIS · SÃO PAULO · MELBOURNE · ORLANDO · RALEIGH · PHOENIX · JEJU · WARSAW · WASHINGTON · PORTO

Andorra	
Argentina	Buenos Aires
Australia	Adelaide, Alice Springs, Brisbane, Cairns, Canberra, Melbourne, Perth, Sydney
Austria	Vienna
Bahamas	Nassau
Bahrain	Manama
Belgium	Brussels
Bermuda	Hamilton
Brunei	
Canada	Calgary, Edmonton, Halifax, Kamloops, Montreal, Niagara Falls, Ottawa, Toronto, Vancouver, Victoria, White Rock

Cayman Islands	George Town
Channel Islands	Jersey - St. Helier
PR China	Beijing, Chunquing, Guangzhou, Hangzhou, Hong Kong, Macau, Shanghai
Cyprus North	Laykosia
Cyprus South	Nicosea
Denmark	Copenhagen
Egypt	Cairo
England	Ascot, Banbury, Bath, Birmingham, Blackpool, Bognor Regis, Bolton, Bournemouth, Bradford, Brighton, Bristol, Burton, Cambridge, Canterbury, Carlisle, Coventry, Dartington, Deal, Dover, Durham, Exeter, Falmouth, Folkestone, Gateshead, Gloucester, Hastings, Henley-on-Thames, Herne Bay, Hove, Lands' End, Leamington Spa, Leicester, Liverpool, London, Luton, Maidenhead, Maidstone, Manchester, Margate, Marlow, Newcastle, Newquay, Newton Abbot, Northampton, Norwich, Nottingham, Penzance, Plymouth, Poole, Portsmouth, Preston, Ramsgate, Reading, Salisbury, Sheffield, Whitstable, York
Finland	Helsinki
France	Aix-en-Provence, Antibes, Cannes, Courchevel, Dieppe, Le Havre, Lyon, Marseille, Nice, Paris, St. Paul de Vence
Germany	Berlin (East), Berlin (West), Frankfurt, Hamburg, Munich, Stuttgart

Greece	Athens, Los, Kos, Rhodes
Hungary	Budapest
Iceland	Reykjavik
India	Mumbai
Indonesia	Jakarta
Ireland Northern	Belfast
Ireland Southern	Cork, Dublin, Waterford, Wexford, Wicklow
Israel	Jerusalem, Tel Aviv
Italy	Florence, Milan, Naples, Positano, Rome, Venice
Jamaica	Kingston, Montego Bay, Negril, Ocho Rios, Port Antonio
Japan	Kyoto, Niigata, Osaka, Tokyo
Jordan	Amman, Petra
Kuwait	Kuwait City
Liechtenstein	Vaduz
Luxembourg	
Madeira	Funchal
Malaysia	Kuala Lumpur, Penang
Maldives	
Mexico	Amatlán, Cabo San Lucas, , Cancún, Ciudad del Carmen, Cuernavaca, Culiacán, Dolores Hidalgo, Guadalajara, Guanajuato, Irapuato, Jalpa, León, Los Mochis, Mexico City,

	Monterrey, Pachuca, Playa del Carmen, San José los Cabos,, Tepoztlán, Tijuana, Tlaquepaque, Villahermosa, Xochimilco
Monaco	Monte Carlo, Casablanca
Netherlands	Amsterdam, Nunspeet, Rotterdam, Stenden, Utrecht
New Zealand	Auckland, Christchurch, Wellington
Norway	Bergen, Lillehammer, Oslo, Stavanger, Trondheim
Oman	Muscat
Philippines	Manila
Poland	Krakow, Warsaw
Portugal	Lisbon, Madeira, Sintra
Qatar	Doha
Russia	Moscow, St. Petersburg
Saudi Arabia	Jeddah, Oman, Riyadh
Scotland	Ayr, Dunfermline, Dunbarton, Edinburgh, Glasgow, Gleneagles, Perth, Stirling
Sierra Leone	Freetown
Singapore	
South Africa	Cape Town, Johannesburg, Kalahari, Kruger National Park, Port Elizabeth, Pretoria, Stellenbosch, Tswalu
South Korea	Busan, Seoul

Spain	Barcelona, Madrid, Majorca, Malaga, Palma, Seville
Sweden	Gothenburg, Malmö, Stockholm
Switzerland	Basel, Davos, Geneva, Gstaad, Lausanne, Stein-am-Rhein, Zurich
Taiwan	Taipei
Thailand	Bangkok
Trinidad & Tobago	Port-of-Spain, Scarborough
Turkey	Antalya, Bodrum, Istanbul, Izmir
United Arab Emirates	Adu Dhabi, Dubai
USA	Atlanta, Baltimore, Bellingham, Boston, Chicago, Colorado Springs, Dallas, Denver, Detroit, Eugene, Houston, Kansas City, Las Vegas, Long Beach, Los Angeles, Miami, Miami Beach, Minneapolis, Mt. Olympus, New Jersey City, New York, Oakland, Philadelphia, Portland, Sacramento, Salt Lake City, San Antonio, San Diego, San Francisco, San Jose, Santa Barbara, Seattle, St. Paul, Tacoma, Tampa, The Grand Canyon, Topeka, Washington, West Palm Beach
Vietnam	Ho Chi Minh City
Wales	Aberystwyth, Cardiff, Newport, Portmeirion

• • • •

Appendix B

Book Titles Written By Tony Buzan

- Age Proof Your Brain
- Brain Child
- Brain Sell
- Brainsmart Leader
- Brain Training for Kids
- Brilliant Memory (BBC Bites)
- Bruk Hodet Bedre! – An Operation's Manual for the Brain (Norwegian edition only)
- Buzan Bites:
  - Memory
  - Mind Mapping
  - Speed Reading
- Buzan's Book of Mental World Records
- Buzan's Book of Genius
- Embracing Change
- Evolving Brain
- Get Ahead
- Grass Roots Leaders
- Head First
- Head Strong
- How to Mind Map
- IBM Deep-Blue Versus Garry Kasparov
- Karate – Wado Ryu:
  - Introduction I
  - Introduction II
  - Introduction III
- Language Revolution:
  - French Beginner
  - French Beginner Plus
  - French Word Power
  - Italian Beginner
  - Italian Beginner Plus

- Italian Word Power
- Spanish Beginner
- Spanish Beginner Plus
- Spanish Word Power
- Lessons From the Art of Juggling
- Make the Most of Your Mind
- Master Your Memory
- Memory Vision
- Mind Map Handbook
- Mind Maps at Work
- Mind Maps for Business
- Mind Maps for Kids - An Introduction
- Mind Maps for Kids - Max your Memory and Concentration
- Mind Maps for Kids - Study Skills
- Modern Mind Mapping for Smarter Thinking
- My Pets
- Poetry\;
  - Concordea
  - Requiem for Ted
  - Spore One
  - The Younger Tongue
- Sales Genius
- Super Self
- Super-Creativity

- Teach Yourself Literature Guides – Romeo and Juliet
  - A Midsummer Night's Dream
  - The Merchant of Venice
  - Julius Caesar
  - Twelfth Night
  - Macbeth
  - The Tempest
  - Pride and Prejudice
  - Jane Eyre
  - Wuthering Heights
  - Great Expectations

- Far From the Madding Crowd
- The Mayor of Casterbridge
- Pygmalion
- A Portrait of the Artist as a Young Man
- Hobson's Choice
- Of Mice and Men
- Animal Farm
- An Inspector Calls
- The Crucible
- A View From the Bridge
- Lord of the Flies
- To Kill a Mockingbird
- The Owl Service
- Roll of Thunder, Hear My Cry
- Poems of Sylvia Plath
- Poems of Seamus Heaney
- A Choice of Poets

- Teach Yourself Revision Guides – GCSE
  - Mathematics Intermediate Level
  - Mathematics Higher Level
  - English
  - Modern World History
  - Geography
  - French
  - Science: Double Award
  - Science: Single Award
  - Biology
  - Chemistry
  - Physics
  - Information Technology
  - Spanish
  - German
  - Standard Grade – Biology
  - Standard Grade – Chemistry
  - Standard Grade – Physics

- Success at Key Stage 3 – English
- Success at Key Stage 3 – Mathematics
- Success at Key Stage 3 – Science

- GCSE Exam Practice:
  - Science
  - Geography
  - Maths
  - French
  - Business Studies
  - English
  - Modern World History
- The Age Heresy
- The Brain Club Manifesto
- The Brain User's Guide
- The Buzan Licensed Instructor's Manual
- The Buzan Study Skills Handbook
- The Genius Formula (audio book)
- The Memory Book
- The Mind Map Book
- The Most Important Graph in the World
- The Power of Creative Intelligence
- The Power of Physical Intelligence
- The Power of Social Intelligence
- The Power of Spiritual Intelligence
- The Power of Verbal Intelligence
- The Speed Reading Book
- The Sussex University Reading Manual
- Ultimate Book of Mind Maps
- Use Your Head
- Use Your Memory

• • • •

APPENDIX C

Magna Memoria - Manifesto for the Mind

Our ability to remember is being eroded. This is especially significant and dangerous as Memory is at the heart of everything we do - all communication, all creativity, all physical movement and all thinking - Indeed at the very heart of our existence.

What is the antidote? To strengthen our powers of Memory. The organisation of a World Memory Sports Council and a World Memory Championship represent the logical steps to focus attention on Memory.

Reasons to hold a World Memory Championship

Executive Summary

1. To promote Memory as a new Mind Sport, and in so doing to expand opportunities for Mentathletes and Warriors of the Mind in all countries.

2. To redefine the art and the science of Memory by establishing new norms, benchmarks and records, and to provide certification and ranking for these norms.

3. To reintroduce Memory as a fundamental skill for early childhood education, thereby reinvigorating faith in, and enjoyment of, Memory.

4. To reverse the global misconception that Memory deteriorates with age and demonstrate, by example, that it will continually get better.

5. To demonstrate that Memory is the basis of creativity.

6. To recover, validate and preserve for future generations the mnemonic systems of earlier human cultures and to revive the traditions of oral Memory.

7. To create a global community of like-minded individuals fascinated by exploring the power and potential of Memory and the human mind.

Introduction To The Charter

The Charter includes five major divisions, stating our major goals, which concern:

I. Society and Philanthropy

II. Science

III. Creativity

IV. Education

V. Heritage and the Future

This full document is a Manifesto for Memory. It explains the reasons behind establishing National and World Memory Championships. It is designed to give vivid insight into the wholesome and necessary needs for resurrecting the art and science of Memory.

It is also designed to shed light on the need for unleashing that extraordinary, largely untapped, and crucial resource for the future benefit of humanity: the Power of the Human Brain.

The principles of the Manifesto have been proclaimed at a significant moment in the history of The World Memory Championship: the culmination of its second decade, with the Championship in London UK celebrating the 21st in the series since the foundation year, 1991.

The Great Memory Charter

1) Social and Philanthropic

I. To introduce a new Mind Sport in the field of mental combat based on the fundamental cognitive function of the Human Brain – Memory.

II. To create Memory competitions which are truly global and human. The World Memory Championship competitions are open to all people, regardless of age, race, religion, education, language, creed, gender or physical ability, and which promote the positive human values of understanding, mutual respect, open exchange, co-operation and harmony, leading to a greater probability of world peace.

III. To open up fresh and significant opportunities for Mentathletes by providing recognition, employment and financial opportunities.

IV. To create a global community and network of like-minded individuals; a community fascinated by the exploration of the power and potential of Memory and the Human Mind.

V. To provide deeper understanding of Memory and to spread this information globally as a resource for the benefit of all those who wish to understand and improve their own performance and Memory skills.

VI. To defend the human brain against the dangers of relying on excessive tools and props.

VII. To empower the individual by giving a competitive edge, and to enhance the sense of self worth and confidence, thus permitting a more successful contribution to society.

VIII. To wield Memory as a weapon against ageism, showing that Memory, properly used, can help to stave off senility, senescence and Alzheimer's Disease.

IX. To release people and the planet from the tyranny of linear, black-and-white, boring thinking. To demonstrate further that Memory is colourful, imaginative, dynamic, the protector of heritage and the driving force for all scriptural, Biblical, classical, epic and oral traditions in every founding civilisation.

X. To create a social network, centred around an official website solely dedicated to Memory Championships and Memory.

2) Scientific

I. To monitor, measure and extend the frontiers of Memory, while exploring its infinite universes and establishing its true nature and functions.

II. To supply both support and data for academic research into Memory.

III. To establish for Memory, both on a national and global scale, new benchmarks and ongoing records.

IV. To provide certification of levels of achievement in the art and science of Memory, authenticated by an international Guild of trained and qualified arbiters.

V. To establish similarly a rating system and norms that allow competitors in national and international competition to achieve global ranking.

VI. To establish, as in chess, International Master and Grand Master titles.

3) Creativity

I. To demonstrate that Memory is the twin of Creativity, that Memory is an intrinsically creative act, and that investing Energy (E) into Memory (M) produces greatly enhanced Creativity (C) as in Tony Buzan's formula $E+->M=C\infty$

II. To demonstrate that metaphor, described by Aristotle as "The highest level of thinking", and which is the essence of all poetry and creativity, is also the essence of Memory.

III. To provide a mental playground in which imagination and association, the twin pillars of creativity, learning and Memory, provide both the tools and impetus for exploring the universes of the mind.

4) Educational Impact

I. To convince governments worldwide that Memory is a worthy subject to be approved and taught academically, from early childhood to kindergarten, through primary and secondary schools, to colleges and universities.

II. The Spanish philosopher Santayana stated "Those who fail to learn the lessons of history are doomed to repeat it." Developing Memory skills strengthens the remembrance of the lessons of history.

III. To inspire young people of the world to take on new and self-improving mental challenges.

IV. To inspire, similarly, older generations to enhance their own Memory and mental skills.

V. To make all students of any age aware that by developing mental skills, particularly Memory, they can dramatically reduce study time, improve their grades and make learning and studying enjoyable.

VI. To provide educational beacons to help and inspire teachers to realise and nurture the previously untapped potential of human performance in Memory, Creativity and Learning.

5) Heritage and the Future

I. To give hope for the future.

II. To create new Brain Stars and Warriors of the Mind in the field of Mind Sports and Memory.

III. To present these Brain Stars as role models for everyone, incorporating the spirit of "mens sana in corpore sano".

IV. To revive the mnemonic systems of previous tribes, nations and civilizations, which for posterity need to be rediscovered, re-evaluated and reinvigorated.

Conclusion

Memory Sport, in its 21st year, is now entering a mature phase, in which every single one of the stated objectives has, to varying degrees of completeness, now been achieved. Memory as a new Mind Sport has been established on a global basis and is now energetically and enthusiastically expanding in more than 37 countries.

The original psychological and academic estimates of the limits of human potential in Memory are now extinct. Memory's frontiers have significantly expanded.

In 1995, paying homage to the initial award of the chess Grandmaster title by Tzar Nicholas II, the Mind Sport of Memory was granted Royal patronage by Prince Philip of Liechtenstein.

Rating systems and norms for both national and international competitions are now in place and can be accessed on the internet. In conjunction with this, worldmemorychampionships.com has been created and is already a major resource for enthusiasts, competitors and the media.

Hundreds of local, school, national, regional and world-level competitions have already been held, including 21 World Memory Championships, with participation from the following countries:

- Brazil
- The Czech Republic
- Canada
- China
- Cyprus
- Denmark
- England
- Finland
- Germany
- Japan
- Hong Kong
- India
- Indonesia
- Israel
- Italy
- Lithuania
- Malaysia
- Mexico
- Mongolia
- Nigeria
- Norway
- The Philippines
- Poland
- Scotland
- Singapore
- Slovakia
- South Africa
- Sweden
- Thailand
- Turkey
- United States of America
- Uzbekistan
- Wales.

On the educational front, Memory is now being introduced as a subject in schools around the world, and Memory championships for schools are already a feature in the academic firmament.

A rising number of Brain Stars have become media personalities, bestselling authors and role models.

We do solemnly publish and declare that the global community and network of like-minded individuals, free from all boundaries and restrictions, is now established and is alive, growing and vibrant.

www.worldmemorysportscouncil.com

The Competitors' Pledge:

I agree to act at all times as an Ambassador for the Mind Sport of Memory and actively to promote the benefits of becoming a Mental Athlete.

I pledge to conduct myself in a civilised and dignified fashion at all times, representing Memory Sport, my nation and myself.

I pledge to uphold the principles of fair play and transparency in accordance with the rules and regulations of the Sport of Memory and in the spirit of the Magna Memoria.

The Arbiters' Pledge:

As an Official Arbiter, I pledge to act at all times as an Ambassador for the Mind Sport of Memory.

I pledge to conduct myself in a civilised and dignified fashion at all times, representing Memory Sport, my nation and myself.

I pledge that all my decisions will be unbiased, fair and balanced, and that I will treat all competitors equally.

I commit to act honourably, and to promote the benefits of becoming a Mental Athlete.

I pledge to uphold the principles of fair play and transparency in accordance with the rules and regulations of the Sport of Memory and in the spirit of the Magna Memoria.

Floreant Dendritae!

• • • •

Appendix D

Creations / Accomplishments/Awards and Themes

Tony's prodigious creative output in manifold fields:

- he invented Mind Maps;
- he authored / co-authored 120 books;
- he wrote and presented in 1974 the ground-breaking ten-part BBC Television series Use Your Head;
- he completed and had published 4 volumes of poetry;
    - o The Younger Tongue;
    - o Spore One;
    - o Concordea;
    - o Requiem for Ted;
- he wrote 4,000 poems, some of which are now being published on the web;
- he co-founded, with John Carder Bush and Jeremy Cartland, the Salatticum Poets;
- he took up the piano and guitar, reaching first grade in both;
- he took up photography as a hobby;
- in addition to inventing Mind Maps, he has created thousands of them himself;
- he created New Memory Systems;
- he pioneered new approaches to Speed Reading, Comprehension and Study, including the Buzan Organic Study Technique;
- he created a new learning system (TEFCAS-trial-event –feedback -check-adjust-success) based on Scientific Method which removes the false concept of 'failure' from learning, replacing it with 'Experiment'.
- he created a new Reading Taxonomy, to help guide teachers around the world to teach students how to read;
- he developed new language learning systems, which were published by Collins in 2008 under the title 'Language Revolution';

- he developed new approaches to Thinking, Thinking Systems and Intelligence;
- he wrote and presented many other television series and features, including:
    - o The Enchanted Loom;
    - o The BBC Brain Bites Series;
    - o The Happy Dictionary Programme for CCTV (China);
- he wrote hundreds of newspaper and magazine articles;
- he wrote and presented thousands of hours of radio programmes;
- he created new moves on the dance floor, and was often awarded the 'best-in-disco' title;
- he composed his first piece of classical music with the guidance of Geoff Wayne, the composer of the music for War of the Worlds;
- he created and co-founded:
    - o The Brain Trust Charity;
    - o The World Memory Championships;
    - o The World Memory Sports Council;
    - o The Schools Memory Championship;
    - o The Brain of the Year Award;
    - o The Mind Sports Olympiad;
    - o The Festival of the Mind;
    - o The Mind Body and Spirit Festival in London;
    - o The World Council for Creativity;
    - o The World Council for Intelligence;
    - o The World Council for Mind Maps;
    - o The World Council for Speed Reading;
- he studied art and learnt the basics of both drawing and painting;
- he shattered the conventional boundaries of the Torrance Creativity Test;
- he generated many new words and expressions including:
    - o "Mind Maps";
    - o "Mental Literacy";
    - o "Goethendipity" – the art of directed serendipity;

o "Visio-technologist" – those who combine the art and science of vision with the art and science of technology to create new forms;

o "Neuronosphere" – the place where we live!

o "Holanthropy" – the study of the complete human, specifically the effects of the body on the mind, and the mind on the body;

o "Meta-Positive Thinking" – a comprehensive new methodology for thinking positively, which removes all the lurking 'failures' in many traditional 'positive' thinking forms;

- he designed his own house, The Gates of Dawn, including all the furniture in it;
- he designs and creates his own clothes;
- His corporate and keynote themes include:
  - Business and Mind Mapping;
  - Intellectual Capital:
  - Multiplying the intellectual power of organisations
  - Creativity and Innovation;
  - The application of the multiple Intelligences to business success;
  - Brain Training;
  - Speed Reading and Knowledge Management;
  - Talent Management;
  - Presentation skills in the age of multimedia;
  - Good Thinking;
  - Communication and presentation skills;
  - Memory (personal and corporate).
  - Leadership in times of crisis

Credit crunch, financial downturn, falling sales, rising prices, budget cuts – these are issues being urgently addressed by companies all over the world. Tony has always maintained that investing in the Brain Power of employees is the best investment a business can ever make.

He addresses these issues particularly in his *Leadership in Times of Crisis* course, in which he contends that the cascading growth in global bankruptcies, has been caused not by any standard economic reasons, but by a series of underlying bankruptcies: the bankruptcy of intelligence; the bankruptcy of ideas; the bankruptcy of thought.

The excellence of Tony's Corporate, Academic and Government work has received many accolades, including:

- In 1995 awarded by Royal Decree the title of International Arbiter Of Mental World Records
- Dean of the Liechtenstein Global Trust Academy
- Lifelong Dean of the Renaissance Academy
- The Eagle Catcher Award, awarded by Electronic Data Systems (EDS) 'for attempting the impossible and achieving it;
- Made Dean of the Young Presidents' Organisation Floating University;
- Invited as special Guest Lecturer to the Oxford Union; Institute for Management Studies Distinguished Lecturer Award;
- Innova award from Mexico;
- Special Recognition Award by President Vicente Fox of Mexico for length and excellence of service in helping Mexico with educational and good governance initiatives;
- YPO Leadership Award;
- Lifetime Achievement Award, the American Creativity Association, for Services to Global Creativity and Innovation.
- The Brand Laureate Award
- Founding Member of the Inaugural International Board of
- Advisers, University Putra Malaysia, Graduate School of Management; Honorary Fellow of the Academy for Leadership in Higher
- Education - Ministry of Higher Education, Malaysia;
- External Adviser to the 32 campuses of TecMilenio in Mexico, where 40,000 students are being taught a 100 hour Mind Mapping and Mental Literacy Course. 6,000 have already graduated;

- Special Adviser to the Pathlight School in Singapore. This is a school devoted totally to the education of autistic children, where Mind Maps are used as a learning tool. As visitors enter the school, they are met by a giant Mind Map which summarises the functions, aims and goals of the school, and which was largely illustrated by the children themselves.
- Guest Lecturer for the London School of Economics (LSE) Doctoral Student Induction Programme;
- Appointed by Dr. Anthony Seldon, Master of Wellington College, as Thinker in Residence.

In making the appointment Dr. Seldon said:

"Education is about much more than exam scores; it is about teaching the whole child, and this involves being taught how to think and reason independently. I want to thank the man who has been the most inspirational person on my thinking about the process of learning throughout my career as a teacher, which has lasted 25 years. That man is Tony Buzan… the best teachers are those who make learning fun, and Mind Maps are fun!"

In his role as Wellington College's first Thinker in Residence, Tony is delivering lectures to teachers, all students, support staff, parents and governors on Thinking, Study Skills, Memory and Creativity, as well as becoming engaged in special educational projects.

In December 2009 of this most extraordinary educational year for Tony, he was honoured by being appointed a Freeman of the Guild (now a Company) of Educators. " In which the pledge was I shall be true to the art and mystery of the profession known as Education giving of my skills and knowledge without limitation in the profession to which I have been called... "

The Guild honoured Tony by requesting that he give the annual Franklin Lecture, which had in the previous year been given by Dr.

Anthony Seldon, and which is one of the most prestigious global lectures on the educational calendar. The lecture was attended by many dignitaries, including the Lord Mayor of London.

In 2010, Tony was further honoured:

- he was appointed guest lecturer at the London School of Economics (LSE) for their new and revolutionary course LSE 100 a course on thinking skills specifically designed for all students entering the social sciences at LSE;
- he was then made Visiting Professor of Thinking at the Stenden University of Applied Science in the Netherlands,
- and finally… Individual Nomination for the Nobel Peace Prize

• • • •

Acknowledgements

T hanks to all those who contributed stories, information or tributes to Tony. Above all I would like to thank Tony Buzan, with whom I have spent thousands of hours over more than two decades. Tony has generously made available to me his personal papers, anecdotes, his complete photographic archive and everything a biographer could possibly need to know, including many hours of recorded interviews with him. To do full justice to it all would probably take multiple volumes of Encyclopaedia Britannica dimensions.

Next I would like to thank in particular Aditi Bland, who has helped me format and finalise the script. Rhian Connell, Jenny Redman and Sue Flint, from Tony's office, unflinching when confronted with my demands for additional details or to fill gaps. Special thanks to Jennifer Goddard for her expert editing and bringing it all together.

Of course, the unfailing support of Nicky and Jonathan Oppenheimer has been vital to the project.

Stephen Brough has been supportive, while Anthony Arnott of Eoson was always there when needed.

Finally, I would like to thank all of the following, who have contributed in various ways to the completion of this volume:

- Isobel Abulhoul
- Sean Adam
- Joe Adams
- Dr. Roger Blackwood
- Libby Blackwood
- Michael Boulton
- Pauline Boulton
- Lord Charles Brocket
- Belinda Budge (of Harper Collins)
- Yvonne Burne OBE
- John Bush
- Kate Bush
- Barry Buzan
- Deborah Buzan
- Jean Buzan
- Jeremy Cartland
- Jonathan Case
- Jorge Castaneda
- Claudia Castaneda
- Philip Chambers
- Eric Cheong
- Stewart Collins
- Tony Connell
- Professor Michael Crawford
- Chris Day
- Sally Farmiloe

- Nathalie Fitzgerald
- Angela Folley
- Chris Folley
- Sjoerd Gehrels
- Lorraine Gill
- Michael Gelb
- Jennifer Goddard
- Andrew Greystoke
- Andrea Greystoke
- John Harlow
- James Harrison
- Christopher Hedley-Dent
- Jude Hedley-Dent
- Alan Hooker
- Sheila Hooker
- Richard Hoppe
- Edward Hughes
- Samantha Jackson
- Bill Jarrard
- Masanori Kanda
- Annette Keene
- Alexander Keene
- Ken Kennedy
- Frieda Kennedy
- Prince Mohsin Ali Khan of Hyderabad
- Princess Asra Khan
- Brian Lee
- Jenny Lee
- Prince Philipp of Liechtenstein
- Princess Isobel of Liechtenstein
- Jock Lowe
- Bertie McIntosh
- Neil Massa
- Jackie Massa
- Jo Metcalfe
- Jeremy (Jezz) Moore

- Richard Morris
- Neelam Morris
- Vanda North
- Dominic O'Brien
- Robert Parsons
- Emma Payne
- Tanya Phonanan
- Mark Rowles
- Robert Sandall
- Julian Simpole
- Kirpal Singh
- Lorri Spragg
- Cllr Frances Stainton
- Jane Stephenson
- Dr Andrew Strigner
- Henry Toi
- Sir Brian Tovey
- Lady Mary Tovey
- David Taylor
- Pam Taylor
- Alper Utku
- Filiz Utku
- Hilary Walsh
- Susan Whiting
- John Whiting OBE
- Sutanto Windura
- Thomas Woodcock, Garter King of Arms
- Vivienne Wordley
- Klaas Wybo van der Hoek
- Lian Yang
- YoYo Yang
- Yudenia Ayala
- Ben Zephaniah
- David Zhang
- and finally, Chris and Gaile Griffiths of Think Buzan Ltd who were responsible for launching iMindMap onto the world stage.

Closing Poems by Jean Buzan

Mirror Image

I look in the mirror

And what do I see?

A woman years older than me.

It must be my mother

Returned from the grave,

For I am much younger than she.

This woman is plumpish,

And I'm very thin.

Her eyebrows can scarcely be seen.

Her neck's full of wrinkles

And mine is quite smooth -

What can this anomaly mean?

Did I enter a time warp

And speed years ahead?

And where have the years between fled?

If time goes that fast

For the rest of my life,

Tomorrow I'll surely be dead!

Jean Buzan (20/05/1916 – 24/09/2010)

Where Is My Child?

Where is my child, that tiny boy
Who daily gave me so much joy?
That little voice for 'Mummy' calls,
Those happy games with bats and balls.
I search the world but he has gone!
I cannot find my precious son;
Here is a book and here a toy --
A pair of shoes worn by my boy.
He isn't dead -I would have known;
It seems that all he's done is grown.
A lovely man now owns his name
But no way is that the same.
When a person dies it's plain
You'll never see that one again.
But my small child I'll never see
And he's not dead - so where is he?

Jean Buzan (20/05/1916 – 24/09/2010)

• • • •

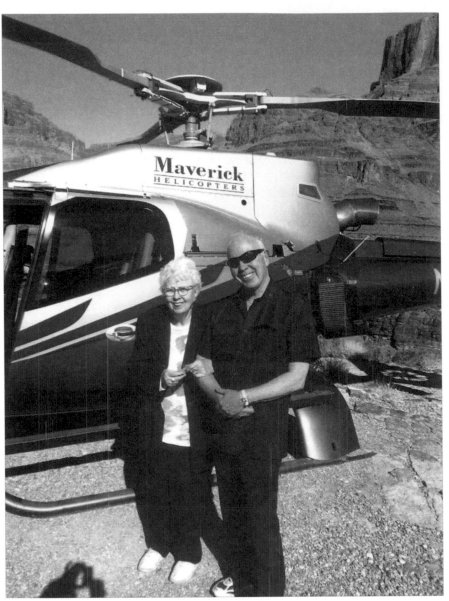

Tony and mother Jean Buzan

O N SUNDAY JUNE 2, 2013, on his 71st birthday, TONY BUZAN WAS AWARDED THE INAUGURAL GOLD MEDAL OF THE AVICENNA SOCIETY BY PROFESSOR DR AHMED ALI KHAN.

AD 980 – June 1037 - **Avicenna** was a Persian polymath, who wrote almost 450 treatises on a wide range of subjects, of which around 240 have survived. In particular, 150 of his surviving treatises concentrate on philosophy and 40 of them concentrate on medicine.

His most famous works are *The Book of Healing*, a vast philosophical and scientific encyclopaedia, and *The Canon of Medicine*, which was a standard medical text at many medieval universities. His corpus also includes writing on philosophy, astronomy, alchemy, geology, psychology, theology, logic, mathematics and physics, as well as poetry. He is regarded as the most famous and influential polymath of the Islamic Golden Age.